Sunset

Lawns & Ground Covers

By the Editors of Sunset Books and Sunset Magazine

Border of evergreen candytuft (Iberis sempervirens) accentuates gentle curve of lawn in this perfect marriage of ground cover and grass.

Lane Publishing Co. ■ **Menlo Park, California**

Book Editor
Fran Feldman

Research & Text
Michael Bowker
Philip Edinger

Contributing Editors
Gloria Mellinger
Susan Warton

Coordinating Editors
Deborah Thomas Kramer
Gregory J. Kaufman

Design
Joe di Chiarro

Illustrations
Jane McCreary

Photographers: William Aplin: 95 left; Automatic Rain Company: 57 center left; Glenn Christiansen: 36; Roger DeWeese: 12 top; Derek Fell: 5, 6, 15 top, 81, 82, 83 top, 85 top left, 86 top, 88 bottom, 90 bottom, 91, 93, 96, 119, 135, 136, 141, 142, 143, 145, 153, 156, 157; Gerald R. Fredrick: 83 bottom, 125, 139, 146; Saxon Holt: 87 top, 88 top, 89, 108, 152; Horticultural Photography: 14 bottom, 84; Michael Landis: 7 bottom, 8 top, 9 top left and bottom, 13, 27, 31, 60, 63, 65; Renee Lynn: 41, 67; Michael McKinley: 7 top, 10 bottom, 15 bottom; Stephen Marley: 113, 114, 150; Ells Marugg: 87 bottom left and right, 95 right, 115, 116, 117, 120, 124, 129, 133, 144, 147, 154, 155; Norman A. Plate: 9 top right, 11, 86 bottom, 92 top; Bill Ross: 85 top right, 94 bottom, 134; Chad Slattery: 127; David Stubbs: 16; Michael S. Thompson: 1, 24, 94 top, 111, 112, 121, 122, 126, 128, 131, 132, 137, 140, 149, 151; Darrow M. Watt: 10 top, 85 bottom; Russ Widstrand: 28, 34, 42, 43, 46, 118; Tom Wyatt: 8 bottom, 12 bottom, 14 top, 19, 20, 22, 23, 25, 26, 44, 49, 50, 51, 52, 53, 54, 55, 57 top, center right, and bottom, 58, 59, 84, 90 top, 92 bottom, 102, 104, 138, 148.

Photo stylist: JoAnn Masaoka Van Atta: 8 bottom, 12 bottom, 49, 53, 54, 55, 57 top, center right, and bottom, 58, 59, 90, 92 bottom, 138, 148.

Greening Your Garden

Although their other plantings may vary, most gardens include one feature in common—a green carpet of lawn or ground cover.

The carpet may be small or expansive, square or asymmetrical, flat or sloped, smooth or irregular. Blanketing the area may be one or several types of grasses and ground covers, chosen from the myriad varieties available.

This book will acquaint you with the plants and their requirements so you can cultivate a lush lawn or ground cover that's appropriate for your own situation. By choosing plants suitable for your climate, planting with care, and then providing the right watering and maintenance, you can enjoy the showiest landscape in the neighborhood.

For his invaluable and expert help with the manuscript and photographs, we wish to thank Dr. Ali Harivandi, Turfgrass Specialist, Cooperative Extension of Alameda County, University of California, Berkeley.

For their help with the text, we also thank Dr. M.C. Engelke, College of Agriculture, Texas A&M University, Dallas; Dr. C. Reed Funk, Research Professor in Turfgrass Breeding, Department of Soils and Crops, Cook College, Rutgers University, New Brunswick; Dr. Victor A. Gibeault, Extension Environmental Horticulturist, Department of Botany and Plant Sciences, University of California, Riverside; Dr. Anthony J. Koski, Assistant Professor of Turfgrass, Department of Horticulture, Colorado State University, Fort Collins; and Dr. William A. Meyer, Turf Seed, Inc., Hubbard, Oregon.

Special thanks also to Jim Borneman and Bob Pearson of Automatic Rain Company; Gus Selke of Cole & Weber; Russ Hayworth of Foster Turf; Bill Polk of Irrometer Company, Inc.; Jim Traub of Kensco Supply; John Holmquist and Dave Witzke of KKW, Inc.; Lou Sapudar and Mathew Narog of Lawn Clinic, Inc.; Madrone Landscape Group.

Also Orchard Supply Hardware; Ken Lyons, Cathy Morrow, and Kitty Tebrugge of Pursley Turf Farms; Dea L. Morrison of Rain Bird Sprinkler Manufacturing Corporation; Bill Trask of Sleepy Hollow Nursery; John McShane of Stover Seed Company; Rob Edelstein of Systematic Irrigation Controls, Inc.; Dennis Nord and Jack Prust of The Toro Company; and Bill Stepka of Traditional Landscape Art.

Finally, we extend our thanks to Marianne Lipanovich for scouting and assistance with photography, to Rik Olson for the maps, and to Scott Atkinson and Rod Smith for preliminary editorial research.

Cover: Serpentine lawn winds gracefully through flanking ground cover beds in a living tapestry of tones and textures. Landscape architect: Richard Moore. Cover design by Susan Bryant. Photography by Norman A. Plate.

Editor, Sunset Books: Elizabeth L. Hogan

Second printing May 1990

Contents

Lawns   **4–79**

Lawns in the Landscape   7

Presenting the Grasses   17

Planting a Lawn   29

Watering Your Lawn   47

Lawn Maintenance   61

Ground Covers   **80–157**

Ground Covers at Work   83

Ground Covers—The Basics   97

Ground Covers A to Z   109

Plant Index   158

General Subject Index   159

Special Features

Grasses at a Glance   18
Climate Map for Grasses   21
Tough Turf for Play Surfaces   24
A Selection of Native Grasses   27
A Lawn Design Primer   30
How to Read a Grass Seed Label   39
Seed Versus Sod   44
Tips for a More Water-efficient Lawn   48
If It's Not Weeds, Pests, or Disease   69
Lawn Weeds, Pests & Diseases   70
Lawn Maintenance Calendar   79
Using Organic Amendments   99
Plant Hardiness Zone Map   110

Lawns

Whether grown from seed or sod, used for croquet or display, cultivated in a small plot or a vast, rolling green, your lawn plays a prominent role in your landscape. More than any other kind of greenery, lawns are a basic fixture in residential gardens across a diverse climatic range.

Although not hard to achieve, a healthy, lustrous carpet of grass requires the right grass choices and a regular program of watering and lawn care to sustain its green glory. A lawn's appearance usually reflects the quality of its maintenance. Basic feeding, watering, and mowing don't demand extensive effort, but each task helps to create and preserve a beautiful, flourishing lawn.

Welcoming guests into the garden, a carpet of bluegrass displays the look of unabashed luxury for which lawns are famous.

Lawns
in the Landscape

Verdant Vistas

For garden-party glamor or a magnificent view, nothing can match the sweeping expanse of a picture-perfect, emerald green lawn.

Stately home *requires a broad lawn to balance its imposing size. This one rolls richly over terraced slopes, contrasting with wide steps and walls of stone. Landscape architect: Thomas Church.*

Keep off the grass? *That isn't always easy to enforce. Concrete squares provide an attractive alternative that protects St. Augustine blades as it directs foot traffic.*

Swirling gracefully *between house, steps, and border plantings, this lush lawn is planted with perennial ryegrass cultivar Pennfine.*

Lawns in Miniature

Small-scale lawns create pockets of lush, cool green that require less upkeep and water. And they fit well on many urban and suburban lots.

Circle of tall fescue demands less water than a larger lawn would, yet still splashes vibrant color in an entry garden. Landscape designer: Charlene Yockum.

A swatch of green tall fescue sets off paving, flowers, and foliage in a luxuriant patchwork landscape. Its velvety influence seems to soften adjacent driveway and garden path. Landscape designer: Richard Plaxco of Geared for Growing.

Swath of bluegrass sets off house and its landscaping from encircling border of trees, shrubs, ground covers, and blooms.

A backyard oasis, this curve of vivid fescue brightens a water-thrifty desert garden. Landscape designer: Ric Wogisch.

Stepping-stones skip across a 10-foot-wide lawn of bluegrass cultivar A-34, edged by brickwork and combined with drought-tolerant plantings. Design: Konrad Gauder of Landsculpture.

Situational Problem Solvers

Lawns flow smoothly through complex landscapes, contributing design continuity and soft, rich texture as they also solve practical problems.

Cushioning turf *under structure softens impact of falls. Rugged mix of Kentucky bluegrass and ryegrass handles foot traffic. Landscape design: Barbara Vendt, Con Mara Gardens. Play structure: Columbia Cascade.*

Spreading trees shade *carpet of lawn, an inviting place to linger on warm summer afternoons. Grass frames circular flower beds at bases of tree trunks. Landscape architect: Thomas Church.*

Retaining walls cascade down a hillside garden to overlap this inviting lawn, used as a family play space. Landscape architect: John Herbst, Jr.

…Situational Problem Solvers

Flowing bluegrass visually calms and unites this complex garden, while accentuating its man-made dry creek bed and individual trees and shrubs. Landscape architect: DeWeese Burton Associates.

Serpentine curves and graceful slopes add interest to this spacious lawn; border plantings and path repeat undulating theme. Landscape architect: Peter Wright Shaw Associates, Inc.

Turf Innovations

More than just a smooth stretch of mowed grass, a lawn shows off its versatility when planted by an innovative gardener in surprising locations.

Hardscape meets softscape *in this unique garden walk that alternates bands of bluegrass with brickwork.*

Checkerboard hybrid *of lawn and patio results from planting tufts of grass inside open-ended concrete blocks. Grass grown here is a varietal called Warren turf A-34.*

Landscape Drama

With ribbons, circles, and other accents of green, decorative lawns show off nearby landscape elements to their brightest advantage.

Island of green at center of a driveway, this plot of Kentucky bluegrass mixed with Bermuda grass dresses up surrounding pavement and provides a soft pad under swing. Landscape architect: James Chadwick.

An emerald border outlining a stone-and-gravel path, this graceful lawn accents diverse foliage and flowers displayed along its edges.

Promenade of lawn, *a blend of bluegrass and ryegrass, draws stroller toward pergola. Vivid perennials border grassy path, heightening garden's drama.*

Rich greenery *enhances vibrant blooms of azaleas. Lawns often play role of a catalyst, making nearby flowers appear to explode with reds, yellows, or whites.*

Presenting the Grasses

Of the many hundreds of grasses that grow in the Northern Hemisphere, only about 40 types are usually cultivated as lawns. Many of those have numerous varieties developed to give you a multitude of choices.

Grasses vary greatly in their performance, appearance, watering needs, and maintenance requirements. Moreover, each grass has its own climate considerations. This chapter presents 18 of the most common grass types, each with a photo and description to help you make the right choice for your lawn.

Understanding Grasses

Grasses have these anatomical points in common: leaves grow alternately in two rows up the sides of jointed stems. The space between the joints may be hollow or pithy. A sheath surrounds the stem above each joint. Follow the sheath up and you come to a collarlike growth, the auricle, that clasps the stem at the top of the sheath. The blade grows outward, and usually upward, from this collar.

The particular arrangement of sheath, auricle, and blade helps botanists identify lawn grasses in the absence of flowers or a seed spike. Other aids to identification include the shape of the leaves, thickness of the stem, color, and means of spreading—stolons, or runners, above ground or rhizomes below ground.

Grass blades elongate from the lower end—when you mow off the tips, the leaves renew their length from the root end or new blades sprout from the base. This is why grasses perform so well as closely cropped ground covers.

Climate Considerations

The two basic kinds of grasses are cool season and warm season. Cool-season grasses withstand cold winters, but most types languish in hot summers. They're used mainly in northern latitudes.

Warm-season grasses grow vigorously during hot weather and go dormant in temperatures below freezing. If you find their winter brownness offensive, you can overseed (see page 18) with certain cool-season grasses. But grasses in the same group can perform differently in various climates. To choose the grass best adapted to your region, turn to the climate zone map on page 21. If you're unsure of the grass type you want or the best one for your area, consult a reputable nursery or your County Cooperative Extension office.

Cultivars, Blends & Mixtures

Lawns can be composed of a single grass type, called a cultivar, a blend, or a mixture. When a single *cultivar*, a grass that's named and grown on a regular basis for sale, is used, the lawn is the most uniform in appearance, giving you the maximum expression of whatever characteristic you select.

The main disadvantage of using a single type of grass is that it can be wiped out if it's susceptible to a pest or disease in the area.

Hardy Kentucky bluegrass offers rich, deep color, good wearability, and high tolerance to cold.

Using a *blend*, several cultivars of one species, or a *mixture*, composed of two or more different species, is safer. Seed companies prepare blends and mixtures for specific situations—one grass's strengths compensate for another's weaknesses in areas such as resistance to disease, drought tolerance, and wearability. Thus, a lawn can look good even when one grass type is suffering.

Overseeding

The major drawback of warm-season grasses is their unattractive dormancy during cool weather—they turn brown in winter. In many cases, cool-season grasses are seeded over warm-season grasses approaching dormancy. This maintains a green lawn all year but increases water use and maintenance.

Choosing a Grass

The following section presents the most common cool- and warm-season grasses. Dichondra is also included, although it isn't technically a grass. Native grasses, gaining in popularity because of their drought tolerance and low maintenance, are discussed on page 27.

With each grass description is a sampling of available cultivars. Not all the listed cultivars are available everywhere, and you may find additional ones in your area. Moreover, new named varieties appear on the market frequently; keep in mind that they may exhibit characteristics different from older cultivars.

A grass's root depth may be an important factor in your choice of grass type: shallow-rooted grasses need to be watered more often for shorter periods of time than deep-rooted grasses, which require deep watering less often.

In the grass descriptions that follow, "shallow" refers to roots up to 8 inches deep, "intermediate" to roots from 8 to 36 inches deep, and "deep" to roots deeper than 36 inches. These ranges refer to grass roots growing under ideal conditions and may vary a great deal depending on your maintenance practices.

Grasses at a Glance

For playing, running, or simply formal display, there's nothing comparable to a lush and healthy lawn. Cultivating such a lawn requires choosing the right grass type for your climate and your particular situation.

The chart below shows you at a glance each grass type's tolerance to certain conditions. For example, if you want a lawn that doesn't require massive amounts of water and chemicals, look for grasses with high tolerance to drought, pests, and disease. For a detailed description of each grass, refer to the individual listings that follow. To learn which grasses are best adapted to your climate, see the climate map on page 21.

	Tolerance to						
	Cold	Heat	Drought	Shade	Disease	Pests	Wear
Cool-season Grasses							
Colonial bent grass							
Creeping bent grass							
Kentucky bluegrass							
Rough-stalk bluegrass							
Chewings fescue							
Creeping red fescue							
Hard fescue							
Tall fescue							
Annual ryegrass							
Perennial ryegrass							
Warm-season Grasses							
Bahia grass							
Common Bermuda grass							
Hybrid Bermuda grass							
Centipede grass							
Dichondra							
Seashore paspalum							
St. Augustine grass							
Zoysia grass							

High   Moderate   Low

Bahia Grass

Paspalum notatum
Warm season

Introduced to the United States from Brazil in 1913, Bahia grass is a low-growing turf that spreads by runners. Its extensive, deep root system can help control erosion.

■ *Pluses:* Good in sandy or infertile soils. Tends to stay green longer in winter than other warm-season grasses. Some drought tolerance.

■ *Minuses:* Coarse and moderately aggressive; considered a weed in fine lawns. May turn yellow from chlorosis; dollar spot and mole crickets may also be problems. Frequent mowing required to remove seed heads.

■ *Regions:* Southern U. S. coastal areas, particularly Florida and the Gulf states.

■ *Sun/Shade:* Grows in sun or partial shade.

■ *Water:* Tolerates some drought but grows best with abundant water.

■ *Wear:* Very good wearability.

■ *Planting Methods:* Seed, sod.

■ *Mowing:* Mow 2 to 3 inches high; fast-growing seed stalks require frequent mowing.

■ *Fertilizer:* Apply ½ pound actual nitrogen per 1,000 square feet each month during active growing period.

■ *Cultivars:* Argentine, Paraguay, Pensacola.

Colonial Bent Grass

Agrostis tenuis
Cool season

Colonial bent grass is a fine-textured turf grass that produces high-quality lawns, ideal for golf course fairways. Its roots extend to an intermediate depth.

■ *Pluses:* Tolerates acidic, infertile soils and doesn't require much fertilizer. Also fairly drought tolerant.

■ *Minuses:* Does not perform well in extreme summertime heat. Depending on cultivar, is somewhat susceptible to pests and fungal diseases.

■ *Regions:* Coastal areas of northeastern U.S., Canada, Pacific Northwest, and California.

■ *Sun/Shade:* Needs sun but will tolerate moderate shade.

■ *Water:* Light to moderate watering required.

■ *Wear:* Moderate wearability.

■ *Planting Method:* Seed.

■ *Mowing:* Mow ½ to 1 inch high.

■ *Fertilizer:* Apply ⅛ to ¼ pound actual nitrogen per 1,000 square feet each month during active growing period.

■ *Cultivars:* Astoria, Bardot, Exeter.

Creeping Bent Grass

Agrostis palustris
Cool season

A fine-textured grass, creeping bent produces a high-quality lawn that, with constant care, is ideal for putting greens and lawn bowling. Its roots grow to an intermediate depth.

■ *Pluses:* Wears well and tolerates some heat.

■ *Minuses:* Needs ample water and constant care. More susceptible to pests and fungal disease than colonial bent.

■ *Regions:* Northeastern U.S. and Canada; coastal areas of Pacific Northwest and western Canada.

■ *Sun/Shade:* Likes full sun but will tolerate some shade.

■ *Water:* Frequent watering required.

■ *Wear:* Very good wearability.

■ *Planting Method:* Seed.

■ *Mowing:* Mow ¼ to ½ inch high. Use a reel mower that's designed for close cutting.

■ *Fertilizer:* Apply ¼ to ½ pound actual nitrogen per 1,000 square feet each month during active growing period.

■ *Cultivars:* Emerald, Penncross, Penneagle, Pennlinks, Providence, Seaside.

Common Bermuda Grass

Cynodon dactylon
Warm season

Common Bermuda grass produces a medium- to fine-textured turf that spreads rapidly by surface and underground runners. This deep-rooted grass survives low maintenance, but extra care makes a more attractive lawn.

■ *Pluses:* Drought and heat tolerant; disease resistant. Outstanding wearability.

■ *Minuses:* Turns brown in winter but when well fertilized, some strains may remain green longer. Root system invasive if not confined; difficult to eradicate. Won't tolerate shade.

■ *Regions:* Southern U.S., Gulf Coast, and mild-weather western coastal areas.

■ *Sun/Shade:* Requires full sun. Poor shade tolerance.

■ *Water:* Needs less water than most grass types; tolerates drought well.

■ *Wear:* Excellent wearability.

■ *Planting Method:* Seed.

■ *Mowing:* Mow ¾ to 1 inch high, cutting ½ inch or less each time.

■ *Fertilizer:* Apply ½ to 1 pound actual nitrogen per 1,000 square feet each month during active growing period.

Hybrid Bermuda Grass

Cynodon
Warm season

Tough and heat loving, hybrid Bermuda grass makes a lawn that's finer textured and greener than common Bermuda grass. Tifway is a good cultivar for home lawns; Tifdwarf is best for golf greens. All are deep-rooted grasses.

■ *Pluses:* Drought and cold tolerant; doesn't turn brown in winter as readily as common Bermuda grass. Very resistant to diseases and pests.

■ *Minuses:* May tend to build up heavy thatch. Root system can be invasive. Won't tolerate shade.

■ *Regions:* Southern U.S., Gulf and East coasts, and mild-weather western coastal areas.

■ *Sun/Shade:* Requires full sun.

■ *Water:* Drought tolerant but needs regular watering to look good.

■ *Wear:* Excellent wearability.

■ *Planting Methods:* Sod, sprigs, plugs.

■ *Mowing:* Mow ½ to 1 inch high, cutting ½ inch or less each time. Use a reel mower. If allowed to grow longer, lawn tends to yellow.

■ *Fertilizer:* Apply ½ to 1 pound actual nitrogen per 1,000 square feet each month during active growing period. May require more for good appearance or recovery from wear.

■ *Cultivars:* Midiron, Midway, Ormond, Santa Ana, Sunturf, Tifdwarf, Tifgreen, Tiflawn, Tifway.

Kentucky Bluegrass

Poa pratensis
Cool season

A moderate- to fine-textured, hardy grass, Kentucky bluegrass is the most widely planted cool-season grass. Blue green in color, its blades have characteristic boat-shaped tips. Rhizomes of this shallow-rooted grass knit into firm turf.

■ *Pluses:* High cold tolerance. Many cultivars resistant to leaf spot, smut, and rust.

■ *Minuses:* Needs ample amounts of water. Some cultivars don't tolerate intense heat or shade.

■ *Regions:* Northern U.S. and Canada, and mountain and cool-weather areas of South and Southwest.

■ *Sun/Shade:* Likes full sun. Some cultivars tolerate a fair amount of shade.

■ *Water:* Requires frequent watering. Some cultivars won't tolerate drought conditions.

■ *Wear:* Good to excellent wearability.

■ *Planting Methods:* Seed, sod.

■ *Mowing:* Mow 1½ to 2 inches high.

■ *Fertilizer:* Apply ½ to 1 pound actual nitrogen per 1,000 square feet during active growing period. Some improved, established varieties do well with less.

■ *Cultivars:* Adelphi, America, Bensun (A-34), Blacksburg, Bristol, Challenger, Cheri, Columbia, Eclipse, Enmundi, Glade, Kenblue, Majestic, Midnight, Newport, Nugget, Parade, Plush, Rugby, Sydsport, Touchdown, Vantage, Windsor.

Climate Map for Grasses

The map below is divided into seven climate zones, each of which is characterized by particular climate conditions. Grasses that grow well in each zone are listed.

Keep in mind that the map is only a guide. Specific areas within a zone may vary in rainfall, temperature, altitude, terrain, and soil. Areas bordering the dividing lines are transitional: the grasses that flourish in those areas may be different from those that do well throughout the rest of the region. For help, consult your local nursery or County Co-operative Extension office.

■ *ZONE 1: West and Pacific Northwest.* Climate is cool and humid. Rain is plentiful, except during summer in West. Lawns seeded from cool-season grasses—bent grasses, fine and tall fescues, Kentucky bluegrass, and perennial ryegrass—do well in this area.

■ *ZONE 2: Southwest.* Temperatures are high. Rainfall is scarce and soils are dry. Lawns here need additional irrigation. Bermuda grass is used primarily, with some zoysia and St. Augustine. With adequate irrigation, tall fescue can provide year-round turf where temperatures are not too severe. Perennial ryegrass is excellent for winter overseeding of dormant warm-season grasses. Seashore paspalum is used in Southern California, dichondra in mild-winter areas.

■ *ZONE 3: Mountains, Great Plains, and Central Plains of Canada.* Climate is dry and semiarid, with wide temperature fluctuations. Drought-tolerant native grasses (buffalo grass, crested wheatgrass, and blue grama) do well. With irrigation, fine fescues and Kentucky and rough-stalk bluegrasses succeed in northern areas, and tall fescue (and occasionally Bermuda and zoysia) in southern areas. Dichondra does well in mild-winter western areas.

■ *ZONE 4: Northeastern U. S. and Eastern Canada.* Summers are hot and humid, winters cold and snowy. Rainfall is abundant and soils are often acidic. Colonial and creeping bent grasses, Kentucky and rough-stalk bluegrasses, and perennial and annual ryegrasses are common; fine fescues are used in northern areas.

■ *ZONE 5: North and South (transition zone).* Summers are warm and humid, with abundant rainfall. Winters are generally mild but can be severe. Bermuda grass, tall fescue, and zoysia grass perform well. Kentucky and rough-stalk bluegrasses, perennial and annual ryegrasses also are used.

■ *ZONE 6: Central South.* Climate is warm and humid with abundant rainfall; winters are mild. Bermuda grass, centipede grass, tall fescue, and zoysia do well. Kentucky bluegrass is used in cooler areas, St. Augustine in southern areas.

■ *ZONE 7: Florida, Gulf Coast, and Hawaii.* Climate is semitropical to tropical with a year-round growing season. Rainfall is generally very high. Bahia, Bermuda, centipede, St. Augustine, and zoysia grasses grow well throughout most of the region. Bent grasses, fine fescues, and ryegrasses are useful for winter overseeding of dormant warm-season turfs.

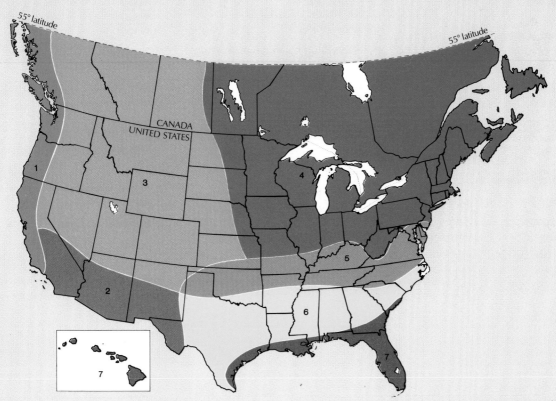

Rough-stalk Bluegrass

Poa trivialis
Cool season

Rough-stalk bluegrass is a bright green, fine-textured turf. Like Kentucky bluegrass, its blades have boat-shaped tips. A shallow-rooted grass, it does well in wet, shady areas. Some recommend its use in mixtures, but it may become weedy.

■ **Pluses:** Outstanding shade tolerance. Minimal fertilizer requirements.

■ **Minuses:** Needs ample amounts of water. Poor wearability. Can turn yellow during cool periods and develop brown spots in summer. Susceptible to fungal diseases. Can become a weed in wet soil.

■ **Regions:** Northern U.S. and Canada, and mountain and cool-weather areas of South and Southwest.

■ **Sun/Shade:** Outstanding shade tolerance.

■ **Water:** Requires frequent watering. Doesn't tolerate drought conditions.

■ **Wear:** Poor wearability.

■ **Planting Method:** Seed.

■ **Mowing:** Mow 1½ to 2 inches high.

■ **Fertilizer:** Apply ¼ to ½ pound actual nitrogen per 1,000 square feet each month during active growing period.

■ **Cultivars:** Colt, Laser, Sabre.

Centipede Grass

Eremochloa ophiuroides
Warm season

This light green, medium- to fine-textured grass spreads by stolons, crowding out weeds. Its root depth varies from shallow to deep.

■ **Pluses:** Does well in infertile or acidic soils. Requires little maintenance. Resistant to chinch bugs and rhizoctonia.

■ **Minuses:** Vulnerable to chlorosis. Poor wear and cold-weather tolerance; cold causes browning.

■ **Regions:** Southeastern U.S., Gulf Coast, and Hawaii.

■ **Sun/Shade:** Likes full sun but tolerates some shade.

■ **Water:** Requires frequent watering. Shallow-rooted varieties not drought tolerant.

■ **Wear:** Takes only light wear; shallow-rooted types damage easily.

■ **Planting Methods:** Seed, sod, sprigs, plugs.

■ **Mowing:** Mow 1 to 2 inches high.

■ **Fertilizer:** Apply less than ¼ pound actual nitrogen per 1,000 square feet during active growing period. Don't overfertilize.

■ **Cultivars:** Centennial, Centiseed, Oklawn.

Dichondra

Dichondra micrantha
Warm season

A perennial lawn plant or ground cover, dichondra is a soft, bright green, ground-hugging plant that behaves like a grass. It produces a lush mat of small, broad leaves that resemble miniature lily pads. Shallow rooted, it spreads by rooting surface runners.

■ **Pluses:** Looks thick and luxurious. Depending on desired appearance, can be mowed infrequently. Will tolerate heat and some shade.

■ **Minuses:** Needs ample amounts of water and constant vigilance against such pests as cutworms, flea beetles, snails, and slugs. Weeds are difficult to eradicate and can be invasive.

■ **Regions:** Mild-winter areas of western and southwestern U.S.

■ **Sun/Shade:** Likes full sun but tolerates some shade.

■ **Water:** Requires frequent, thorough watering, which encourages deep root growth and increases drought tolerance.

■ **Wear:** Tolerates ordinary lawn traffic, not heavy play.

■ **Planting Methods:** Seed, sod, plugs.

■ **Mowing:** Mow ¾ to 2 inches high.

■ **Fertilizer:** Apply ½ to 1 pound actual nitrogen per 1,000 square feet each month during active growing period.

Chewings Fescue

Festuca rubra commutata
Cool season

Chewings fescue is an aggressive, bunch-type fine fescue that can overtake other grasses. It's very tolerant of shade and mixes well with Kentucky bluegrass. Its roots grow to an intermediate depth.

■ **Pluses:** Good for overseeding shady areas of dormant Bermuda grass when mixed with perennial ryegrass. Excellent shade tolerance. Good drought tolerance.

■ **Minuses:** Vulnerable to fungal diseases during spells of hot, wet weather. Poor wearability; slow to reestablish after root damage.

■ **Regions:** Northern U.S. and Canada, and cooler elevations elsewhere. Particularly adapted to cool coastal areas of Northeast and Pacific Northwest.

■ **Sun/Shade:** Excellent shade tolerance.

■ **Water:** Not especially thirsty. Drought tolerant.

■ **Wear:** Takes only very light traffic.

■ **Planting Method:** Seed.

■ **Mowing:** Mow 1 to 2½ inches high.

■ **Fertilizer:** Apply ¼ to ½ pound actual nitrogen per 1,000 square feet each month during active growing period. Don't overfertilize.

■ **Cultivars:** Banner, Enjoy, Highlight, Jamestown, Longfellow, Mary, Shadow, Tamara, Victory.

Creeping Red Fescue

Festuca rubra rubra
Cool season

A fine-textured fescue, creeping red has narrow, dark green blades. It grows well on slopes and banks, creating a lush effect when not mowed. Planted alone, it grows in clumps; in mixtures, it compensates for weaknesses in other grasses. Roots grow to intermediate depth.

■ **Pluses:** Most shade tolerant of good lawn grasses. Where winter wear is limited, good for overseeding dormant warm-season grasses. Drought tolerant.

■ **Minuses:** Poor wearability; slow to recover when damaged. Vulnerable to fungal diseases during hot, wet weather. Spreads slowly.

■ **Regions:** Northern U.S. and Canada, and high elevations elsewhere. Good in cool coastal areas of Northeast and Pacific Northwest.

■ **Sun/Shade:** Excellent shade tolerance.

■ **Water:** Low to moderate watering needs; overwatering encourages disease. Drought tolerant.

■ **Wear:** Poor wearability.

■ **Planting Method:** Seed.

■ **Mowing:** Mow 1½ to 2½ inches high.

■ **Fertilizer:** Apply ¼ to ½ pound actual nitrogen per 1,000 square feet each month during active growing period. Don't overfertilize.

■ **Cultivars:** Boreal, Dawson, Ensylva, Flyer, Fortress, Illahee, Pennlawn, Pernille, Ruby, Shademaster.

Hard Fescue

Festuca longifolia
Cool season

A clumping, fine-textured grass, hard fescue grows more slowly than other fescues, requires little maintenance, and mixes well with other grasses. Its roots reach an intermediate depth.

■ **Pluses:** Excellent shade and drought tolerance; does well even in poor soil. Good disease resistance. Newer cultivars mow well.

■ **Minuses:** Some cultivars are difficult to mow evenly; shredded tips can discolor.

■ **Regions:** Northern U.S. and Canada, and high elevations elsewhere. Particularly adapted to cool coastal areas of Northeast and Pacific Northwest.

■ **Sun/Shade:** Excellent shade tolerance.

■ **Water:** Very drought tolerant. Don't overwater.

■ **Wear:** Moderate wearability. Clumps recover slowly from damage.

■ **Planting Method:** Seed.

■ **Mowing:** Mow 1½ to 2½ inches high.

■ **Fertilizer:** Apply ¼ to ½ pound actual nitrogen per 1,000 square feet during active growing period. Don't overfertilize.

■ **Cultivars:** Aurora, Reliant, Scaldis, Spartan, Tournament, Waldina.

Tough Turf for Play Surfaces

For most people, the scent of bruised grass brings on a flood of memories—twilight games of hide-and-seek, the absorbing joy of a close volleyball game, the crack of a bat followed by the lazy hiss of a grounder.

Turf is everyone's favorite activity surface. It's springy, resilient, and renewable, and it even smells good. Yet many lawns are underutilized because their owners think only about appearance, forgetting that grass can be hard-working and still look great.

Planning a play area. As you design your landscape, consider how best to use the different areas around your home. You may want to keep the portion visible to the outside world ornamental and use back or side sections for sport. Be sure to keep in mind the proximity of trees and shrubs to activity areas—shade will affect the grass choice, and overhanging branches can snare balls and birdies.

Durable and attractive, *perennial ryegrass stands up to wear, performs well on play surfaces.*

The choice of a grass variety or blend will depend on climate, sun-shade ratio, and, of course, the sport at hand. In general, any wear-resistant grass can do recreational duty, although some grasses are better for specific applications than others. For example, the fine texture of colonial bent grass makes it an excellent choice for a putting green, but any harder use would destroy it.

The most desirable quality in a sporting turf is the ability to rebound quickly from damage. Drought resistance, moderate thatch (for resilience), deep roots, and density are other desirable characteristics.

Best bets. Among the favorite turf grasses for athletic surfaces are warm-season Bermuda and zoysia grasses and cool-season perennial ryegrass.

■ *Bermuda grass* is perhaps the most widely adaptable athletic turf grass; it's used on baseball fields, golf course fairways, and football fields. Resistant to drought, pests, and disease, Bermuda grass is tough and deep rooted. Its major drawback is low shade tolerance.

■ *Zoysia grass* may be a better choice than Bermuda for shady yards. A heat-loving turf grass, zoysia is dense, fine textured, and drought tolerant. It wears almost as well as Bermuda grass but turns brown sooner in areas with cool fall weather.

■ *Perennial ryegrass,* a cool-season grass, is also a good choice for recreational use. It offers excellent wearability and moderate shade tolerance.

Other hard-working turf grasses. Other grasses work well in certain situations, although they may not be the most desirable types for athletic surfaces.

■ *Bahia grass,* a warm-season grass, has an expansive, deep root system. Because of this, it's good for unstable slopes or loose soils in large play areas. It tolerates a fair amount of shade and stays green longer than other warm-season grasses. However, it doesn't form a very dense turf, and the tall seed stalks require frequent mowing.

■ *Tall fescue* is a cool-season grass that can also be useful for unstable slopes or loose soils in large play areas. It stays green all year, is fairly tough, and tolerates moderate shade. Its clumping habit, however, can cause balls to take bad hops. Heavy play may wear down the grass enough to require annual reseeding.

Tall Fescue

Festuca arundinacea
Cool season

Tall fescue is a dense, clumping grass that stays green year-round. It's used for erosion control and athletic surfaces. Newer cultivars tend to be less coarse and more attractive than older ones and are used for lawns.

■ **Pluses:** More heat tolerant than other cool-season grasses. High water user but will survive drought conditions longer and better than bluegrass or perennial ryegrass. Some resistance to disease and pests.

■ **Minuses:** Some cultivars considered a fast-growing weed in mixtures. Clumping can result in an irregular surface in shade and during hot weather.

■ **Regions:** Transitional zones with mild winters and warm summers; in mild-temperature regions of Southwest.

■ **Sun/Shade:** Moderate shade tolerance.

■ **Water:** Needs infrequent, deep watering but does well under drought conditions.

■ **Wear:** Moderate wearability.

■ **Planting Methods:** Seed, sod.

■ **Mowing:** Mow 1½ to 2 inches high for athletic use; otherwise, mow 2 to 3 inches high.

■ **Fertilizer:** Apply ¼ to ½ pound actual nitrogen per 1,000 square feet during active growing period.

■ **Cultivars:** Adventure, Apache, Arid, Bonanza, Falcon, Jaguar, Olympic, Pacer, Rebel, Tempo, Trident.

Seashore Paspalum

Paspalum vaginatum
Warm season

This glossy, deep green, medium-textured grass is native to Australia. It was introduced to the United States as an alternative to Bermuda grass in dry coastal areas. A deep-rooted grass, it stays green in mild-winter climates.

■ **Pluses:** Spreads quickly but is easy to contain. Requires little maintenance. Tolerant of heat, drought, and salty soils. Resistant to pests.

■ **Minuses:** Browns during cold weather. Produces tough stems in late summer that turn brown after scalping (to avoid, don't feed from spring to fall).

■ **Regions:** Cool coastal areas of Southern California.

■ **Sun/Shade:** Likes full sun but tolerates some shade.

■ **Water:** Requires a moderate amount of water (more than Bermuda grass).

■ **Wear:** Good wearability.

■ **Planting Method:** Sod.

■ **Mowing:** Mow ¾ to 1 inch high.

■ **Fertilizer:** Apply ½ to ¾ pound actual nitrogen per 1,000 square feet each month during active growing period.

■ **Cultivars:** Adalayd (Excalibre), Futurf.

Annual Ryegrass

Lolium multiflorum
Cool season

Annual ryegrass, though coarse in texture, is used for overseeding dormant warm-season grasses, providing an attractive alternative to brown lawns from fall to late spring; most die out with heat. Roots are shallow.

■ **Pluses:** Germinates and establishes quickly. When mixed with slower-germinating varieties, it offers protection from wind and foot traffic while other varieties are becoming established.

■ **Minuses:** Clumping makes an uneven surface; rapid growth rate requires frequent mowing. Can become weedy. Intolerant of extremes in temperature. Requires frequent watering.

■ **Regions:** Good in transitional climate zones with mild winters and warm summers, and in South, Northeast, and Pacific Northwest.

■ **Sun/Shade:** Likes full sun. Poor shade tolerance.

■ **Water:** Moderate to high water requirement. Not drought tolerant.

■ **Wear:** Moderate wearability.

■ **Planting Method:** Seed.

■ **Mowing:** Mow 1½ to 2 inches high.

■ **Fertilizer:** Apply ¼ to ½ pound actual nitrogen per 1,000 square feet each month during active growing period.

■ **Cultivars:** Agree and Oregreen (hybrids of annual and perennial ryegrasses).

Perennial Ryegrass

Lolium perenne
Cool season

Shallow rooted with deep green, glossy blades, perennial ryegrass has a finer texture than annual ryegrass. Because it establishes itself quickly, it, too, is used to overseed warm-season lawns.

■ *Pluses:* Outstanding wearability. Fast germination and quick growth.

■ *Minuses:* Fibrous leaves on some cultivars tear when mowed, but improved cultivars mow cleanly. Can delay germination of other grasses. Sensitive to extreme cold and heat.

■ *Regions:* Cool-climate areas of Midwest and West, and coastal areas of Northeast.

■ *Sun/Shade:* Likes full sun but tolerates some shade.

■ *Water:* Requires frequent watering.

■ *Wear:* Excellent wearability.

■ *Planting Methods:* Seed, sod.

■ *Mowing:* Mow 1½ to 2 inches high.

■ *Fertilizer:* Apply ¼ to ½ pound actual nitrogen per 1,000 square feet each month during active growing period.

■ *Cultivars:* All Star, Birdie II, Blazer II, Dasher II, Derby, Diplomat, Fiesta, Gator, Loretta, Manhattan II, Omega II, Palmer, Pennant, Pennfine, Prelude, Regal, Tara, Yorktown II.

St. Augustine Grass

Stenotaphrum secundatum
Warm season

This deep-rooted, extremely coarse-textured grass with broad, dark green blades spreads rapidly by surface runners that root at the joints. New cultivars are finer textured.

■ *Pluses:* The most shade tolerant of all the warm-season grasses. Aggressive, crowds out most weeds. Tolerates steady traffic and salty conditions. Excellent heat resistance.

■ *Minuses:* Can produce heavy thatch. Some varieties susceptible to chinch bugs and St. Augustine grass decline (SAD) virus. Looks ragged in winter.

■ *Regions:* Coastal areas of Southeast, Gulf states, Florida, and Southern California.

■ *Sun/Shade:* Will grow in sun. Tolerates even dense shade well.

■ *Water:* Requires frequent watering.

■ *Wear:* Takes hard use.

■ *Planting Methods:* Sod, sprigs, plugs.

■ *Mowing:* Mow 1½ to 2 inches high; use a reel mower. If mowed too low, weeds can be a problem.

■ *Fertilizer:* Apply ½ to 1 pound actual nitrogen per 1,000 square feet each month during active growing period.

■ *Cultivars:* Bitter Blue, Floratine, Floratum, Seville, Sunclipse.

Zoysia Grass

Zoysia species
Warm season

Zoysia grass is fine textured with wiry blades. Deep rooted, it spreads slowly by creeping rhizomes and stolons to make a dense turf. Some cultivars make good play surfaces.

■ *Pluses:* Good resistance to most pests except billbugs; very good drought and heat tolerance. Very attractive when well tended.

■ *Minuses:* Slow to get established and propagate, although newer types spread faster. Goes dormant sooner than other warm-season grasses and may stay brown longer.

■ *Regions:* Southern U.S. coastal areas and Southern California.

■ *Sun/Shade:* Moderate shade tolerance.

■ *Water:* Low water requirement once established. Drought tolerant.

■ *Wear:* Good wearability.

■ *Planting Methods:* Sod, sprigs, plugs.

■ *Mowing:* Mow 1 to 2 inches high.

■ *Fertilizer:* Apply ¼ to ½ pound actual nitrogen per 1,000 square feet each month during active growing period.

■ *Cultivars:* Bel Air, El Toro, Emerald, Jade, Meyer, Midwest, Sunburst.

A Selection of Native Grasses

Native grasses, unlike the more commonly used turf grasses, are indigenous to North America. Because they haven't been bred for uniformity like the introduced species, they exhibit variations in height and color, and look more natural and informal in the landscape.

Although not used historically on lawns, native grasses are gaining in popularity because of their tolerance to drought and low maintenance requirements. They need to be watered from germination to establishment, but once established, require minimal watering, fertilizing, and mowing. They also help control wind and water erosion by stabilizing loose earth, so they're useful on hillsides and banks.

Native grasses are green only during their growing season, which can be rather short, and don't offer the high quality of the more traditional turf grasses.

Beach grass (Ammophila breviligulata) is an erect, hardy grass that grows well in coastal areas, on dunes and beaches, and in sandy, arid soils inland. It establishes deep roots and spreads widely by underground rhizomes. Its leaves are tough and coarse.

Blue grama (Bouteloua gracilis) is a hardy, pale green pasture grass with slightly fuzzy blades. It tolerates wide temperature fluctuations and thrives in the arid, windy areas of the Central Plains states. It's very drought tolerant and requires little maintenance.

Blue grama offers moderate wearability but recovers slowly from damage. It's slow to germinate and become established, and goes dormant in hot weather.

Buffalo grass (Buchloe dactyloides) has great potential as a lawn grass; current research in many areas of the country is yielding ever-improving cultivars that make buffalo grass competitive with many of the established turf grasses.

Buffalo grass is a pale, fine-textured prairie grass that germinates quickly and makes a dense sod. It survives intense heat but turns golden in winter. Other advantages that make buffalo grass a potential favorite include excellent drought tolerance, very good wearability, and low maintenance requirements. Because it only grows to 4 to 5 inches in height, it needs very little mowing.

Buffalo grass is indigenous to the prairie states and to Texas and Arizona, but it can be grown elsewhere. Because of its shallow roots, it does well where there are frequent, short afternoon rains. It grows well in alkaline soils but doesn't like sandy soils.

Crested wheatgrass (Agropyron cristatum), a light bluish green, medium-textured grass, grows well in mountainous areas and is used extensively for roadside erosion control in Colorado. It germinates fairly quickly and grows successfully in a wide range of climates, from extremely hot to below freezing. It prefers some moisture but will survive drought, and is adapted to alkaline soils.

Crested wheatgrass grows in thick clumps. It goes dormant and turns brown in hot weather.

Carpet of buffalo grass *survives on rainfall. A deep irrigation in spring greens it up; one in fall keeps it growing later in year.*

Planting a Lawn

Verdant, emerald green expanses of lawn are so commonplace in the landscape that it's hard not to take them for granted. In cities, they offer a restful contrast to the miles of paving that assault the eyes and bring special beauty to a hard-edged landscape. In small towns, they link structures one to another and contribute to a feeling of openness and warmth.

But it's important to remember that planting a lawn—whether you're starting from scratch or replacing an existing lawn—is a project that requires an investment of time and money, as well as a firm commitment to conscientious maintenance.

Is it worth it? You bet. Turf is beautiful, useful, and, if installed and maintained correctly, fully in keeping with the new spirit of water conservation. It will help to improve the quality of life for you and your family for many years to come.

In fact, preparing soil and planting grass is well within the ability of the average home owner who's willing to put some time and energy into the task. All of the steps, as outlined in this chapter, are straightforward and not difficult. As you read, remember that the two most important keys to success are good planning and attention to detail.

Getting Started

It's important to be realistic about the amount of time and money you're willing to spend on planting your lawn. Even if you decide to do most of the work yourself, you may want to call in a landscaping professional for advice on specific issues—for example, on the types of grasses that grow well in your local area. A professional can also advise you on how to deal with any grading or soil problems.

Working with Professionals

You can choose from a number of qualified lawn experts, including landscape architects, landscape designers, landscape contractors, nursery personnel, and professional gardeners. Most professionals can be hired on a limited or hourly basis.

Regardless of whom you approach, look for evidence that the person listens carefully to your ideas and problems and is responsive to them. It's always a good idea to ask for references and talk to former clients. Try to see some of the professional's work, if possible. It's also best to get more than one estimate if the cost will be significant.

If you hire someone to plant your lawn and do the necessary preparation work, you'll probably want to have a clear contract for specified services, including guarantees that your design will be followed and that work will be completed by a certain date. One way to ensure the promptness of the work is to include a per-day late penalty clause in the contract. Before the professional team begins work, check with your in-

(Continued on page 32)

Pallets of freshly cut sod await installation. With sod, you can transform bare earth into a lush green lawn in just a few hours.

A *Lawn Design Primer*

Grass is one of the most common plants in the landscape. By itself, a single grass plant seems innocuous and, in fact, rather plain. But there is strength in numbers. Thousands of plants together form one of our oldest friends—the grass lawn.

A lawn does more than cover up dirt. A cool green expanse of grass, with its uniform texture and color, bestows a polished look on any patch of ground. It makes the structures around it look better, too. There's a certain formality to a lawn that's pleasing to the eye as well as the senses.

You'll seldom have an opportunity to be so creative, or to enjoy such practical, long-term benefits from your creativity, as when you plan and design a new lawn and landscape, or remodel an old one. A vital, functioning landscape transcends mere decoration to become a unique expression of your personality and life-style.

Careful planning at the design stage is the key to achieving the effect that will make a difference between a plain lawn and one that is graceful, fits into the surrounding landscape, and meets your family's needs. Creating a good design takes attention to some basic design principles and clear thinking about your needs.

Basic Landscaping Principles

A lawn doesn't have to be a simple square or rectangle, with four perfectly straight sides. As the photographs in "Lawns in the Landscape" on pages 7–15 demonstrate, lawns and plantings can take different shapes. For example, you may want to design a nearly circular lawn surrounded by plantings, such as the one shown on the facing page. Or you can curve a lawn to follow the lines of a freeform swimming pool. Let your imagination—and good design sense—experiment with different shapes and sizes.

Keep in mind that whether you're planning a large, formal landscape or something much more modest, observing the four basic landscaping principles will ensure that your entire garden design is visually pleasing.

Unity. A unified landscape is all of one piece, rather than disjointed groupings and scatterings of features. No one element stands out; instead, all the parts work together.

Strong, observable lines and the repetition of geometric shapes contribute significantly to the unity of your landscape, as does simplicity—for example, using just a few harmonious colors and a limited number of plant varieties. Be prepared to give up the idea of having every one of your favorite plants around you and avoid designing too many distinct units that will have to be tied together.

Start with your lawn; think of it as a neutral element, a blank canvas on which you'll assemble your landscaping units to provide balance, proportion, and variety.

Balance. To balance a landscape is to use mass, color, or form to create equal visual weight on either side of a center of interest. In a formal landscape, balance may mean simply creating one side as a mirror image of the other.

In informal styles, balance is just as important, but more subtle: a large tree to the left of an entryway can be balanced by a grouping of smaller trees on the right. Likewise, you can balance a concentration of color in a small flower bed on one side of a lawn with a much larger and more diffuse mass of greenery on the other side.

Proportion. In a well-designed landscape, the various structural and plant elements are in scale with one another. Start with your house; it will largely determine proportion in your landscape. When choosing trees and shrubs, keep their ultimate sizes and shapes in mind.

Variety. Break up a monotonous landscape by selecting plants in a variety of shapes, shades, and textures; or add interest by juxtaposing different materials.

Designing for Practicality

As you think about the design of your lawn and plantings, try to be perfectly clear about what you want your landscape to give you, and what you're prepared to give it. Whatever you plant now will have to be maintained for many years to come. Don't make the mistake of sowing the seeds of a shade-intolerant grass in an area where the sun cannot easily penetrate. (For help in identifying the characteristics of various grasses, see the chapter beginning on page 17.)

Organizing space. Patterns of turf around your house can both accommodate and display other plants. Low and lush, grass is the perfect foil for flowering trees and shrubs, as well as for bright annuals or perennials. Grass also draws the eye around a landscape and is the perfect space organizer—you can shape it to help define an area or direct traffic around it.

Keep off the grass? If you have young children, don't think that you'll be able to keep them and the neighborhood kids off your lawn. Instead, choose a grass that will stand up to wear and recover quickly from injury or abuse. Likewise, if you expect to entertain frequently out-of-doors, make sure your grass can take the additional wear and tear.

Your natural environment. Don't try to fight your environment by choosing plantings that, although attractive, are unsuited to your microclimate.

Although soil can be amended and improved (as explained in this chapter) if it lacks certain nutrients or suffers from a bad grade or poor drainage, there's not much you can do if you live in an area where rainfall is scarce. With today's emphasis on water conservation, due in part to recurring drought conditions and in part to a simple shortage of water to serve increasing populations, choosing drought-tolerant grasses and plantings is essential. The availability of a myriad of grass cultivars means that you can plant a grass both you and your microclimate can live with.

Think also, while you're still in the planning stage, about your water delivery system (see pages 47–59). Now is the perfect time to put in an underground sprinkler system. Or are you satisfied to use a simple hose and hose-end sprinkler? If you're irrigating by hand, you may want to keep your lawn area small for ease of watering.

If towering trees dot your landscape, plant a grass type that's appropriate for the amount of shade they cast. Remember, too, that grass will compete with tree roots for available water and nutrients, so you may have to water more deeply and fertilize more often.

Thinking about lawn care. A lovely lawn need not make a slave of its owner. If you much prefer playing a set of tennis to mowing the front lawn, be selective about the type of grass you plant. Some require more frequent mowing than others.

The same is true of other gardening chores. Grasses that are disease and insect resistant will require less care than grasses that aren't. Fertilizer requirements vary, too.

Structural elements. Designing mowing strips and other edgings (see page 48) along the perimeter of your lawn will make lawn management easier. A mowing strip accommodates the wheels of your mower, enabling you to cut right to the edge of the grass and eliminating trimming chores.

Edgings neatly contain your lawn—and any plantings on the other side. If you plant a grass that grows by stolons, or runners, edgings will help keep growth within bounds.

Small circle of lawn *ringed by trees and low-growing plants offers shade and color, as well as play space. Landscape designer: Alan Rollinger.*

(Continued from page 29)

surance agent to find out who is liable in case of injury or property damage.

Most professional companies will require a deposit before they'll begin any work on your property, but before you make the final payment, be sure the job has been completed to your satisfaction.

The following professionals offer expertise in specialized areas.

Landscape architects hold one or more degrees in their field and are trained and often licensed to design both commercial and residential landscapes. Many are willing to offer you a simple consultation, either in their office or at your home, for a modest fee.

Landscape architects alone are licensed to prepare designs for a fee, which may be an hourly rate, a flat sum, or a percentage of construction costs.

Landscape designers usually limit themselves to residential landscape design. They're unlicensed and meet no specific educational requirements, although many are extremely skilled and experienced. In some states they're barred from certain kinds of structural designing.

Landscape contractors are trained, and in some states licensed, to install landscapes, including plantings, pavings, structures, and irrigation systems. Some also offer design services, which may be included in the total price of materials and installation. They can also interpret and implement the plans of a landscape architect.

Nursery personnel often provide design services, usually at no charge if you buy their plants. In addition, some nurseries have highly skilled personnel who are available for outside consultations or who are able to recommend good local professionals.

Professional gardeners may do everything from mowing and raking to planting and highly skilled maintenance; fees vary accordingly. There is no special training required for gardeners. In some states, gardeners are prohibited from

installing landscapes unless their fees fall below a certain limit.

Legal Considerations

Your city or county building department personnel can help you determine which codes and ordinances will affect your landscaping plans, and what permits and inspections are required. If you're simply planting a lawn, you probably won't need a permit.

Laying a Solid Foundation

As in any building project, constructing a solid foundation—in this case, a seedbed—is essential to creating a long-lasting lawn.

If you're replacing an existing lawn, you'll first have to remove the old grass. The most efficient way to do this is to use a sod cutter (available at most equipment rental stores). This machine slices just under the old lawn; you can then pick up the old grass and cart it away to a disposal site.

If you're starting your lawn from scratch, however, the first step involves grading your soil—moving soil so it's at the proper height and slope to ensure adequate drainage for the lawn.

Improving drainage by working with the soil to channel and collect excess water away from the lawn is the next step—and one that's often overlooked by gardeners preparing their own lawn seedbeds.

Here's a closer look at those steps. Even if you don't do this work yourself, it's important to understand the process so you can make sure the company you hire is doing it right.

Grading

The work of grading progresses hand-in-hand with the other aspects of install-

ing your landscape. Generally, you'll need to begin with rough grading, bringing the areas of your yard to the desired finished level. Then, after you've installed any underground watering system, you'll need to re-establish the rough grade. The final stage is the finish grading.

If the grading is simple and you have the time and inclination to do it, you can save money and have the satisfaction of having literally shaped the land you'll live with for years to come. But many special situations require that you obtain professional help or, at least, advice.

For example, if an area around existing trees is to be graded, call in a tree expert who understands how to grade without damaging the trees. If steep or unstable slopes are to be smoothed out, call in a landscape architect or civil engineer—someone who can foresee all the implications and who is familiar with legal requirements. In short, rely on the expertise of professionals for major grading of any unstable area.

If your landscape is nearly flat, be sure that it has adequate surface drainage: a minimum slope of nearly 3 inches per 10 feet of unpaved ground. A steeper gradient is better for slow-draining, heavy soils. Also be sure that runoff is directed away from adjacent property and toward a storm sewer or drainage ditch.

Before you start digging, check with your building department for any permits you may need. When you're digging, it's essential to know the location of any underground lines for gas, water, sewer, electricity, telephone, or other utilities. If your home isn't connected to a sewer, locate the septic tank and drainage field.

Rough Grading

The goal of rough grading is to remove or add enough soil in each area of your yard to bring the soil surface to the height and slope you want, thus ensuring proper water drainage.

Eliminating high spots. Excavate any high places in your yard so the level of the soil will be at the desired height and slope. When you dig, put the topsoil (usually the top 6 to 8 inches of soil) and subsoil in separate piles. You'll use them later for filling.

Filling low spots. Fill low spots in your yard by adding soil to bring the level up to the desired height and slope. Partially fill any deep holes with subsoil, leaving room for a final layer of topsoil so plants can grow. Use just topsoil to fill shallow areas.

Getting the Grade You Want

As you grade, you'll need a reliable method to ensure that you get the grade you want. During rough grading, you can simply estimate the grade visually; for greater accuracy, use a carpenter's level.

Visually estimating. Establishing the grade by "eye-balling" is often all that's required. Inspect the grade closely to be sure any slope goes in the proper direction—away from structures and toward areas where water can drain away without causing problems. Also look for high and low spots.

Estimating with a level. Using a level is more accurate than visually estimating. Set the level on an 8-foot-long 2 by 4 placed on the ground. With a tape measure, determine how far you have to raise one end of the board to center the bubble in the level. That way you can get a rough idea of how much the ground slopes.

Improving Drainage

Good drainage is vital for growing healthy lawns. Methods for solving drainage problems range from the relatively easy one of improving the composition of the soil to more complex solutions that include digging trenches or installing a drainage chimney, dry well, or catch basin.

Unless your lawn has obvious topographical problems, consider the simple solutions first.

Working with the Soil

Grading the soil for the proper slope, as explained at left, is a basic way to improve drainage. Sometimes, this will eliminate all drainage problems. But if you have a layer of hardpan, or tight, compacted soil, in your yard, you'll need to take more drastic action, as described on page 35.

Another way to ensure good drainage is to improve the texture of the soil itself by adding amendments to it (also see page 35).

Channeling Excess Water

Often, you can improve the drainage in one area by channeling excess water to another place for disposal. To channel water below the surface, use drainage trenches containing gravel or flexible drainpipes.

Before you begin digging, check for the location of any underground utilities. You'll probably be able to dig a trench up to about 2 feet deep yourself. Anything deeper may have to be excavated by a pipeline contractor.

Use a trench shovel and pick for digging; a trench shovel will keep the sides of the trench straight and square.

Gravel-filled trenches. These trenches can catch and channel excess water running off hillsides, roofs, and concrete paving around swimming pools.

Dig the trench a foot deep and 6 to 12 inches wide, depending on the volume of water to be handled. Fill the trench with gravel or small stones. Unless the trench is part of your lawn, don't cover it with soil.

Flexible drainpipes. Flexible plastic drainpipes are easy to install and effectively carry runoff water away from the yard. Dig a trench about 4 inches wider than the drainpipe's diameter and at least a foot deep; slant it at least 3 inches for every 10 feet of trench.

Put coarse gravel or small stones 2 inches deep in the trench and lay flexible pipe on top, as shown above, at right. If you use perforated pipe, lay it with

the drain holes to the side so soil won't seep in and clog the pipe. Fill the trench with gravel. If it's part of the lawn, cover it with a layer of soil.

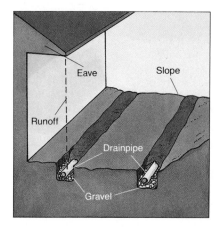

Flexible plastic drainpipes in gravel-filled trenches carry water away from lawn.

Collecting Excess Water

Drainage chimneys, dry wells, and catch basins aid drainage by gathering excess water and providing for its disposal.

Drainage chimneys let water pass through impervious soil layers to more fast-draining soil below. Dry wells allow water from drainpipes to settle slowly into the ground. The pipes from catch basins carry excess water to a disposal area, such as a storm drain.

Drainage chimneys. Use a posthole shovel or power posthole digger to dig 8- to 12-inch-wide holes spaced 2 to 4 feet apart down through poorly draining soil to gravel or sandy soil. Dig as many chimneys as you need. Fill each with small rocks or coarse gravel to let water pass through quickly.

Dry wells. Dig a 2- to 4-foot-wide hole 3 or more feet deep. (Keep the bottom of the hole above the water table.) Then dig trenches for drainpipes that will carry water into the dry well from other areas. Fill the dry well with coarse gravel or small rocks and cover with an impervious material, such as heavy roofing

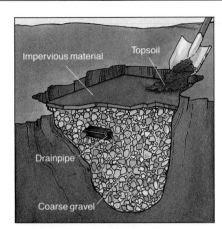

Dry well lets runoff water soak into fast-draining soil above water table.

mineral particles, as well as their relative number, chiefly determine the structure of the soil.

Clay particles are the smallest mineral component, sand particles the largest, and silt an intermediate size. Clay and sand give their names to two soil types. A combination of clay, sand, and silt forms the basis for the soil referred to as loam.

Clay soils. Also called adobe, gumbo, or just "heavy" soils, clay soils are composed of microscopically small mineral particles. These tiny particles are flattened and fit closely together. Spaces between particles (for air and water) are also small. But because small clay particles offer the greatest surface area per volume of all soil types, clay soils can contain the greatest volume of nutrients.

When clay soils get wet, drainage—the downward movement of water—is slow. This means that loss of soluble nutrients by leaching also is slow. And because of its high density, clay soil is the slowest to warm in spring.

To test for a clay or claylike soil, pick up a handful of wet soil and shape it into a ball. Clay will feel slippery; when you let it go, it won't crumble (as shown below), and if you squeeze it, it will ooze through your fingers in ribbons.

Sandy soils. Sandy soils are the opposite of clay: particles are bigger and are rounded rather than flattened, allowing for larger pore spaces between particles than clay soils have. Consequently, sandy soils contain a lot of air, drain well, and warm quickly.

In a given volume of sandy soil, the surface area of particles is less than that in the same volume of clay. The volume of soluble and exchangeable nutrients in sandy soil is therefore correspondingly less. And because sandy soil drains quickly and hence leaches out nutrients faster than clay, plants need watering and fertilizing more often than those in clay soils.

If you squeeze a handful of moist sandy soil into a ball, it will form a cast but barely hold together.

Loam. Loam, a gardener's term for soil intermediate between clay and sand, contains a mixture of clay, sand, and silt particles. In addition, loam is well supplied with organic matter. Considered the ideal gardening soil, loam drains well (but doesn't dry too fast), leaches only moderately, and contains enough air for healthy root growth.

If you pick up a handful of loam, it will form a pliable ball that breaks apart with a gentle prod.

paper; conceal with topsoil, as shown above.

Catch basins. To drain water from a low-lying area, dig a hole for a catch basin at the lowest point. Then dig a trench from the hole for a drainpipe that will carry the water to a disposal place, such as a storm drain.

Either set a ready-made concrete catch basin (available at building supply stores) into the hole and fill in with soil, or form and pour the concrete base and sides yourself. Set a grate on top.

Preparing the Soil

An understanding of your soil is perhaps the most important aspect of growing a healthy lawn. This knowledge will guide you in planting your lawn, as well as in watering and caring for it.

Once grass is established, you can aerate and fertilize it, but the actual soil base can't be reworked without a major renovation. Carefully prepared soil provides a strong foundation for your lawn.

Soil Types

Soil is a mass of mineral particles mixed with air, water, and living and dead organic matter. The size and form of the

Moist clay soil, formed into a smooth ball, doesn't crumble when you let it go.

Soil Problems & Remedies

Although an amazing variety of soils support thriving lawns, many were not always so hospitable to the plants they now host.

The best way to determine what nutrients your soil needs is to run a soil test. This will tell you how much nitrogen, phosphorus, and potash you need to add to your soil, as well as its pH balance. Physical problems, such as shallow soil, will be visible to the naked eye.

Testing Your Soil

You can have a professional laboratory test your soil, or you can do it yourself with a home test kit (available at most lawn-care centers). Professional soil tests are more accurate and extensive, but they're also more expensive. To find a professional testing center, ask your County Cooperative Extension office.

Gather the soil to be tested from at least four different areas in your yard; dig to a depth of 2 to 3 inches. Mix the soil together before testing it or sending it to the laboratory.

Do-it-yourself kits are easy to use; they involve gathering soil samples and mixing them in test tubes with special solutions provided in the kit. Most kits come with a color chart against which you measure the color of the soil-solution mixture. Often, you'll have to estimate for shades between the colors shown on the color chart.

Chemical Problems

These conditions—acidity, alkalinity, and other related problems—are invisible to the gardener's eye but are revealed by poor plant performance.

Acid soil (pH 6.9 and lower) is most common in regions where rainfall is heavy; it's often associated with sandy soils and soils high in organic matter. Most plants grow well in mildly acid soil, but high-acid soil is inhospitable.

Add lime to such soils only if a soil test indicates that it's needed and only in the quantity recommended by a local expert. If you attempt to raise your soil's pH with lime, be sure that any fertilizers you use thereafter do not have an excessive acid reaction.

Alkaline soil (pH 7.1 and higher), common in regions with light rainfall, is high in calcium carbonate (lime) or certain other minerals, such as sodium. Many plants grow well in moderately alkaline soil; others will not thrive there because the alkalinity reduces availability of elements necessary for their growth.

If a soil test shows that your soil is highly alkaline, liberal additions of such organic amendments as peat moss, ground bark, or sawdust (see page 36) or fertilization with acid-type fertilizers

can help decrease alkalinity. For soil with a very high pH, use soil sulfur.

Salinity is an excess of salts in the soil. These salts may be naturally present in the soil, or they may come from water (especially softened water, which has a high sodium content), from fertilizers and chemical amendments, or from manures with high salt content.

Where these salts are not leached through the soil by heavy rainfall or deep irrigation, they reach high concentration in the root zone, inhibiting germination of seeds and stunting growth.

Periodic, thorough leaching of the soil with water will reduce its sodium content. But to carry out this leaching, drainage must be good.

Chlorosis is a systemic condition in which newer grass growth turns yellow. The condition is usually caused by a deficiency of iron.

Iron deficiency is only occasionally the result of a lack of iron in the soil; more frequently, it's due to high alkalinity, poor drainage, or some other substance (usually lime) making the iron unavailable to the plant. To correct chlorosis, treat the soil with iron sulfate; or use iron chelate, which has the ability to hold iron in a form that's available to plantings.

Nutrient deficiency may be the problem if the soil drains well, has ample water and the proper pH, yet still has failed to sustain plant growth well. It's most likely that nitrogen is missing from the soil. For information on combatting nutrient deficiency, see "Lawn Fertilizers," page 63.

Physical Problems

The most common physical soil problem is drainage. (Grading and more complex solutions for getting rid of excess water are described on pages 32–34.) But more often, poor soil conditions lie at the root of drainage problems.

Shallow soil (hardpan). A tight, impervious layer of soil, called hardpan,

can cause problems if it lies at or near the surface. Such a layer can be a natural formation or man-made, such as when builders spread excavated subsoil over the surface and then drive heavy trucks or bulldozers over it. If the subsoil has a clay content and is damp, it can take on a bricklike hardness when it dries.

A thin layer of topsoil may conceal hardpan, but roots cannot penetrate the hard layer, and water cannot drain through it. Grass will fail to grow, be stunted, or die.

Whatever the cause, time spent in correcting the problem at the outset will pay long-range dividends. The best method of dealing with a thick layer of hardpan is to scarify the soil, that is, rip it to a depth of about 18 inches with a chisel-toothed plow. This is work performed by a professional and only if the area is large and the problem severe.

If the hardpan layer is thin, you may be able to improve the soil by having it plowed to a depth of 12 inches or more.

Adding new soil. If you're adding soil to fill in low spots or raise the level of your lawn area, don't add it as a single layer on top of existing soil. Instead, add a portion of new soil (up to half, depending on projected new depth) and mix it thoroughly with existing soil by spading or rotary-tilling. Then add the remaining new soil to bring the level up to the desired height and mix it thoroughly into the previously tilled soil.

This extra work prevents the formation of an "interface"—a dividing-line barrier between two dissimilar soils that can slow or stop the downward movement of water.

If you purchase topsoil, try to find material that closely approximates your existing soil. Look for crumbly texture and avoid very fine-textured clays and silts. Try to steer clear of saline soils and soil that contains seeds of noxious weeds or residue from herbicides.

Amending the Soil

Adding organic or inorganic (mineral) amendments to your soil before plant-

Organic or natural-material amendments, *tilled into soil before planting, improve soil composition, resulting in healthy plant growth. Among popular choices are commercial compost, shown at left, which typically consists of sludge mixed with wood by-products; aged sawdust, in center, which won't steal nitrogen from soil the way raw sawdust does; and aged redwood sawdust, at right, the longest-lasting sawdust product.*

ing improves soil quality, encouraging healthy root growth. (A soil test, as described on pages 34–35, will indicate which nutrients are present or needed.) Typically, an inch-thick layer of amendment (about 3 cubic yards per 1,000 square feet of soil) is added.

Organic Amendments

Vital to the fertility of all soils—and particularly needed in sand and clay—is organic matter, the decaying remains of once-living plants and animals.

Organic soil amendments immediately improve aeration and drainage of clay soils by acting as wedges between particles and particle aggregates. In sandy soil, organic amendments help hold water and dissolved nutrients in the pore spaces, so the soil will stay moist and hold dissolved nutrients longer.

As the organic matter decomposes, it releases nutrients, which add to soil fertility. But the nitrogen released by decaying matter isn't immediately available to plants. First, it must be converted by soil microorganisms (bacteria, fungi, and molds) into ammonia, then into nitrites, and finally into nitrates, which can be absorbed by the roots of the plants.

The microorganisms that do this converting are living entities themselves and need a certain amount of warmth, air, water, and nitrogen in order to live and carry on their functions. Soil amendments, by improving aeration and water penetration, also improve the efficiency of those organisms in making their nitrogen available.

The final product of the action by soil bacteria and other organisms on organic materials is the creation of humus. By binding minute clay particles into larger units, or "crumbs," this soft, sticky material improves aeration and drainage. And in sandy soil, humus remains in pore spaces and helps hold water and nutrients.

Types of organic amendments. Even the best of soils will benefit from the application of an organic amendment. Included among organic soil amendments are weed-free compost and manure, sawdust and wood shavings, ground bark, peat moss, leaf mold, and many other plant by-products, such as rice hulls and hay.

Several examples of organic amendments are shown above.

When you add organic amendments to your soil, be generous and mix them in deeply and uniformly. The mixing will add some air to the soil, and the amendments will help keep it there.

Cautions. The organisms that break down organic materials need nitrogen. If they cannot get all that they require from the organic material itself, they'll draw upon any available nitrogen in the soil, stealing the nitrogen vital to root growth; the result can be a temporary nitrogen depletion and reduced plant growth.

Most organic amendments either naturally contain enough nitrogen to satisfy the soil organisms or have been nitrogen fortified. But if you're using raw wood shavings or a similar noncomposted, low-nitrogen amendment, you'll need to add nitrogen.

After application, use 1 pound of ammonium sulfate for each 1-inch-deep layer of undecomposed organic material spread over 100 square feet. A year later, apply half as much ammonium sulfate, and in the third and fourth years, use a quarter as much.

Inorganic Amendments

Various inorganic soil amendments may be useful in special situations. But because they provide no nourishment for soil microorganisms, they're no substitute for organic amendments. Use inorganic materials only to supplement organic amendments when a specific need arises.

Included under inorganic amendments are lime and gypsum, both sold as fine powder or granules to be scattered over the soil surface and dug or tilled in. Although lime is the traditional remedy for raising the pH of overly acid soils, both lime and gypsum may improve some clay soils by causing the tiny clay particles to group together into larger "crumbs." This creates more space between particle aggregates, with a corresponding improvement in aeration and drainage.

Which material you use depends on the pH of your soil. Where soil is high in sodium, applications of gypsum will react with the sodium and clay particles to produce the larger soil "crumbs." If your soil is acid, lime will be useful.

Lime will add calcium to soil, and gypsum furnishes both calcium and sulfate; either material may be used as a nutrient supplement in soil deficient in those minerals.

Before using either lime or gypsum, check with your County Cooperative Extension office for advisability and guidelines.

Applying Amendments

Before you add any amendments, analyze the moisture content of the soil by picking up a handful and compressing it. If the soil crumbles to powder, it's too dry to work; soak it deeply, wait a few days for it to dry out, and test again. If the soil sticks together in a solid lump, it's too wet; in this case, wait for it to dry out and test it again. If it breaks apart into small clumps, it has the right moisture content and can be prepared.

If you're adding bulk amendments, use a shovel and wheelbarrow to make piles throughout the yard. Then rake them over the entire surface in an even layer 2 to 4 inches deep. Finally, evenly scatter fertilizer and, if necessary, a soil modifier such as lime or gypsum.

Although you can dig in soil amendments by hand using a sharp, square-edged spade, a power tiller (available at lawn-equipment rental outlets) is the tool of choice when you have a large area to cultivate.

Start by tilling in one direction; when you've tilled the entire area, make another run at right angles to the first direction. Dig up a spadeful of soil to see if the amendments are well combined. If necessary, till one or two more times to make certain the amendments and soil are thoroughly mixed.

Final Soil Preparation

Once you've completed the preliminary steps—grading, improving drainage, and amending the soil—you're ready for the installation of any underground watering system and for final grading.

Underground irrigation systems. When properly installed and operated, an in-ground irrigation system conserves water and is a far more efficient way to deliver water to your new lawn than is a hose-end sprinkler. You can have a professional install your system, or you can do it yourself. (For complete instructions, turn to pages 51–58.) No matter who does the work, it's most efficient to install the system just prior to the finish grading.

Finish grading. The goal of finish grading is to make the surface smooth enough for planting. After rough grading and tilling, the soil may be uneven, with shallow mounds and ruts in places. Use a leveler to smooth out the surface and make it even.

Finally, rake the soil, removing any debris, stones, or large clumps of soil the rake turns up. Then use the back side of the rake to smooth the surface of the soil and level it out.

Putting in Edgings

Edgings, whether made from wood, brick, or concrete, separate your lawn from other landscape elements and give a finished look to the areas they surround. They can even add decorative accents without distracting from the main focal point. Edgings are also helpful in keeping any surrounding ground cover or other plantings from invading your lawn, and vice versa.

Install lawn edgings after you've prepared the soil and re-established the rough grade.

A very practical edging you may want to consider is a mowing strip that separates the lawn from adjoining surfaces. The strip neatly contains the turf and also provides a surface for mower wheels so the blades can easily trim the edge of the grass. (For an example of a mowing strip, see the photograph on page 63.)

Mowing strips can be made from brick, poured concrete, or masonry blocks. Wood is the least-used material for mowing strips because it can be easily damaged by the mower.

Wood Edgings

Wood is a popular and easy material to use for edgings. It's best to use Construction Heart redwood or Select cedar, but remember that these labels don't always guarantee quality. Avoid redwood containing streaks of lighter sapwood, as well as cedar with large knots. Pressure-treated fir is another long-lasting alternative, but make sure the boards have been commercially treated.

For straight edgings, use solid 2-by lumber; for curves, use benderboard.

Solid-lumber edgings. Using a mason's line stretched tightly between stakes, dig a narrow trench deep enough so the top of the edging will be flush with the ground and any adjacent paving. To join boards for a long edge, either splice them with 2-foot lengths of 1 by 4s or 2 by 4s, or butt the boards at a stake and nail them when you set them in the trench.

Try to offset the splicing boards slightly so that they won't be visible on the part of the edging that shows above the ground.

Set the board on edge in the trench and drive 12-inch-long stakes (1 by 2s,

2 by 2s, or 1 by 3s) into the soil alongside the board, no more than 4 feet apart. The stakes should be slightly higher than the edging. (Place all the stakes on the side away from the lawn so they won't interfere with the use of an edging tool later on.)

Nail the stakes to the edging board, bracing the board from behind with a heavy hammer head or crowbar (this will also clinch the nails). To keep boards from splitting, blunt the nails or drill pilot holes.

Saw off the stakes at a 45° angle so the tip of each stake is level with the top of the edging board, as shown below, at left. Replace the soil and tamp it; it should be level with the top of the edging.

Benderboard. Perfect for gentle curves, benderboard is thin and flexible, usually ⅜ inch thick by 4 inches wide. To determine the arc of your curve, use a homemade string compass, as shown in the inset below, marking the line with a sprinkling of agricultural lime.

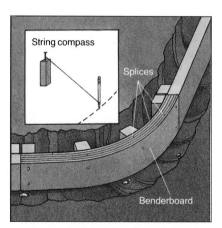

Layer benderboard to form curved edging; determine arc with a string compass (see inset).

Dig a narrow trench as described for solid-lumber edgings (see at left). Then drive in 12-inch-long stakes every 3 feet or so (the stakes should be slightly higher than the edging will be) to mark the inside of the curve.

Soak the benderboard in water, bend it around the stakes, and nail it in place, unless the stakes are on the lawn side of the edging. In that case, clamp the bend-

erboard to them instead of nailing, since you don't want stakes on the lawn side to stay in place permanently.

Bend additional boards around the outside of the first board, staggering any splices, until you've built up the curved edging to the same thickness as your straight edging. (If your inside stakes are just temporary, drive and nail stakes along the outside board.)

Don't try to force the benderboards into sharp curves—some boards will bend more easily than others, but a 6-foot radius is about as tight as you can get without breaking the boards.

Nail all thicknesses of boards together between stakes to keep them from warping or separating and pull out any temporary stakes on the inside of the curve. Saw off the stakes and fill the trench as described for solid-lumber edgings.

Masonry Edgings

Masonry makes a strong, permanent edging. You can install either a simple brick-in-soil edging or one made from concrete.

Brick-in-soil edgings. Very firm earth is required to hold these edgings in place.

To install, mark off and dig a narrow trench. Then simply place the bricks side by side, on end, in the trench. Use a bubble level to get the tops even. You can bury the bricks completely so their ends will be flush with your finished lawn. Or you can tilt the bricks at a 45° angle to give a sawtooth effect.

After the edging is set, pack soil tightly and firmly against the bricks.

Concrete edgings. Excellent for areas where your lawn borders a paved patio or driveway, these edgings are made from poured concrete.

To install such an edging, dig a trench and line the bottom with gravel. Around it, construct a temporary wood form that's your desired width and as high as the adjoining pavement. Pour concrete into the form and use a screed to level it. Cure the concrete for at least 3 days

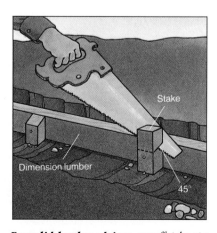

For solid-lumber edgings, saw off stakes at a 45° angle so tips are level with top of edging.

How to Read a Grass Seed Label

The label on a grass seed package is your key to choosing a high-quality seed. It can also help you avoid a product that could actually damage your lawn. A good sack of seeds is one that has your preferred seed type, a high percentage of germination, and a low percentage of crop seed, inert matter, and weed seed. There should be no noxious weed seed.

The label below, at right, describes a typical grass seed mixture. Here's how to interpret it.

Grass Seed Type

Grasses are separated into two basic groups, fine and coarse textured. Fine-textured grasses are bluegrass, fine fescue, Bermuda grass, perennial ryegrass, and bent grass. All other grasses, including tall fescue and annual ryegrass, are considered coarse textured.

Some gardeners prefer fine-textured grasses because they provide an esthetically pleasing lawn. If you want a fine-textured, picture-perfect lawn, look for a mixture in which fine-textured grasses account for more than 50 percent of the mix. (The mix percentage should be clearly marked on the label.) Whenever coarse-textured grass is included in a mix, it should be between 40 and 50 percent of the total; otherwise, your lawn will not have an even texture.

Cultivars will be stated; these varieties have been specially developed for color, texture, drought tolerance, or disease resistance and are usually an indication of quality.

Mix percentages. The seed mixture percentages listed on the label can be misleading. Remember that these percentages are according to weight—not number of seeds.

For example, there are about 230,000 annual ryegrass seeds per pound and about 2.2 million Kentucky bluegrass seeds per pound. Therefore, if the percentage on the label indicates the seed package holds 50 percent annual ryegrass and 50 percent Kentucky bluegrass, you'll actually be purchasing nearly 10 times more Kentucky bluegrass seed than annual ryegrass seed.

Germination. The germination percentage, listed with the seed type, must also be factored into the equation. The percentage of germination represents the portion of seed that will germinate under optimum conditions. To determine a seed sack's real seed mixture, multiply the germination percentage by the percent of the grass type.

Be aware that the older the seed, the lower the percentage of actual germination. Check the package for the "test" and "sell by" dates.

Other Ingredients

The items listed under this heading are potential troublemakers. It's not always possible to keep these to a "zero" percentage, but in cases of crop seed, weed seed, and noxious weeds, try to get seed containers with as close to "zero" percentage as you can.

Crop seed. Usually listed first, crop legally is anything grown commercially by a farmer. Crop can be more of a problem in a lawn than weeds, since any chemical control you might use to kill certain crops could kill your grass, too. Crop can also include other turf grasses that might spoil the color or texture of your lawn.

Inert matter. This is simply filler, chaff, ground corn cobs, leaves, or even sand. It's generally harmless, but it should total no more than about 3 percent.

Weed seed. These are seeds from plants that don't belong in your yard. Again, the lower the percentage of weed seed, the better. Every grass seed package will contain a few weed seeds because of the harvesting techniques used in producing the seeds, but most of these weeds can't tolerate regular mowing and will be eradicated in a few months.

Noxious weeds. In most areas, it's illegal to sell seed that contains some noxious weeds—and for good reason. These can be highly invasive. Insist on a label that says "no noxious weeds."

A Typical Grass Seed Label

Fine-textured Grasses:	Origin	Germination
49.09% Pennant Perennial Ryegrass	Oregon	90%
24.68% Enjoy Chewings Fescue	Oregon	90%
24.41% Newport Kentucky Bluegrass	Oregon	85%
Coarse kinds: None		

Other Ingredients:

0.06% Other crop	1.73% Inert matter
0.03% Weed seed	No noxious weeds

by covering it with straw, burlap, or plastic sheeting to keep it moist.

Planting from Seed

Growing grass from seed not only provides you with the satisfaction of having started your lawn yourself, but also is much less expensive than laying sod. (For a comparison between seed and sod, see page 44.) Since the seed you plant will provide the foundation for your lawn in the years ahead, buy the highest-quality grass seed you can.

Choosing Grass Seed

The seed you select is crucial to the success of your new lawn. Your choice will depend on many factors, among them the availability of water, the proportion of sun and shade on your lawn, local climate conditions, and even how you plan to use your lawn.

Grasses are categorized as cool season or warm season. Most cool-season grasses can withstand winter cold, but many types languish during hot, dry summers. Warm-season grasses, on the other hand, grow vigorously during hot weather and go dormant in cool or cold weather. Note that many warm-season grasses are only grown from sod, sprigs, or plugs. Bahia and centipede grasses and many varieties of Bermuda are also available as seed.

Grass seed is sold straight, in a blend, or as a mixture. A straight is when only one species of grass is present. A combination of improved varieties of the same species is called a blend. When seeds have been combined from different grass species, it's called a mixture. To learn how to read a grass seed label, turn to page 39.

For information on the grasses that grow well in your locale, it's best to consult a local lawn expert. The three best sources are reputable garden centers, your County Cooperative Extension office, and professional landscapers. A comprehensive description of the most common turf grasses begins on page 19.

How Much Seed Do You Need?

The amount of seed you need for planting varies according to the type of grass you choose and your local environment. Read the seed container carefully—the amount of seeds per pound in various mixes and blends can vary considerably.

The label will often indicate how much area the seeds will cover on either a new lawn or an established one. Or it may tell you—usually in pounds of seed per 1,000 square feet of lawn—how many pounds are required.

Sowing Seed

The best time to plant grass seed in most areas is in the fall, early enough so that the grass has enough time to get established before having to face the rigors of cold weather. The next best time is the spring, after all chance of frost has passed and before the weather turns hot. Outlined below are the steps in the planting sequence. They're illustrated on the facing page.

Step 1: Seeding. Pick a windless day for sowing and sow seed as evenly as possible; a spreader or mechanical seeder will help. (If the seedbed is dry, irrigate and let the top inch of soil dry out before sowing any seeds.)

If you hand-scatter seeds, sow half of them as you walk across the area and the other half as you walk at right angles to the first route. Scatter the seeds at the rate that's recommended on the label of the package.

Step 2: Fertilizing. Using a mechanical spreader, apply a lawn fertilizer evenly over the surface of the new lawn, following the directions on the fertilizer bag. Don't use a fertilizer that's combined with a weed killer or weed preventer; otherwise, the grass seed will not grow.

Step 3: Raking. Use a steel rake to lightly scratch the seeds into the soil; don't stir the seed deeply, and don't try to cover every seed with soil. Then level the soil, if necessary.

Step 4: Mulching. If you expect hot, dry weather or drying winds, put down a thin, moisture-holding mulch, such as peat moss or screened, aged sawdust. To keep peat moss from blowing away (and to overcome its reluctance, when dry, to take up water), soak, knead, and pulverize it first. After mulching, roll the surface with an empty roller to press seed into contact with the soil.

Step 5: Watering. Water thoroughly, taking care not to wash out the seed, and then keep the seedbed moist with frequent but short irrigations until all the grass is sprouted. This may require watering 5 to 10 minutes each day (two or three times a day during warm periods) for up to 3 weeks.

You can use an underground watering system to do the job. Hand-sprinkling is difficult because you may have to walk on the new lawn; also, water distribution may be uneven.

Step 6: Mowing. Before mowing, check that your mower blades are sharp and the sod is dry enough so that the wheels of the mower will not tear the turf. For mowing instructions for a new lawn, see page 63.

Hydroseeding

This increasingly popular method of planting grass, a "one-step" operation, is now offered by most commercial landscaping companies. A selected combination of grass seed, fertilizer, and fiber mulch is mixed with water and shot through a hose onto your lawn. By applying all these elements at one time, hydroseeding can save you time and effort if you're planting a large area.

Hydroseeding costs more than planting from seed but less than planting sod. Like planting from seed, hydroseeding should be done in the fall or spring.

Seeding a New Lawn

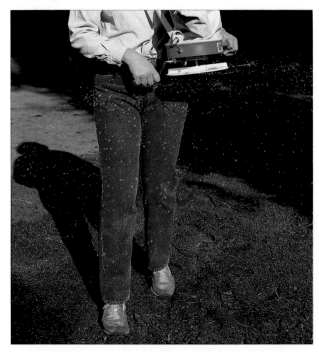

Sow grass seed *as evenly as possible over lawn area, using a broadcast spreader (as shown) or a mechanical seeder; or sow seeds by hand. Do not seed on a windy day.*

After sowing grass seed, *spread recommended lawn fertilizer over entire area, following directions on fertilizer bag. Be careful to apply fertilizer evenly.*

Using a steel rake, *lightly rake area, scratching grass seed into soil. Try not to disturb soil grade; if necessary, gently level surface.*

Spread a thin mulch *over surface, if necessary to protect newly seeded lawn against effects of dry weather.*

If soil has been mulched, *roll entire area with an empty roller to press grass seed into contact with soil.*

If you choose to have your lawn hydroseeded, make sure the company that does the job knows exactly what type of grass and fertilizer you want on your lawn. Both cool-season and warm-season grasses can be planted by hydroseeding, since both seeds and sprigs (see page 44) can be "shot" from the hydroseeder's hose.

Putting Down Sod

Laying sod allows you to perform landscaping magic. In just a few hours, you can convert bare soil into sparkling turf. Sodding is, essentially, the transplanting of living grass with some roots attached. The sod is rolled out on your prepared seedbed much like a carpet is rolled out on a bare floor.

Unlike seed lawns, a sod lawn can be installed almost any time of the year and will establish itself within 2 weeks. It's more expensive than sowing seeds, but it provides an instant green cover that's just as long-lasting as grass planted from seed. (For a comparison between seeding and sodding, see page 44.)

The relatively high cost of purchasing sod makes it important that you shop carefully for the right sod and the right grass variety. You also must determine how much sod you need and take care to install it correctly.

You can purchase sod through a nursery or directly from a sod grower. If you don't have a favorite nursery, look in the Yellow Pages under "Sod & Sodding Service."

Shopping for Sod

Whether you order directly from a sod farm or go through a nursery, find out how long the sod company has been in business. If the nursery has repeatedly ordered sod from the same company and has received no complaints, that's probably a good sign. Reputable sod producers guarantee the quality of their product and offer advice on how to plant and care for a new lawn.

Laying a Sod Lawn

Thoroughly incorporate amendments into soil with a power tiller. Clean surface of any roots, weeds, or rocks. Then scatter fertilizer, roll, and level soil.

Unfold sod strips and lay them brick-bond fashion, pressing edges tightly together. Soil should be moist but not wet when strips are laid.

Using a heavy, sharp knife, cut sod smoothly around sprinkler heads, along adjoining surfaces, and around trees or other obstructions.

Use a roller half-filled with water to press sod roots firmly against soil. Water every day (more often if weather is hot) for 6 weeks.

What to look for. One of the main differences between good and bad sod growers is weed and disease control. The good ones maintain very high standards in the field and supply sod that's virtually free of weeds and pests. Ask if the soil has been fumigated.

To check the quality of sod, unroll a few pieces. The sod should be moist, not dry or dripping wet. It's generally about an inch thick, but that can vary widely. Just make sure that it's an even thickness from one end to the other.

The sod should also be freshly cut. If you're in doubt, reach into the middle of a pile of sod. If the sod feels hot, it may not be suitable to use.

Pieces should be cleanly cut, not shaggy. They should be moist so they mesh readily when installed. You should also see root activity on the soil side.

Next, check the grass blades. They should be dense, like a dark green carpet, and be mowed to a uniform length. Poke around in the blades; if the sod is infested with grass weeds, you may find seed heads, even if it's been mowed short.

Plastic netting is used by some sod growers to reduce the time needed for a harvestable crop. Since it holds grass and soil together, netting also allows growers to cut sod thinner and so, they claim, root into your soil faster.

For home gardeners, netting may be a nuisance. Where the grass wears thin in shady areas or where the mower cuts too deeply, netting can become exposed, tangle mowers, or catch shoes. If you're using a sod with netting, make sure the soil is perfectly level before you plant. Otherwise, high spots will soon wear thin and expose the netting.

Choosing a variety. Depending on the supplier and your climate, you can choose from many kinds of turf. For information on the grass types that are available as sod, see the grass descriptions beginning on page 19.

Most suppliers offer purebred sods, which are strictly one type of grass. Although not as common as purebred sods, mixtures are also available.

Sod raised at a sod farm near your home usually has a better chance of doing well in your yard than sod from a different environment.

How much do you need? Determining the amount of sod you will need is simple. Just measure the size of your lawn to determine the square footage and buy that amount of sod, plus about 10 percent more to be on the safe side.

Sod generally comes in strips from 5 to 9 feet long. Each strip typically weighs about 30 pounds.

Ordering sod. Arrange to pick up sod or have it delivered the morning you intend to lay it. If the sod sits around too long, the grass starts to yellow and go shaggy. It will probably recover, but the lawn will be weak and slow to become established.

Laying Sod

Before you can install a sod lawn, the seedbed must be properly prepared (see pages 32–40). This work must be done in advance of purchasing the sod, because once the sod arrives at your home, it should be installed immediately.

The finished grade before installing sod should be 1 inch below the surrounding surfaces. The turf farm where you purchase the sod may recommend adding fertilizer before the sod is rolled out; the farm normally will provide the correct fertilizer.

The steps for laying sod are described below and are shown on pages 42–43.

Step 1: Soil preparation. After adding amendments and thoroughly working them into the soil, scatter fertilizer (if required), rolling it with a roller half-filled with water. Level soil again to 1 inch below surrounding surfaces.

Step 2: Laying strips. On moist soil, lay the sod strips brick-bond fashion, pressing the edges tightly together.

Step 3: Trimming sod. Use a heavy knife to cut sod around trees, sprinkler heads, and lawn edges. Make sure that cut edges fit snugly.

Step 4: Rolling the lawn. Roll the entire lawn with a roller half-filled with water to smooth out rough spots and press the roots of the sod firmly against the soil.

Step 5: Watering. Water daily (more often if the weather is hot) for 6 weeks.

Sprigging

Also called stolons or runners, sprigs are pieces of grass stem and root that are used to start lawns in place of seeds or sod. In fact, sprigging or sodding are the only methods of planting some grasses because they do not produce viable seed.

Warm-season grasses, such as hybrid Bermuda, St. Augustine, zoysia, and centipede, are most often planted by sprigging. Cool-season grasses, which include bent grasses, fescues, ryegrasses, and Kentucky bluegrass, aren't planted by this method.

It takes longer to establish a lawn by sprigging than it does by laying sod, but sprigging is considerably less expensive. Once a "sprig" lawn is established,

---

Seed Versus Sod

Before you begin the finish grading on your lawn, you'll need to decide whether you want to plant grass seed or roll out a carpet of sod. There are advantages and disadvantages to each planting method.

The pros and cons of seed. Although lawns grown from seed require more work to install and much more care to establish, they do have several advantages over sod. The principal advantage is that seeded lawns are much less expensive to plant.

The wide variety of seed that's available is another important advantage: it allows you to choose the grass or mixture of grasses that will do best in your own lawn.

Finally, because seeded lawns establish deep roots to anchor the turf, they're generally more durable than sod for heavy use and may last longer.

The pros and cons of sod. Ease of installation is probably the primary advantage of sod, but running a close second is the fact that such lawns don't require a lot of care to establish. You must water them, of course, but you don't need to fight weeds, seedling diseases, washouts, or birds as you do with seeded lawns. In fact, when you lay sod, you bury the weed seeds already in your soil, usually for good.

Another very persuasive argument for sod is that it covers the ground immediately. You get an instant reward for your effort, and you don't need to worry about tracking dirt or mud into your house for several weeks. In addition, you can plant a sod lawn just about anytime (but not if the ground is frozen), unlike sowing seeds.

For areas under trees, sod lawns have still another advantage. Because sod already has roots, it doesn't have to compete with established tree roots for nutrients and water in the beginning. Grass seedlings do compete, often unsuccessfully.

On the other hand, sod is much more expensive than seed and isn't available in as many varieties of grasses. Because it introduces a layer of foreign soil, sod may not bond well to the soil beneath it. Sometimes, in fact, a sod lawn can fail to thrive.

it looks no different from a mature lawn started by sod, seed, or plugs.

Shopping for Sprigs

Sprigs most often come by the bushel, but you can also buy sod and carefully tear it apart and plant the runners.

The advantage of making your own sprigs from sod is that you can view the plants before making your purchase. The disadvantages are that this method takes time and effort, and sprigs can easily be damaged during the process.

It's usually best to purchase sprigs from a sod farm or from a reputable mail-order firm. The sprigs will be shipped to you in bags or cartons. It's very important to keep the sprigs cool and moist until planting time. Set unplanted sprigs in shady areas as you plant the others—sunlight can quickly damage sprigs, even if they're properly stored in containers.

Planting Sprigs

Sprigs can be short or long stemmed, but they must contain an intact root system, or at least two to four joints from which roots can develop. As in sowing seeds, care must be taken to plant sprigs at the right time, using the right methods and the right number of runners.

When to plant. Since sprigs come from warm-season grasses, the best time to plant is in early spring, after the danger of freezing weather is over. Warm weather provides the optimum growing conditions for those grasses.

How to plant. The fastest way to plant sprigs is to scatter them evenly by hand over the prepared seedbed and then roll with a cleated roller (usually available at nurseries that sell sprigs). If you can't find one, sprinkle a fine layer of topsoil over the sprigs. If you're planting a very large area, consider the method called hydroseeding (see page 40).

Another quick way to plant sprigs is to place them in the prepared soil and press down gently with a notched stick.

You can plant the sprigs individually, but this takes a great deal of time and is only advisable if your lawn is small. Placing sprigs 6 inches apart, make a small hole, put one end of a sprig in it, and press the soil back around it.

Fertilize the area and sprinkle the surface with water. Keep the area moist until the sprigs start growing.

How many to plant. The number of sprigs you need to plant per square foot of your lawn depends on the type of grass you're planting.

To establish hybrid Bermuda, handcast at the rate of 4 to 6 bushels per 1,000 square feet of lawn; plant St. Augustine, zoysia, and centipede grasses at the rate of 6 bushels per 1,000 square feet. If you're row-planting the runners, use about a third to half fewer sprigs than if you hand-cast.

Plugging

Like sprigging, plugging is a method of planting that allows grass runners to spread horizontally along the surface of the soil. Plugging is simply that—digging round or square holes into the lawn and inserting sod plugs.

Plugging is generally used only for warm-season grasses, such as centipede, St. Augustine, and zoysia. The plugs (2 to 3 inches across) are sold 18 to a tray, which will plant 50 square feet, and have an active root system that's ready to grow when placed in the soil.

If a plugged lawn is properly maintained, it will quickly fill in the rest of the lawn, providing a cover as lush and green as those started from seed, sod, or sprigs. Plant the plugs early, just before warming begins in the spring.

Buying Plugs

You can buy plugs by mail order, or you can buy sod and cut the plugs yourself. Nursery-grown plugs are cultivated under sterile conditions, ensuring that the

plugs will be virtually free of pests and disease. Cutting the sod takes more time and may damage the grass, so it should be done with care.

Be sure the seedbed is prepared beforehand (see pages 32–40) so you can plant the plugs when they arrive. Although they won't wilt as fast as sprigs, plugs still need to be planted quickly. In the event of a delay, be sure to keep the plugs watered.

How to Plug

The soil should be moist but not wet before you begin plugging. You can cut holes with a shovel or spade, but it's much easier to use a round steel plugger or a plug auger suitable for use with a drill; look for these tools at equipment rental outlets. The pluggers make a clean, straight-sided hole that's the correct size and depth for the grass plug.

Cut the holes, spacing them as recommended for the type of grass you're using (generally 12 to 18 inches apart). Offset the rows checkerboard fashion. Remember: The closer the plugs are planted, the quicker your lawn will fill in.

If recommended, add a small amount of fertilizer to the holes before inserting the plugs. Plug-starter fertilizer has been specially formulated to provide quick growth of the plugs. The fertilizer has a small measuring container so that the correct amount is supplied to each plug.

Plant the plugs firmly, being sure that no air pockets are left around the plugs. The runners should be perfectly flush with the ground. Fertilize, if necessary, and scatter the soil removed from the hole around the plug. Water immediately. Continue watering on a daily basis for the first 2 weeks to prevent the plugs from drying out. Then you can water every other day for a month.

Once the plugs have rooted into the soil, begin mowing. The more the plugs are mowed, the more rapidly they'll spread. Always mow at the recommended height.

The plugs should be fertilized with a good granular fertilizer every 6 to 8 weeks until full coverage occurs.

Watering Your Lawn

Keeping a lawn lush, green, and healthy looking takes an understanding of your lawn's specific water needs—and an efficient watering system.

The first step is to become familiar with your microenvironment. Then you can decide on the best watering schedule for your lawn, as well as the most practical way of delivering that water.

Watering Guidelines

Perhaps the most common question asked by gardeners is "How often and how much should I water my lawn?" Unfortunately, there is no easy answer to this question. A general rule of thumb is to water infrequently but thoroughly. But because every lawn situation is different, you need to consider several site-specific factors—soil, microclimate, grade, and grass type—in order to determine your lawn's water requirements.

An understanding of those factors and the ability to "read" your lawn's water needs can eliminate much of the guesswork.

Your Microenvironment

When you apply water to soil, the water moves down through it by progressively wetting soil particles. As each particle acquires a film of water, any additional droplets move down to wet lower layers. Although water moves primarily downward, it also moves laterally (to a much lesser extent), particularly in claylike soils.

When you soak your soil, you're wetting each layer, as the water moves downward through it, to a condition known as field capacity. In this condition, each soil particle holds the maximum amount of water film it can against the pull of gravity; the amount of air space in the soil then is low.

As plant roots and evaporation draw water from the soil, the films of water become thinner, and there's more space for air. The film eventually becomes so thin that a plant will wilt. Field capacity depends on soil type, as explained below.

Other factors, as well, determine your lawn's watering needs, including your property's microclimate, its grade, and the type of grass you have. Because every lawn is different, each factor has to be considered independently.

Soil types. The three basic types of soil are clay, sand, and loam (to learn the differences and how to recognize each type, turn to page 34).

Each soil type interacts differently with water. Clay soil, with its fine particles, can hold more water than sandy soil which has fewer, coarser particles. Field capacity for loam falls somewhere between clay and sandy soils.

Because of its high holding capacity, clay soil can be watered less often than the other types. But when you do water, you'll have to sprinkle for a longer time and at a lower rate. An inch of water will

Providing the right amount of water at the right time helps ensure a healthy lawn.

47

penetrate only 4 to 5 inches in clay soil, while the same amount of water will penetrate 6 to 10 inches in loam and 12 inches through sandy soil.

In addition, clay soil absorbs water very slowly; for this reason, it must be irrigated slowly. Sandy soil, on the other hand, holds little water and dries out quickly; consequently, plants in sandy soil need supplemental water more often than they would if grown in another soil.

Loam falls in between the extremes of clay and sand. It has both large and small particles and will absorb and hold water moderately well.

Microclimate. Your watering schedule needs to reflect temperature changes, humidity levels, wind, and the amount of sun or shade on your property.

■ *Hot weather* causes plants to use water so rapidly that shallow-rooted ones sometimes cannot absorb water from the soil fast enough to prevent wilting. In such weather, you need to water more often than usual.

■ *Humid, cool weather* benefits lawns and allows you to water less frequently.

■ *Wind* robs your lawn of water in two ways. First, when you turn on a sprinkler on a windy day, much of the water may be carried away before it can penetrate the soil. Second, wind steals water that the plants draw up and release through their leaves. In still weather, the air around the leaf surface is humid, so the loss of moisture is not as great. Windy weather causes a more rapid water loss from leaves.

■ *Shaded lawns* need less water than unprotected lawns, unless grass is competing with tree roots for available water. If part of your lawn is constantly shaded while another section is in full sun, the two areas will require separate watering schedules. If you're designing an underground sprinkler system (see page 51), be sure to put the areas on separate circuits.

Grade. The steeper your lawn, the more often you'll have to water due to runoff. But water for shorter periods of time so the water has a chance to soak in.

Grass type. Grasses with deeper root systems generally require more water with each sprinkling to moisten the lower soil layers than grasses with shallower root systems. But you can water deep-rooted grasses less frequently, since the soil will lose moisture more slowly.

For information on the depth various grasses can send their roots under ideal conditions, see "Presenting the Grasses" beginning on page 17.

Watering Lawns— How Much & How Often

Recent studies have shown that home owners consistently apply at least twice as much water as their lawns actually need. Learning how and when to water can reduce your water bill substantially. It can also benefit your lawn.

Overwatering yields a shallow-rooted lawn and can leach fertilizers and nutrients out of the root zone. It causes grass to grow faster, so you have to mow more often, and can also encourage disease.

On the other hand, a little water wets only a little soil and won't dampen soil to any depth. This will produce a shallow root system and require you to water lightly each day during the growing season.

Tips for a More Water-efficient Lawn

Here are some good lawn practices that will help you conserve water.

■ *Water early in the morning.* Little moisture is lost to evaporation or wind, and the grass and soil will then be ready for the day's demand. Also, water pressure is usually highest at that time. Although night watering also keeps losses from evaporation to a minimum, it can create a moist habitat for pests and disease-causing organisms.

■ *Don't sprinkle during mid-day heat,* even if your lawn is showing signs of stress at that time.

■ *Plant a drought-tolerant grass* if you live in an arid climate or one prone to frequent droughts. For information on grasses, see the chapter beginning on page 17.

■ *Aerate your lawn* (see page 66) if you have a water runoff problem due to compacted or heavy clay soil. Or run sprinklers at full rate until runoff begins and then shut them off for about an hour to let the soil absorb some of the water. Repeat the process.

■ *With new lawns,* daily sprinkling is needed. In hot weather, it may be necessary to water twice daily to allow sod roots to grow or seeds to germinate.

■ *Dethatch your lawn* (see page 65) to allow water to penetrate into the soil more easily and reduce wasteful runoff.

■ *When mowing cool-season grasses,* set your mower higher than normal during dry times so that soil will stay moist for a longer time. Mow warm-season grasses at the highest recommended cut.

■ *Avoid overfertilizing* —it promotes more vigorous growth that will use more water. Don't fertilize your lawn unless it's showing signs of nutrient deficiency.

■ *Keep after weeds;* they compete with grass for whatever water is available.

Lawn Audit

A lawn audit allows you to determine how much water your lawn is getting, and how evenly it's being watered.

Generally, the most effective watering plan is to soak the soil deeply and not water again until the top inch or two begins to dry out. Watering deeply allows grass roots to extend deeper into the soil; although you'll have to apply more water to moisten the lower soil layers, you can water less often, since the soil will lose moisture more slowly.

Allow the soil to partially dry between waterings; this replenishes oxygen in the soil, necessary for healthy root growth.

The best way to find out about water penetration is to use a sampling tube, a device that removes cores of soil for close examination. You can also test water penetration by probing the soil with a thick piece of wire or a long screwdriver. Such a probe will usually move easily through moist soil but will stop when it reaches firmer, dry soil.

If the top inch or two of the soil is dry, it's time to water. Other signs of a thirsty lawn are grass blades that fold up, exposing their bottoms, and loss of resiliency (walk across your lawn—if your footprints remain for more than several seconds, you need to water).

In addition to these observations, there are several scientific methods you can turn to for help in determining a more precise watering schedule.

Measuring Evapotranspiration

The easiest way to determine if your lawn is getting enough water is to measure evapotranspiration (ET). ET, measured in inches or millimeters, is the amount of water that evaporates from the soil plus the amount that transpires through the leaves of the plant, in this case, grass. It's not easy to get a precise figure, but if you know how much water is leaving the soil, you can predict how much you need to replace it.

ET figures vary from place to place, day to day, season to season, and year to year. But if you know the average for your general area and make adjustments to fit your lawn and the weather, you can water much more efficiently.

Many communities have guidelines based on ET figures to help gardeners determine how long to water. Rates are less in spring and fall than during the summer. To find out if there's an ET chart for your area, contact your County Cooperative Extension office.

In order to use the chart, you'll need to perform a lawn audit to find out how much water your lawn is getting from your present watering system. Even if an ET chart is unavailable, a lawn audit can tell you how uniformly your system is delivering water to your lawn.

Performing a lawn audit. Begin by placing a grid of equal-size containers or coffee cups around your lawn, as shown at left. Then run your watering system for 15 minutes. With the water off, measure the depth of the water that has accumulated in each container, keeping track on a piece of paper. (If you're using an ET chart, note the lowest amount and choose the water depth closest to that figure.)

If there's more than a ¼-inch difference between containers, you may want to make some changes in your system, whether it's adjusting or changing sprinkler heads or experimenting with the positioning of hose-end sprinklers. Once you've achieved a more consistent watering pattern, rerun the test.

Adjusting the figures. Although ET charts tend to recommend watering twice a week, more frequent, short sprinklings may be best in very hot, dry climates, in areas with very sandy soils, or for lawns that are very shallow rooted. Shorter sprinkling times, even if separated by only an hour, are also better where runoff is a problem.

Moisture Sensors & Probes

Both moisture sensors and soil probes can tell you when water is really necessary. Sensors, available in both automatic and manual versions, measure soil moisture pressure; a selection of sensors is shown on page 50.

Probes, which range from soil-coring tubes to an ordinary screwdriver, are less accurate than sensors but can still provide a good indication of how much water your soil is getting.

Moisture sensors. Moisture sensors gauge the moisture condition of the soil in a variety of ways. The type that measures moisture tension is called a tensiometer; it's a sealed, water-filled metal tube with a porous ceramic tip at one end and a pressure gauge at the other.

Other sensors measure temperature or the electrical conductivity of the soil. Your local nursery can help you figure out what the moisture content of your lawn should be.

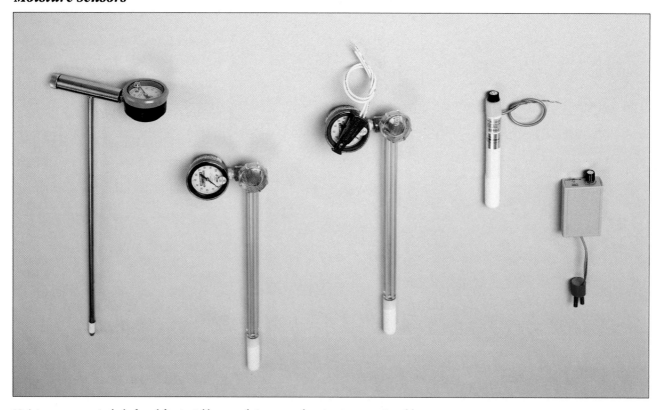

Moisture sensors *include, from left, a portable sensor that goes anywhere; two permanent models, a manual one that can be used anywhere and an automatic one that's wired to a controller; and two electronic sensors.*

Be sure to place the sensor in a representative area of lawn or in a spot that tends to dry out first. Also, its tip must be the approximate root depth of your grass.

Portable tensiometers, which are inserted into the grass, register moisture tension in about 5 minutes. These types can be used around trees and shrubs and in containers, as well as in lawns.

Manual or automatic tensiometers are generally intended for permanent placement. Use the manual kind if you don't have automatic sprinklers; check each time before you water.

The automatic version is designed to act as a master switch between your watering system's controller and valves; it allows watering only when the moisture level of the soil drops below a preset value. If you use this type, instead of scheduling an irrigation every 3 or 4 days, you need to set the controller to water every day. The system will click on only when the moisture sensor tells it to.

Electronic models, designed for use only with automatic sprinkler systems, work in different ways. Some monitor soil moisture by combining two measurements—moisture pressure and temperature. Others gauge soil moisture by sensing the hydrogen charge of water in the soil.

Look for sensors at specialty irrigation stores and follow the manufacturer's directions for installation. Whatever kind you choose, check it often to be sure it's working properly.

Soil probes. Although they're less sophisticated than moisture sensors, soil probes can also tell you when to water, as well as let you see what's happening underground. Probes such as soil-coring tubes pull out a cross section of soil so you can see moisture content.

To help you determine if you're watering deeply enough, push a sampling tube into your lawn about 24 hours after watering. (You can't get a good core in mud or bone-dry soil.) If the core is moist only 2 inches deep and roots can grow 6 to 12 inches, you need to water three to six times as long.

Repeat the test in several areas of your lawn; then you'll know how long it takes for your irrigation system to wet soil to the desired depth.

The soil core can also help you tell when it's time to water again. If the core is damp, there's probably enough moisture. If the core is powder-dry more than a few inches deep, you probably need to water more often unless your lawn is very deep rooted and drought tolerant.

Soil-sampling tubes may be hard to find; check companies that sell scientific supplies or irrigation equipment for gardens.

For a quick test of your soil, poke a stiff wire or screwdriver into the soil in several places. If it penetrates easily for 6 or 7 inches, the soil has been properly saturated.

Underground Sprinkler Systems

The most efficient way to water your lawn is to use an underground sprinkler system. If you're putting in a new lawn or reseeding an existing one, consider installing such a system. You can also add a system to an existing landscape, but you'll have a lot of repair work to do on your lawn afterwards.

In most cases, you can install a system yourself; the basic steps—from planning to installation—are outlined in this section. Or you can have a landscaping expert do the work for you. For help in choosing a system or contractor, ask your neighbors for recommendations or look in the Yellow Pages under "Irrigation Systems & Equipment," "Landscape Contractors," or "Sprinklers—Garden & Lawn."

Even if you don't plan to do the work yourself, it's important to understand the basic components of a sprinkler system and the installation procedures so you can adequately operate the system once it's installed.

Basic Components

The parts you'll need to install a system include control valves, pipes and pipe fittings, risers, sprinkler heads, and a controller, or timer. The photo below shows how the components fit together to form an automatic system. For a manually operated system, you don't need control valves or a controller.

Assembling these components and installing them in your yard isn't difficult, but it can take time.

Control valves. These valves, the heart of the system, regulate the flow of water from your water source to the sprinkler heads. They're attached to the controller (see page 52), which automatically opens and shuts the valves.

Since there usually isn't enough water pressure in residential water lines to water the entire lawn at one time and service the house, too, irrigation systems are often separated into circuits. Each circuit is operated by a control valve that services a portion of the lawn or garden.

Circuits operate one at a time so the maximum flow rate isn't exceeded. They

Components of an Automatic Sprinkler System

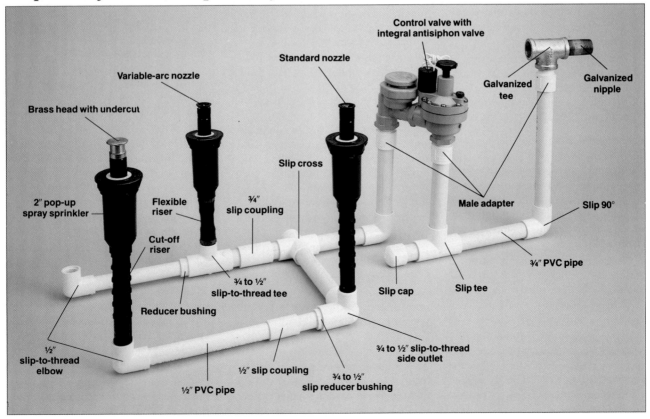

How to "Read" a Sprinkler Head

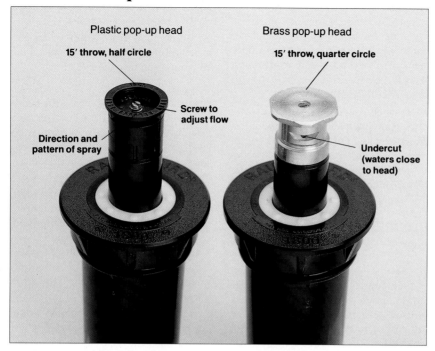

Plastic pop-up head
15′ throw, half circle
Screw to adjust flow
Direction and pattern of spray

Brass pop-up head
15′ throw, quarter circle
Undercut (waters close to head)

also allow for differences in the water requirements of the various areas in the landscape. (For more on designing circuits, see page 54.)

Each control valve should have an antisiphon valve, either integral or separate. Also known as vacuum breakers, antisiphon valves prevent the backflow of water into the main line.

Pipes. Most sprinkler systems use pipes made from polyvinyl chloride (PVC). In areas where the ground freezes, use copper pipe from your water meter to the control valves and PVC pipe for the rest of the system; just be sure to drain all water from the pipes before the first freeze.

PVC pipe comes in several strength designations. Choose heavy-duty pipe for areas where pressure is highest; use thinner, less expensive pipe for lines that are under no pressure.

Pipes in lengths of 10 and 20 feet with flared and standard ends are available. The standard end of one pipe fits into the flared end of the next pipe or into a fitting; a solvent is used to cement the ends together.

A general rule of thumb for sizing pipe is to choose a size that's the same as or larger than the house service line (usually ¾ or 1 inch in diameter). Manufacturers recommend a maximum of 13 gallons per minute (gpm) for ¾-inch pipe and 22 gpm for 1-inch pipe. (To calculate gpm, see the facing page.)

Pipe fittings. Available in a wide assortment of shapes, fittings, like those shown in the photo on page 51, allow you a great deal of flexibility when you're constructing the system. For example, fittings let you connect two pipes together at almost any angle; special fittings also allow you to connect PVC pipe to galvanized pipe and to connect pipes of different sizes together.

Some fittings screw together (always use pipe tape when screwing fittings and pipe together); others are cemented to the pipe with solvent.

Risers. Vertical pieces of pipe, risers connect underground pipe to sprinkler heads. Risers are designed to be used at different heights, depending on what's needed for each sprinkler head. Al-

though most risers are rigid, you can buy flexible risers that bend rather than break when hit.

Sprinkler heads. Manufacturers produce a large number of sprinkler heads in many different spray patterns, including full, half, and quarter circles, as well as rectangular shapes. Heads designed for shrubs, flower beds, and gardens, including drip emitters, are available.

Also on the market are low-precipitation-rate nozzles that reduce runoff, improve spray uniformity, and allow a larger area to be irrigated with a given amount of water. With matched-precipitation nozzles, available for almost every system, a sprinkler in a corner covering 90° of arc puts out a quarter as much as a 360° head—conserving water by allowing coordinated coverage.

The most common types of sprinkler heads used are pop-up heads made from plastic or, less commonly, brass (see at left); use these in open lawn areas where foot traffic and mowing will occur. Other heads are mounted on risers; use these where you need to throw water over shrubs or other plantings.

Some companies offer heads that are adjustable for patterns as well as for distance of throw.

Controllers. Most new controllers are solid state with electronic components (one type is shown on page 58). They offer features unavailable in the older mechanical timers. For example, dual- or multiple-program controllers let you water a lawn on a separate and more frequent schedule than ground covers, shrubs, and trees. You can also connect moisture sensors (see page 49) to such controllers.

The controller directs the watering cycle by automatically activating the control valves for the different circuits so they turn on for a selected period of time, at the hour and day you choose. The number of valves in your watering system determines the size controller you need.

If you think you may add more sprinklers or drip lines later, consider buying a controller with more station terminals than you currently need.

Because irrigation timers operate on low, 24-volt current, they're easy and safe to install. The wiring most often used is 18-gauge jacketed cable; if it's going to run underground, it should be labeled as being approved for burial.

Because each type has different operating instructions, be sure to follow the manufacturer's directions.

Planning Your System

Before you can buy parts and begin work, you'll need to prepare a fairly detailed map of your property that shows the location of all structures, underground utilities, paved areas, and plantings. You'll also need several measurements, such as your water pressure and the output of your service line.

This is a good time to discuss your project with an irrigation equipment retailer or landscape expert. Ask your retailer to provide you with a manufacturer's workbook, which can be helpful in drawing your map and describing the various components available.

Mapping Your Property

Mapping Your Property

The more detailed the sketch of your property and the information about your home's water system, the more confident you can be that the system you eventually buy will do the job you expect it to do.

Making a scale drawing. Using graph paper, plot the location of all structures, walkways and driveways, fences, trees, shrubs, lawns, flower and vegetable beds, and any other obstacles on your property. Be sure to mark where you intend to tap into the house's water supply (at a hose bibb, for example).

Now is the time to check with your local building department for any necessary permits. It's also a good idea to call your utility company if you suspect there may be utility lines buried underground on your property. Be sure to note those on your drawing.

Measuring water pressure. Most sprinklers will not operate efficiently if the water pressure (measured in pounds per square inch, or psi) of your water meter and service line is too low. A minimum of 20 psi is usually required. Your water pressure can be determined by using a pressure gauge (ask your irrigation equipment retailer to loan you one or check local hardware stores).

Measure water pressure at an outside faucet when no water is running in the house. Turn the faucet to be measured completely open. Record psi at each outside faucet location, taking several readings throughout the day, and use the lowest pressure.

If a gauge isn't available, call your water company and ask for the psi average in your neighborhood.

Determining gpm (gallons per minute). To make sure your main water line can handle the sprinkler system, you'll need to calculate the rate at which water travels through your pipes.

Ask your irrigation equipment retailer for help in measuring your main line's gpm. Or simply place a 1-gallon container under an outdoor faucet and count how many seconds it takes to fill the bucket completely. Then divide the total number of seconds into 60 to determine gpm. Write this figure on your plan; you'll use it when plotting circuits.

Note that to use this method of measuring gpm, the outdoor faucet must be the same diameter as your service line.

Plotting Your System

Planning your sprinkler system on paper will help you think the system through, guide you in ordering materials, and serve as a permanent record of where the pipes are buried (for an example, see at left).

You can design your own system or ask your retailer or other professional for help. Base your design on the various components offered by the manufacturer you choose.

Many in-ground sprinkler companies provide detailed planning and installation directions. If you haven't already chosen a manufacturer, ask for recommendations and choose carefully; you'll want to be sure the equipment is of good quality, the service pro-

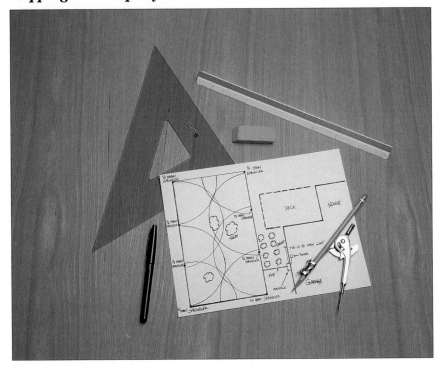

vided is satisfactory, and the components will meet your needs.

Locating sprinkler heads. Make a copy of the scale drawing of your property and sketch in sprinklers in the corners and along the perimeter of your lawn. If you can't get full coverage with those heads, you'll have to place additional ones where needed. (Keep these to a minimum to avoid trenching in an existing lawn and to avoid locating heads in the mowing area.)

Using a pencil compass, draw the pattern needed for each head—quarter-circle heads in corners, half-circle heads along edges, and full-circle heads for center areas. On narrow or odd strips of lawn, use strip spray heads.

Then check the manufacturer's workbook for the radius, or throw, of each sprinkler head. Plan on a 100 percent overlap of spray patterns (spray should extend from sprinkler head to sprinkler head). Spacing the sprinklers too far apart will result in poor water distribution and create brown areas in your lawn.

Plotting circuits. Breaking your system into circuits, each directed by its own control valve, allows you to water lawns, gardens, and shrubs at different flow rates, durations, and times, ensuring that each area of the landscape will get only the water it needs.

The most important factor to remember when you're designing circuits is that the gpm of any one circuit cannot exceed the gpm from your main water line. To determine a circuit's total gpm, use the output chart in the manufacturer's workbook, writing the capacity of each sprinkler next to where it's located on your plan. Add up the figures for each circuit. Attach as many similar sprinklers on a circuit as you can without exceeding the gpm of your main water line.

Don't attempt to place different types of sprinkler heads on the same circuit. For example, standard lawn sprinklers must be on a different circuit from low-spray shrub sprinklers.

Group control valves into what's called a manifold to make operation more convenient and eliminate the need for extra trenching. It also makes it easier to attach the valves to the controller. The entire manifold can be buried underground, but it's a good idea to place an irrigation box around it for easy access. (See page 56 for more information on manifolds.)

Many systems have one manifold in the front yard and another in the backyard.

Where soil freezes, each circuit must be equipped with an automatic drain valve (install one at the low point of each circuit). The valves open automatically to let the pipes drain when the water is turned off.

Adding the piping. Starting at the control valve for each circuit, sketch in the piping that will connect the sprinklers on the same circuit. Try to avoid having pipes that run under driveways or other paved areas.

Assembling a shopping list. Using your drawing, determine the number of control valves you need, the number and lengths of pipes, and the number and types of pipe fittings and sprinkler heads. Know how many stations you'll need on your controller.

Tools you'll need for the actual installation work include a trench shovel and pick, PVC pipe cutters or a hacksaw

Installation Tools

Tools you'll need *to install an underground system include, clockwise from left, a trench shovel, hacksaw, pipe wrench, pick, tape measure, string, mallet, stakes, utility knife, screwdriver, and pipe cutter.*

for cutting pipe (pipe cutters are more efficient and don't leave burrs), a pipe wrench, and a sharp utility knife. (Those and other tools are illustrated on the facing page.) Have primer and solvent on hand for joining pipes and fittings.

Installation

Laying the pipe and building the manifold are two separate procedures that can be done in any order. Once those jobs are complete, you connect the manifold to the pipe and install the risers, sprinkler heads, and controller.

Working with Pipe

As you lay out your pipe lines, you'll doubtless have to cut and fit together sections of pipe. Here's how to do it (the steps are shown at right).

Carefully measure your pipe runs and cut the pipes with a pipe cutter or hacksaw, scraping off any burrs with a utility knife. (To prevent dirt from getting into pipes and to save wear and tear on your back, prop the pipe ends out of the trench when you work on them.)

When you join parts together, you must work quickly. The plastic solvent adheres quite rapidly—and once cemented, joints cannot be broken apart.

First, clean the area to be cemented with a cloth and apply primer to the outside of the standard pipe end and the inside of the flared end or fitting. Then brush solvent evenly over the primer. Place the pipes back in the trench and push the standard pipe end into the fitting or flared end and rotate it about a quarter turn. Hold the pieces together for about 20 seconds until set.

Wait at least an hour (longer in cold weather) before running water through the pipe.

Assembling the System

It doesn't matter whether you install your system from the farthest pipe and work toward the manifold or vice versa. But it is important to determine the

Working with PVC Pipe

Prop PVC pipes out of trench to make them more accessible; make sure ends are clean.

Brush primer on outside of standard pipe end and inside of flared end.

Working quickly, apply solvent evenly over primer coat.

Twist pipes a quarter turn and hold for about 20 seconds until set.

location of your manifold and the tie-in to the main water line before you begin digging.

The steps outlined below are illustrated on page 57.

Digging trenches. Although you can do this job by hand, it can be hard work; you may want to rent a trenching machine or hire someone to do the work for you. Lay out each trench with string and stakes and dig it at least 8 inches deep, using a sturdy trench shovel; use a pick where necessary.

To tunnel under sidewalks or other obstacles, attach a hose to a piece of galvanized pipe and turn on the water full force. The water will soften and tear away the soil. Once the soil is moistened, take the hose out and drive the

pipe through with a sledgehammer. When you're ready to push PVC pipe through the hole, tape the pipe's end with duct tape to keep out debris.

Tapping into the service line. Regardless of where you're tapping into the water line, be sure to turn off the main water supply to the house before beginning work. Three typical situations are illustrated on page 56.

To tap in at an outside faucet, remove the faucet and install a 1-inch galvanized or copper tee; then reattach the faucet. Attach a male adapter to the tee, install a shutoff valve, and run pipe from the valve to the manifold.

If you're tapping directly into the main line, cut out a small piece of the line and replace it with a compression tee. Then install a shutoff valve so you can turn off the water to the irrigation system and still have water to the house. (Some local codes also require you to install an antisiphon valve.)

Wait an hour for the solvent to dry; then flush out the pipe with water until it runs clear.

To tap in at a basement meter, cut into the service line just past the water meter. Install a compression tee and shutoff valve; then drill a hole through the basement wall above the foundation for the outgoing pipe. Be sure to install a drain cap at the lowest point of the system if you live in an area with freezing temperatures.

Assembling the manifold. The manifold, or grouping of control valves, can be assembled on your workbench or other convenient place. On the back of each control valve, screw in a tee fitting and attach a length of PVC pipe. This pipe will connect all your control valves (space the valves at least 3 inches apart for easy access).

Then attach separate fittings to the threaded outlet in the front of each control valve. Later, you'll connect the pipe leading directly to the sprinklers to these fittings.

Be sure to use fittings and pipe the same size as the valves. For future reference, write on the back of each valve the circuit the valve services. You can bury the manifold to keep it out of sight, but if you do, place a box around it for protection.

Laying pipe. Lay out the pipes as level as possible at the bottom of the trenches (some variation won't cause a problem) and make the required connections. If tree roots are in the way, either tunnel under them or cut through them with a saw or ax. Try to keep the inside of the pipes as free of dirt as possible.

Attaching the manifold. Connect the pipes to the manifold, being sure to twist the screw fitting hand-tight only. If you use a wrench, you risk stripping the threads inside the control valve. Also, use pipe tape.

Test the manifold for leaks; if there are any, unscrew the fitting, dry it off,

Three Ways to Tap into the Service Line

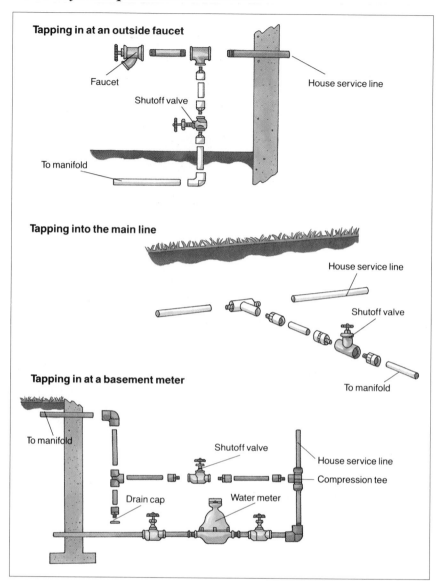

and apply new pipe tape before handscrewing it back into the control valve.

Installing risers. With a tape measure, determine the desired height of each sprinkler head. The top of the pop-up sprinklers should be level with the finished soil. Cut a flexible riser to that length or use a precut riser.

Cut the trench pipe at each sprinkler location. Install a tee fitting and attach the riser, making sure that it's perpendicular to the surrounding terrain. This will ensure proper coverage.

Flushing the system. Don't wait until you've installed your sprinkler heads to flush the system, since dirt and dried solvent inside the pipes can rapidly clog the heads.

To flush your sprinkler system, turn on the water, one circuit at a time. (Make sure the pipe solvent has had at least an hour to dry before flushing, longer in cold temperatures.) You'll be able to see the water gush out of the risers. Wait until the water is clear before shutting it off and installing all of your sprinkler heads.

Installing an Automatic Sprinkler System

To excavate under paving, break up subsoil with a high-pressure hose; then drive a metal pipe through with a sledgehammer.

Shutoff valve allows you to turn off water to irrigation system and still have water inside your house.

Collected into a manifold, valves control flow of water to each circuit of your sprinkler system.

Measure carefully for risers before cutting them to ensure that sprinkler heads will be at desired height.

Flushing the system after attaching risers eliminates dirt and debris that would otherwise clog sprinkler heads.

Automatic tensiometer, buried in ground, activates controller when moisture in turf falls below a preset level.

Attaching the sprinkler heads. Screw the sprinkler heads to the risers, taking care to align them properly so they spray where you want them. If spray direction isn't clearly marked on the sprinkler head, check the manufacturer's workbook or ask your irrigation equipment retailer.

Installing the controller. Mount the controller (shown below) in your garage or another convenient, protected place near a power source. If there's some distance between your controller and the manifold, protect the wires by placing them inside a piece of pipe; bury the pipe in a trench, if necessary.

There are two wires on most control valves: one connects to a common terminal on the controller; the other connects sequentially to its own terminal. Once the wires are connected, set the watering controls (follow the manufacturer's instructions) and plug in the controller. Test the system by electronically opening and shutting each valve in sequence.

This is also the time to check for adequate coverage and attach any additional risers and sprinkler heads that may be needed.

Backfilling trenches. Replace the soil to a depth slightly lower than the original sod line. Flood the trenches with water to settle the soil; then add more soil, mounding it slightly. Sprinkle the mound for additional settling.

Maintenance & Repair

During the warm summer months, check your sprinklers at least once a month for broken or clogged heads. Look for leaks, poor spray patterns, or the resulting dry turf.

Cleaning clogged sprinkler heads. When a sprinkler is clogged, it will usually force water out at odd angles, or the spray will be greatly reduced. Try running a knife blade through the slit where the water is sprayed. If it doesn't clear, remove the head and clean it.

Replacing broken sprinklers and risers. With your hands or a wrench, lift off the broken sprinkler head and replace it with one of the same kind.

If a riser is broken and is difficult to extract, use a stub wrench. If solvent

was used to install the riser, cut it off cleanly and attach an adaptor fitting and another riser.

Work carefully to avoid spilling soil into the line; if the surrounding soil is dry, wet it down first. If soil does enter the line, flush it out by removing all the sprinklers on the circuit and letting the water gush out of the risers.

Hoses & Sprinklers

Despite the increasing sophistication of automated sprinkler systems, nothing beats the garden hose for versatility. You can attach a variety of sprinklers to it, and you can move it almost anywhere you like. With a little care, a good garden hose will last several years. The trade-off, of course, is that garden hoses won't turn on by themselves at 4 A.M.

Hoses

The material a garden hose is made from determines the durability, flexibility, and weight of the hose, as well as how readily it kinks. When you're purchasing a hose, also consider its capacity (its inside diameter) and length.

Materials. Hoses are made from rubber, unreinforced vinyl, vinyl reinforced with fiber-cord netting, or reinforced rubber-vinyl.

■ *Rubber hoses,* which have a dull surface, are the heaviest and toughest of the hoses. Although flexible, they can kink, especially if left in the hot sun. However, they work well in cold temperatures and resist fire better than vinyl hoses (they're recommended in rural areas where wildfires are a danger).

■ *Unreinforced vinyl hoses* are smooth, shiny, lightweight, and inexpensive. However, they kink easily and can burst if the nozzle is shut off. They're also the least durable type, kinking badly in cold and hot weather. In freezing weather, an all-vinyl hose gets so brittle that it can easily break.

A Typical Controller

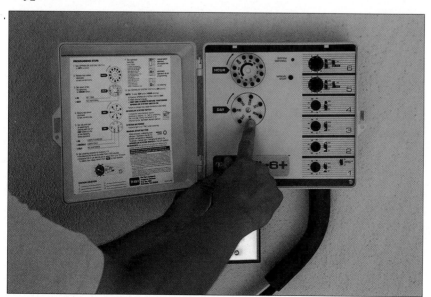

Hybrid controller combines sophisticated solid-state circuitry with ease of use characteristic of older mechanical timers.

■ *Reinforced vinyl hoses* have a textured, shiny exterior. Tough and kink-resistant, these hoses are also lightweight, so they're good choices if you need to move your hose frequently.

■ *Reinforced rubber-vinyl hoses* have a textured, somewhat shiny appearance. They're flexible, kink resistant, medium-heavy in weight, and durable.

Sizes. Commonly available hoses come in ½-inch, ⅝-inch, and ¾-inch inside diameters. (The outside diameter varies with the material used.) Threads are the same on each, so you can use the same nozzle with any size hose.

Although diameters differ by only a fraction of an inch, the volume of water each size hose can carry varies greatly. But there's a catch: using a nozzle or sprinkler minimizes the differences because these devices tend to equalize the amount of water coming out of the hose.

■ *A ½-inch hose* is lightweight and easy to carry and store. It's excellent for watering container plants; to water large trees and shrubs, choose a larger size.

■ *A ⅝-inch hose* is a good size for home gardens. It works well on larger areas even with low water pressure.

■ *A ¾-inch hose* is very heavy when filled with water but will deliver water at a faster rate than the smaller hoses.

Storing hoses. Hose hangers and reels not only make working with hoses easier, but they also help to preserve them by keeping them away from foot and car traffic. A hose hanger attaches to a wall—it's easy to wrap the hose around it in loops. Wall-hung and portable hose reels have handles you use to wrap the hose around the reel.

All types of hoses will last much longer if stored indoors during winter and kept out of the sun when not in use.

Hose-end Sprinklers

Many kinds of sprinklers are available on the market today, and each has its own sprinkler pattern, as shown at right.

Consider the size and shape of the area you want to water when shopping for a portable sprinkler. Here are some of the most popular types.

Impulse, or impact, sprinklers are popular because of their ability to cover large areas at a time. They also offer flexibility—they're easily adjusted to cover smaller areas. Their rotating heads send out a strong jet of water or a gentle mist.

Oscillating sprinklers sweep back and forth in a fan motion, applying water at a relatively slow rate. They're excellent for spot coverage, but they must be moved frequently for best results. Their pattern is similar to that of impulse sprinklers.

Revolving-arm sprinklers are useful but erratic. Most water falls from 4 to 8 feet out.

Cone sprayers, which force water out through holes, soak only a small area. For best results, turn the water down to half-pressure and move the sprinkler often.

Hose-end Sprinklers & Sprinkler Patterns

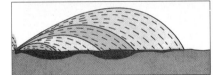

Impulse sprinkler

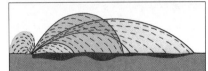

Oscillating sprinkler

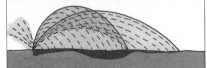

Revolving-arm sprinkler

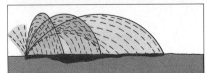

Cone sprayer

Lawn Maintenance

Government statisticians now rank lawn care as the number one leisure activity among home owners. You may sometimes wonder about the statisticians' choice of adjectives, but, if done properly and regularly, lawn maintenance can indeed be an enjoyable activity.

This chapter provides lawn-care information you can use with your turf maintenance schedule (see page 79). Reviewed are lawn mowers and mowing techniques, fertilizers, dethatching and aerating procedures, and techniques for renovating damaged lawns and dealing with lawn ailments.

Mowing

People have different ideas about what a well-groomed lawn should look like. But most would agree that lawns need to be mowed regularly to keep them looking their best.

Lawn Mowers

There are two types of mowers—reel and rotary. Reel mowers, usually five bladed, spin in a circular motion. However, they cut only in a forward motion and, unless powered, are practical only for small lawns.

Rotary mowers are usually tougher than reel mowers and can chop through leaves and twigs, as well as ride over rough terrain. They also cut forward and backward, which can be a definite advantage over reel mowers.

A word of caution: Although reel mowers are considered safer than rotary mowers, any motorized mower is potentially dangerous. Use with care and as directed by the manufacturer.

Reel Mowers

If you can cut your lawn in less than an hour and the terrain is not too hilly, consider buying a hand-pushed reel mower. Because it has no motor, it's less expensive and lasts longer than a motorized one. The only upkeep requirement is sharpening the blades. Moreover, a reel mower is usually much lighter and easier to handle.

Motorized reel mowers are very efficient and are favored for use on fine lawns and golf putting greens. However, they're often more expensive than rotary-mowers and are suitable for use only on smooth, debris-free lawns.

Rotary Mowers

Rotary mowers come in three types. The motorized, push-type rotary mower is the most popular. But it soon may lose its place as the first choice for gardeners to the self-propelled rotary mower. It's similar to the traditional push-type machine, but it moves forward under its own power. The third type of rotary mower is a ride-on, which looks and operates like a miniature tractor.

Fertilizers, such as this water-soluble type, provide essential nutrients to turf, ensuring healthy plant growth.

Hand-pushed rotary mowers. This type has been the most popular lawn mower for the past 20 years. The blades, powered by a small motor, spin parallel to the ground under a metal housing. You furnish the power to move it forward or backward.

These machines are usually very rugged—they can last a long time with a minimum of maintenance. However, they're relatively heavy and it takes some strength to push them. On a hilly or large lawn, you may want to consider another type of rotary mower.

Self-propelled rotary mowers. These are similar to the hand-pushed rotary machines, except they go forward under their own power. You simply walk behind and guide them. Most have variable speed adjustments. They're recommended for large lawns.

Ride-on mowers. For lawns of an acre or more, nothing beats a lawn tractor. These machines come with a variety of features, including a zero-turning radius that allows you to cut easily around trees, fences, and other obstacles.

Ride-on mowers can make mowing fun and easy. However, they're expensive, take up large storage areas, and require skilled maintenance and operation.

Purchasing a Mower

Savvy buyers match the mower with the job. Obviously, a gardener with a small urban lawn doesn't need to purchase a big, roaring ride-on mower. Conversely, a hand-pushed reel mower is going to make an endurance test out of cutting a 2-acre hillside lawn.

Here are some other purchasing tips.

Maneuverability. It's very important to be sure that you can easily handle the mower. You should be able to avoid obstacles with ease and get the whole job done without exhausting yourself. Also, keep in mind that you have to turn most mowers on their sides to sharpen the blades. If the mower is too heavy, you may end up putting off critical maintenance.

Starting systems. Yanking on a stubborn starting cord can be frustrating and can lead to arm and back injuries. Machines equipped with electric starters may be worth the extra cost.

The right handle. Make sure the handle of your walk-behind mower extends between your belt and rib cage. If more than one person is going to do the mowing, find a mower with an adjustable handle.

Using & Maintaining Your Mower

If you aren't mechanically inclined, you may want to consider a simple machine, such as a walk-behind with a 2-cycle engine that requires little maintenance. Or make arrangements with a local mower shop for regular motor tune-ups and to have the blades sharpened.

Winter storage. Before you put your mower away for the winter, check your owner's manual for instructions. Most call for draining the gas and oil, cleaning dried grass from the blade housing, and lubricating moving parts. Remember to disconnect the spark plug before you drain the gas. Once the gas is drained, reconnect the plug and run the engine until the gas in the line is used up. Empty the oil if required.

Just prior to the next growing season, add new oil, replace the spark plug, and clean or replace the fuel filter, if necessary.

Keeping mower blades sharp. Research has shown that lawns cut with a dull-bladed mower are more susceptible to disease and less attractive than ones mowed with a sharp-bladed mower. Mowers with dull blades will use about 22 percent more gasoline each growing season than mowers with sharp blades.

You can sharpen a rotary blade yourself. Remove the blade and sharpen it with a metal file. If heavy grinding is required, take the blade to a mower shop. Reel mowers require more precision sharpening; it's best to have a professional do the job.

Mowing Your Lawn

The rewards for mowing the lawn can extend beyond the nostalgic smell, look, and feel of newly cut grass. Mowing it at the proper height and at the right time can also help the lawn fight pests and diseases. Adjusting the height of the lawn can help it survive periods of drought or severe heat, while timely mowing can protect the fragile crowns from exposure.

When to Mow

Grass types and seasons will dictate how often you should mow. During their respective growing seasons, cool-season and warm-season grasses may require mowing every 2 or 3 days. However, off-season cutting may only be required every 2 weeks or even once a month. A good rule of thumb is not to rely on an established mowing schedule; instead, watch your grass and mow when it needs it.

Allowing your lawn to grow about a third taller than its recommended height before mowing will keep the grass greener and healthier. Letting it grow too tall will force you to cut too deeply into the crowns. This weakens the plants and gives weed seeds a better chance to germinate.

The height of the grass also affects the root system. If the lawn is cut to the correct height, the roots will grow deep and keep the lawn healthy. Scalping the lawn can shock the roots, either killing the plants or leaving them vulnerable to disease and other stresses.

Since grasses need a certain amount of leaf surface to stay healthy, the optimum height of each grass depends on whether it spreads vertically or horizontally. Horizontally spreading grasses, such as Bermuda grass and bent grass, should be cut shorter than vertically growing grasses, like tall fescue and Kentucky bluegrass.

For help in determining the ideal mowing height for your grass type, refer to the grass listings in the chapter beginning on page 17.

Mowing Techniques

If possible, change mowing directions every other time. Mower wheels can create ruts, and the grass may eventually grow lighter or darker in the rutted areas. Also, mowing in only one direction can create an unsightly grain—your lawn may begin to look striped or streaked.

If your lawn is too steep to mow up and down, try mowing at a slight diagonal.

Also, leave the grass clippings in the lawn. Clippings are 75 to 80 percent water and 3 to 6 percent nitrogen, ½ to 1 percent phosphorus, and 1 to 3 percent potassium—the same nutrients contained in most fertilizers. Calcium and other nutrients are also present.

If you don't let the grass get too tall between mowings, the clippings will be small enough to filter down to the soil. As clippings break down, they naturally fertilize the lawn. Lawns where clippings are removed require up to 2 extra pounds of nitrogen per 1,000 square feet per year. Wet clippings tend to clump together, so let your lawn dry before cutting.

Mowing New Lawns

Since the root systems of new lawns are not yet firmly established, go easy on the first couple of mowings. Mow slowly, especially around corners, so the wheels don't tear up the grass. Never cut the grass when it's wet. Let it dry and then water right after mowing.

Be sure not to mow too low: it's better to leave the new grass too high than to risk scalping it. However, when the lawn has grown a third taller than its optimum height, don't be afraid to cut it. Mowing helps the plants spread, and the clippings provide a good natural fertilizer.

Trimming & Edging

Regardless of the mower you use, you'll probably have some trimming and edging to do along sidewalks and driveways, walls, trees, fences, and beds, unless you have a mowing strip, as shown below. On small lawns, hand shears or clippers will usually do the job, but on larger lawns hand-held motorized trimmers and edgers are quicker and easier.

Trimmers. Powered by gasoline or electricity, nylon string trimmers stand midway between mowers and edgers. Nylon filaments are attached to a quickly rotating disk mounted at an angle at the end of a long handle; the spinning filaments cut tall grass and weeds with a whipping action. Caution: Watch out for flying debris when using this type of trimmer.

Gas-powered trimmers that feature reciprocating blades reduce the danger of flying debris. They're lightweight and maneuverable, and their blades stop immediately when the engine is shut off.

Edgers. If your lawn is small and there's little edging to be done, an inexpensive manually operated edger may be all you need. But if you have a number of edges to cut, you may want to consider any of a variety of cordless electric or gas-powered edgers now available.

Most basic of these tools are the various short-handled shears. One type operates by vertical squeezing action: one handle is above the other, and each squeeze closes the blades, which cut as they pass by one another. In another model, one blade remains in a fixed position while the other blade slices across it: the harder you squeeze on the handles, the more tension you apply to the blades. Still another kind operates by horizontal action.

Long-handled, heavy-duty grass shears let you stand up to cut lawn edges and the margins of thick ground covers. They'll even cut right into the sod. Also available are grass shears with wheels at the base of a 3-foot handle. As you wheel it along, you squeeze a handle operating scissors-action blades that cut the grass.

Lawn Fertilizers

Experts don't always agree about the type and amount of fertilizer each lawn needs, but they do agree on one thing—most lawns require it. Lawns are unnatural environments where plants are crowded together. Therefore, they require higher amounts of nutrients than are available naturally. This is especially

Mowing along a Mowing Strip

Wheels of rotary mower ride on a concrete mowing strip, which allows mower to trim grass closely along edge of lawn.

true on lawns where the clippings, a natural fertilizer, are removed after mowing.

Some fertilizers now come mixed with pesticides. Choosing the right mixture and applying it correctly can save you time and money by allowing you to do two jobs in one. Remember—nearly all fertilizers require a thorough watering after application. If left dry, most fertilizers will burn the lawn.

Understanding Fertilizers

Grasses need about 16 different mineral elements to survive. Most of these are available naturally in the soil. However, three primary elements—nitrogen, phosphorus, and potassium—must be added regularly in the form of a fertilizer.

Nitrogen is the key to healthy lawns, since it stimulates leaf growth. Phosphorus is needed for strong root growth, and potassium helps with internal plant development and functions.

Before you choose a fertilizer, you need to test your soil to see which nutrients it needs (see page 34). Home test kits are available at most lawn-care stores. However, results from these kits can be difficult to interpret. If you have questions, you can have your soil checked at a private lab (ask your County Cooperative Extension office for names). Once you know what your lawn needs, you can buy the correct fertilizer.

Regardless of the brand you choose, the package label should contain three numbers, such as 26-3-3, 6-4-2, or 10-10-0. The first number, the most important, refers to the percentage of nitrogen present. The second number refers to phosphorus and the third to potassium. If one of the numbers is zero, that element isn't included.

Choosing a Fertilizer

A bewildering selection of fertilizers is available, including granular types packaged in cartons and sacks, and liquid ones in bottles. In addition, you'll find both organic and synthetic fertilizers, as well as combination products.

Dry granular fertilizers. Most fertilizers sold are in dry form. You sprinkle or spread them onto a lawn and then scratch, rake, or dig them into the soil; or you can apply them in subsurface strips. When the ground is watered, the granules dissolve, beginning their fertilizing action quickly. Depending on the type of nitrogen in the fertilizer, they can last up to several months.

Controlled-release fertilizers are balls of complete fertilizers coated with a permeable substance. When moistened, a small amount of nutrients leaches through the coating until the encapsulated fertilizer is used up. These products last from 3 to 8 months.

Liquid fertilizers. Liquid fertilizers are easy to use, avoid the risk of burning the lawn (as long as you follow label directions for dilution), and are immediately available to roots. However, they're less practical than dry types for large lawns because they're more expensive and must be reapplied more often (their nutrients leach through the root zone rapidly).

Available in a variety of formulas, all liquid fertilizers must be used with water: some are concentrated solutions you dilute in water; others are dry concentrates you dissolve in water.

Organic fertilizers. The word "organic" simply means that the nutrients contained in the product are derived solely from the remains or from a by-product of a once-living organism. Cottonseed meal, blood meal, bone meal, hoof-and-horn meal, and manures are examples of organic fertilizers. (Urea is a synthetic organic fertilizer—an organiclike substance manufactured from inorganic materials.)

Most of these products packaged as fertilizers will be labeled with their nitrogen-phosphate-potassium ratios. Usually, an organic fertilizer is high in just one of the three major nutrients and low in the other two, although some are chemically fortified with the other nutrients.

In general, the organics release their nutrients over a fairly long period. However, they may not release enough of their principal nutrient at the time when the plant needs it for best growth. Because they depend on soil organisms to release the nutrients, most organic fertilizers are effective only when soil is moist and warm enough for the organisms to be active.

Although manure is a complete organic fertilizer, it may be low in some important nutrients. Manures are best used as mulches or soil conditioners.

Synthetic fertilizers. These manufactured fertilizers release their nutrients into the soil quickly and turn grass greener shortly after application. However, the results are temporary unless fertilizer is applied often during the growing season. Synthetic fertilizers can easily burn a lawn, so caution must be used when they're applied.

Combination products. You can buy fertilizers combined with insecticides, weed killers, fungicides, or moss killers. These products are appropriate if you need the extra ingredient every time you fertilize; if not, it's more economical to buy it separately.

When to Fertilize

Fertilizing needs vary with grass type, climate, and the type of fertilizer used. Each fertilizer is labeled with application instructions, but you should also learn to "read" your own lawn so you can recognize when it requires fertilizer. Loss of color is one obvious sign; another is lack of vigor.

Usually, it's necessary to fertilize once or twice in the spring as the growing season begins. If you're using fast-release fertilizer, more frequent applications will be necessary. Many lawns, especially those in warm-climate areas, also require additional fertilization in the fall. Summer applications are risky in most areas, since high temperatures can easily cause a lawn to burn.

For guidelines on how much fertilizer to use on your lawn, see the grass

Fertilizing with a Drop-spreader

Drop-spreader *allows for even distribution of fertilizer; make two passes, one perpendicular to the other, using half the fertilizer during each pass.*

listings beginning on page 19. If you're still in doubt as to when to fertilize, consult a local lawn professional.

Fertilizing Techniques

The three common methods of applying fertilizer are hand-casting, using an applicator, and spraying water-soluble fertilizers through a hose. Regardless of the method you choose, be sure to use the right amount of fertilizer and spread it evenly.

Hand-casting. You can use this method with any type of solid fertilizer. However, it's safest with organic fertilizers, since there's less danger of grass burn.

Hand-cast the fertilizer across the lawn in one direction, applying it at full strength. Then repeat at a 90° angle, using only half as much fertilizer. If you think you've put too much on one area, use a rake to spread it out.

Using an applicator. Hand-operated broadcasters and walk-behind broadcasters and drop-spreaders are commonly used to apply dry fertilizer.

■ *Hand-operated broadcasters* come in different shapes and sizes. A hand crank activates a small hopper that throws the fertilizer out in all directions (one type is shown on page 41).

Start at one end of your lawn and make a run. Then pace off the swath diameter and make your next run parallel to the first. It's best to overlap by about a third. To avoid overfertilizing, stop turning the hand crank as you make your turn at the end of your run.

Be sure to fill the applicator over a driveway or sidewalk so spillage does not burn a patch in the lawn.

■ *Walk-behind broadcasters,* like the one shown on page 67, are pushed from behind like lawn mowers. More accurate than hand-operated broadcasters, they're also more expensive. They're ideal for larger lawns and apply fertilizer evenly. Overlap slightly as you make your runs to avoid creating wheel depressions.

■ *Walk-behind drop-spreaders,* like the one shown above, drop the fertilizer straight down into the turf instead of throwing it out like broadcast spreaders. Therefore, it takes longer to fertilize a yard using a drop-spreader, but they're

the most accurate of all fertilizing applicators.

You can rent this type of applicator; have the rental operator show you how to calibrate how much fertilizer the drop-spreader will apply at one time.

Spraying fertilizers. Water-soluble fertilizers are easily applied using a hose-end sprayer. The fertilizer container should provide a chart showing the water-to-fertilizer mixing ratio.

Divide the lawn in half with a rope or sticks and spray evenly. Try to reach the halfway point in the lawn when the hose container reaches half-empty. Work carefully and quickly so you finish the rest of the lawn as the container empties.

Dethatching & Aeration

When nutrients, water, and air are unable to penetrate the soil because of thatch buildup or soil compaction, bare spots may begin to appear, and grass will no longer thrive. Dethatching and aerating are two practices that can restore your lawn to health.

Dethatching

Thatch is the layer of dead grass, roots, and debris that accumulates between the surface of the soil and the green grass blades above. It's a perfect hideout for insects and prevents water from reaching the soil.

Controlling thatch is one of the most important and overlooked steps in lawn care. Almost every lawn needs dethatching at least once a year. Water and fertilizers are absorbed much more quickly when thatch is cleared away, and diseases and insects have a tougher time getting established. Also, grass seeds germinate more quickly, roots grow deeper, and the lawn remains a deep green longer in the fall and regains its color earlier in the spring.

Some grasses are more susceptible to thatch buildup than others. The creeping grasses, most notably Bermuda grass, St. Augustine grass, bent grass, zoysia grass, and Kentucky bluegrass, develop thatch quickly. A lawn planted with one of those grasses will have to be dethatched more often than a lawn planted with a different grass.

When to Dethatch

Lawn experts recommend dethatching when the thatch depth has reached ½ inch. To check depth, press your fingers into the grass. The depth between the beginning of the brown thatch layer and the soil is your thatch level.

Another indication is when your mower leaves brown streaks and patches in the lawn. This occurs where the thatch is soft and the mower wheels sink in, allowing the blades to scalp the grass.

Timing also depends on climate and type of grass. Fall is preferable for cool-season grasses; dethatch early enough so there's still at least a month of good growing weather during which the grass can recuperate. Cool-season grasses can also be dethatched in early spring.

The best time to dethatch warm-season grasses is late spring, when they can recover quickly.

How to Dethatch

Although you may be able to properly dethatch a small lawn with a heavy rake, the most efficient method is to use a dethatching machine, or vertical cutter. These machines look like lawn mowers, but they slice the turf vertically with knifelike cutters, tearing through thatch layers and low grass runners.

The most common dethatching machine is a front-throw, reel-type mower with a grass catcher. Some manufacturers of lawn mowers are now selling special dethatching attachments that fit on the front of the mower. Generally not as effective as professional dethatching machines, these attachments do help prevent the buildup of thatch.

Since calibration of the depth and width of the cutter blades is crucial, you may want to hire a professional to do the dethatching. Contact a local lawn-care service. If you want to do the work yourself (dethatching a 1,000-square-foot lawn usually takes a little more than 2 hours), you can rent a vertical cutter from an equipment rental company. Note that although the machine is small enough to fit into the trunk of most cars, it is very heavy.

The key to proper dethatching is correct adjustment of the vertical cutter blades. For tough warm-season grasses like Bermuda grass, the cutter blades should be set to slice completely through the thatch layer and about an inch into the soil. To promote heavy thinning, set the blades about an inch apart.

For more fragile grass types, the blades should be set higher and about 3 inches apart. Check with your local lawn-care center for recommended settings. Most rental companies will help you make the blade settings.

When cutting, make several criss-crossing passes to lift and loosen the tough, interlocking runners that hold thatch.

The soil should be damp but not wet when you use a dethatcher.

Aeration

Lawns grown in clay soils or those subjected to heavy foot traffic can easily become compacted. Aeration is simply a method of punching holes into the turf to allow moisture, oxygen, and nutrients to penetrate the soil. It can also help break up thatch, which discourages water absorption and root growth.

When to aerate. The timing and frequency of aeration depend on your soil type. Clay soils compact easily and must be aerated often, generally at least twice a year. Sandy soils need aerating only about once a year. Since aeration schedules are site and soil specific, check with a local lawn-care professional before developing your own schedule.

How to aerate. To aerate your lawn, you can use either a motorized aerating machine or a foot-press aerator that you push into the soil, much like a shovel. (Either tool can be rented from an equipment rental company.) Many professional lawn-care companies also provide aerating service.

Although motorized aerators are more expensive to rent, they're quicker, easier, and usually much more efficient to use than the foot-press types. Whichever tool you choose, aeration holes should penetrate 2 to 4 inches into the soil. Most lawns require a single coverage, but if you have clay soil or if your lawn hasn't been aerated for more than a year, do it twice, the second time at a 90° angle to the first pass.

Back-comb the soil with a rake to level it; or you can break up the turf cores by dragging a metal mat over them and then using them to fill in low spots in the lawn.

Lawn Renovation

Although lawns can have a lengthy life span, there are times when an entire lawn—or a substantial portion of it—must be replanted. When bare spots aren't responding to your normal cultural practices, it's time to renovate.

Renovations aren't difficult and don't require a lot of time, but they can make a big difference in how your lawn looks. Before beginning any work, apply a translocating nonselective herbicide to the lawn to kill all grasses and weeds (follow the manufacturer's directions for use). Wait until the chemical has had enough time to do its work before you proceed.

The steps in the renovation process are outlined below. See the facing page for a look at the process.

Step 1: Dethatching. Use a dethatching machine, available at most equipment rental companies, to slice through the dead grass to allow the seeds, water, and fertilizer access to the soil. The dethatching blades leave slits in the soil that will be filled with new seed after the area is raked and leveled.

Six Steps in a Lawn Renovation

Before renovation, *lawn looks blotchy and unhealthy. Numerous bare spots mark surface.*

Dethatching machine, *or vertical cutter, tears through thatch layers and slices into soil.*

Rake up old grass *and cart it off to a disposal site. (Thatch is not suitable to use as mulch or compost.)*

Power aerator *pulls up turf cores, reducing compaction and permitting water, seed, and air to penetrate soil more easily.*

Walk-behind broadcast spreader, *ideal for large lawn areas, throws grass seed out evenly.*

Apply fertilizer *and, if desired, rake lightly to scratch grass seeds into soil. Water, keeping soil moist at all times.*

On very small lawns, you can de-thatch by mowing close to the ground and using a metal rake to tear up the thatch. For detailed instructions on de-thatching, see page 65.

Step 2: Raking. Use a rake to gather up the old grass and weeds, thereby eliminating unwanted seeds that will compete with the new ones you'll plant. Then rake the area level.

Because thatch decomposes very slowly, it's not a good idea to use it either as mulch or as part of a compost pile.

Step 3: Aeration. Punching holes in the turf, a process known as aeration (see page 66), allows moisture, fertilizer, grass seed, and air to penetrate the soil. Using a power or foot-press aerator, cover the entire area to be renovated.

The aerator pulls plugs of soil, called turf cores, out of your lawn, easing soil compaction and giving the new lawn roots room to grow.

Step 4: Seeding. Put down grass seed or start your lawn with sprigs or plugs. If you're laying sod instead, you may need to test the soil and add any necessary soil amendments. (For help, see the chapter beginning on page 29.)

Step 5: Fertilizing. Apply fertilizer as described on page 65, following the manufacturer's directions.

Step 6: Watering. The lawn must be kept moist at all times. If you're renovating during a summer hot spell, it may be necessary to sprinkle the seed bed several times a day. Once the new grass has grown a third taller than its optimum height, you can mow it. Be careful not to cut it too closely.

Weeds, Pests & Diseases

Although on the surface lawns appear to be peaceful, soft mats to walk on, under the blades a daily battle takes place. Militant weeds, insects, and grass-destroying diseases are constantly attacking your lawn. They'll take advantage of any turf weakness caused by improper watering, too much thatch, soil nutrient depletion, or compaction of soil.

Waging War Against Weeds

Technically, weeds are annual or perennial plants that grow where they're unwanted. Weed seed comes in all packages of lawn seed; it can also be blown in by wind, washed in by water runoff, or carried in by animals and humans.

Types of Weeds

Weeds are classified into two groups: grassy and broad leaved. For a close look at some common grassy and broad-leaved weeds and information on how to control them, see the chart beginning on page 70.

Grassy weeds. Any grass unwanted by the gardener is considered a grassy weed. The most common is hairy crabgrass. Although it's not always the culprit (many other weeds are mistaken for hairy crabgrass), it remains king of the grassy weeds.

Hairy crabgrass seedlings grow 2 to 4 leaves that form large, flat, stem-rooting clumps during summer. The weed looks like a large, green, upside-down spider at maturity, and it spreads very quickly. Other common grassy weeds are Bermuda grass, dallis grass, and quack grass.

Broad-leaved weeds. All nongrassy plants that invade your lawn are considered broad-leaved weeds. Spurge, dandelion, and chickweed are common examples.

Eradicating Weeds

Getting rid of weeds isn't usually a difficult job if weeds are kept to a minimum by such good lawn practices as frequent mowing, watering, and fertilizing. Weeding can be done by hand or with chemical herbicides. Some biological products, such as herbicidal soaps, are also helpful if the infestation is not too extensive.

Since herbicides contain toxic materials, they should always be used with caution. Be sure to read labels carefully and follow directions exactly.

Weeding by hand. Pull the invading weeds out by hand, if possible, or use a weeding tool; take care to pull out the roots as well as the tops. Although hand-pulling takes time and effort, it does ensure that the weed is totally removed and avoids the use of a chemical herbicide.

Using herbicides. If used incorrectly, herbicides can injure or kill desirable turf and commit unwanted poisons into the environment. Any weed killer you purchase should be labeled with its chemical name, the specific weeds it will kill, and the grasses to which it can be applied.

There are a number of ways to apply herbicides. Hose-end applicators, hand sprayers, pressure spray tanks, and watering cans can all be used. Choose the method that allows the most direct and site-specific application.

Avoid spraying on windy days and remember that once a container has been filled with a herbicide, it should not be used for any purpose other than weed eradication. Do not use herbicides on a new lawn until it has grown enough to require two mowings.

Caution: If you have children or pets that play frequently on the lawn, be sure to check how long the poisons remain active.

Lawn Pests

Lawn-damaging pests fall into two categories: those that feed on leaf blades and other above-ground lawn parts and those that feed on roots and other below-ground parts.

Insects

It's important to identify which insects can damage your grass because dozens of harmless insects also inhabit your lawn. And different pests require different chemical treatments and application methods. For detailed information on how to identify and control some of the most common insects, see page 74.

Above-ground insects. Infestations of above-ground feeders are easy to spot if you look closely in the lawn itself. Cutworms, sod webworms (lawn moth larvae), leafhoppers, dichondra flea beetles, and chinch bugs are common above-ground feeders.

Below-ground insects. These insects, which include billbugs and white grubs, feed on grass roots and can devastate large sections of a lawn in a short time.

Gophers & Moles

These creatures can be a source of great frustration to gardeners, wreaking havoc on lawns and escaping all but the most persistent efforts to eradicate them.

Gophers. Serious pests in many areas, gophers resemble little bulldozers, digging a network of tunnels below the surface of lawns. Gophers eat roots, bulbs, and sometimes entire plants by pulling them down into their burrows.

Often, the first sign of gopher trouble is a fan-shaped mound of fresh, finely pulverized earth in a lawn. You may find a hole in this mound or (more often) a plug of earth blocking the exit.

Trapping is the most efficient method of catching gophers. Avoid the temptation of placing a single trap down a hole. Your chances of catching a gopher are much greater when you dig down to the main horizontal runway connecting with the surface hole and place two traps in the runway, one on either side of your excavation.

Once the traps are in place, plug the hole with fresh grass or other tender greens. Place a board or soil over the greens to block all light. Check the traps

often and clear the tunnels if the gopher has pushed soil into the traps. Be persistent: a wily gopher may avoid your first attempts.

Moles. Notorious pests in good soils, moles are primarily insectivorous, eating earthworms, bugs, and larvae, and only occasionally nibbling on greens and roots. Irrigation and rain keep them near the soil surface where they do the most damage as they tunnel, disfiguring lawns, heaving plants from the ground, and severing tender roots.

A mole's main runways, which are used repeatedly, are usually from 6 to 10 inches underground and are frequently punctuated with volcano-shaped mounds of excavated soil. Shallower burrows, created while feeding, are used for short periods and then abandoned.

Trapping is the most efficient control. The spear- or harpoon-type trap is the easiest to set because you simply position the trap above the soil. A clever mole will spring, heave out, or go around a faultily set trap.

Fungus Diseases

Threadlike lawn fungi are parasites that live off grass plants and can turn your lawn yellow or brown in a hurry. Usually, they're detected after most other pests have been eliminated and the lawn has been watered and fed with nitrogen.

Although fungus diseases rarely show all the classic symptoms, the disease information beginning on page 76 will help you identify and control any fungi that attack your yard.

Fungus problems are easier to prevent than to cure. Since fungi cannot develop in the absence of moisture, proper irrigation is the key. Water deeply; then allow the top 2 inches of soil to dry out before watering again. This eliminates the breeding grounds for fungi.

If It's Not Weeds, Pests, or Disease

Sometimes, problems linger in your lawn even after you've systematically eliminated weeds, pests, or disease as a probable cause. Here are some typical problems and their solutions.

■ **Spots on your lawn.** If spots suddenly appear on your lawn, check to see if they bear any relationship to the course you traveled with your chemical dispenser (whether a pesticide, weed killer, or fertilizer). Water the areas heavily to leach the chemicals out; the lawn will eventually recover.

If the spots persist, sight across them to see if they lie low or high in the lawn. If so, they may be getting too much or too little water. Level off a high area with a spade or fill in a low spot. Then reseed.

■ **Excessive puddling or runoff.** Soil compaction not only causes pooling

and quick runoff but also retards root growth. Too much thatch can also keep water from penetrating the soil. A proper maintenance schedule that includes dethatching and aeration (see page 65) may solve the problem.

■ **Persistent yellowing.** Lack of water or sunlight can turn a lawn yellow. Make sure enough water is getting to the area. Trees can both shade a lawn and rob it of nutrients and water. Solutions include thinning the tree to allow more sunlight to reach the lawn and adding extra fertilizer and water on lawn areas that must compete with trees.

■ **Dead spots ringed by healthy grass.** Female dogs are often responsible for stubborn dead spots in an otherwise healthy lawn. Keep the dog off the grass and soak the spots with water. If the spots persist, you'll have to reseed.

Lawn Weeds, Pests & Diseases

Despite your best intentions, some weeds, pests, or diseases will inevitably invade your lawn from time to time. Cultural controls, such as weeding or deep watering, can often eliminate the nuisance. Only if the infestation is extensive should you apply the appropriate chemical control. Take all necessary precautions whenever you use a chemical on your grass. Protect both yourself and your lawn by reading labels carefully and following the manufacturer's directions.

Lawn problems and their remedies are described on the following pages. Remember: The best protection against those problems is a lawn that's carefully maintained. For a year-round maintenance calendar, see page 79.

Common Lawn Weeds

The weeds described below, commonly found in lawns, can be controlled in several ways. You can control them culturally by keeping turf healthy. You can control them physically, by pulling or hoeing them. Or you can control them chemically with herbicides.

When you purchase a weed killer, be sure to read the label carefully. It should give the specific weeds it will control, the types of grasses you can apply it to, and instructions for use. Follow the manufacturer's directions exactly.

BERMUDA GRASS
Cynodon dactylon

■ *Description:* Bermuda grass is a perennial that thrives in warm climates. Although it's a common turf grass, it can also be a persistent weed where it grows unwanted. It spreads underground by rhizomes and above ground by seeds and stolons. Its fine leaves are pointed at the end. It's sometimes mistaken for crabgrass, but its leaves are much finer and smaller.

■ *Controls:* Cultural controls include hand-weeding, the most effective method of eradication on smaller lawns. Be sure to remove the entire underground stem; otherwise, it can start new shoots.

On larger lawns, spray isolated patches with fluazifop-butyl, sethoxydim, or glyphosate; then reseed. Repeat applications may be necessary.

ANNUAL BLUEGRASS
Poa annua

■ *Description:* Bright green annual bluegrass is fine textured and narrow leaved. It produces small, wheatlike seed blossoms that are borne on top of the grass, giving the turf an overall white-flecked appearance. Although annual bluegrass looks great in cold weather, it turns brown when the weather gets hot.

■ *Controls:* Bluegrass will die out by itself in warm weather, but it can be a stubborn weed in spring and fall.

To discourage annual bluegrass, maintain a thick-turfed, deeply rooted lawn. Eradicate by hand or apply bensulide.

CHICKWEED
Stellaria media

■ *Description:* Chickweed, an annual, has leaves that are smaller than postage stamps. They grow in opposite pairs on many-branched stems. This weed thrives in sheltered areas.

■ *Controls:* Keeping turf well drained helps prevent chickweed from growing. Dicamba is effective when applied in spring or fall.

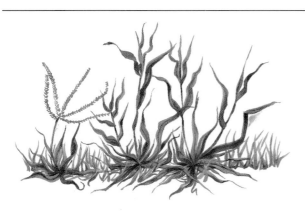

CRABGRASS
Digitaria species

■ *Description:* This is a tough annual summer weed that spreads quickly through abundant seeding. It thrives in lawns that get frequent surface watering, in underfed lawns, and in poorly drained fields.

Hairy crabgrass germinates in spring, sending up small seedlings with two to four leaves that form large, flat, stem-rooting clumps in summer. The undersides of the pale green blades are covered with coarse, tiny hairs. Fingerlike flower spikelets rise from narrow stems.

Smooth crabgrass is similar to hairy crabgrass, except that its leaves and leaf sheaths are smoother, longer, and narrower. Although not as gruesome in appearance as its hairy cousin, smooth crabgrass can infest a lawn with equal speed. Immediate eradication is necessary.

■ *Controls:* Cultural controls include keeping lawns well fertilized and vigorous to provide tough competition for weeds. To dry out crabgrass roots, water lawns deeply but not frequently.

In late winter or early spring before seedlings appear, apply a preemergent, such as DCPA (Dacthal), with a fertilizer spreader.

DALLIS GRASS
Paspalum dilatatum

■ *Description:* This perennial is a common weed during summer, its active growth period. Large, flat stalks grow in crown-shaped rings 4 to 8 inches across. The rhizomes are very closely jointed, and the seed heads are sparsely branched on long stems.

■ *Controls:* Hand-weeding is effective, but reseeding is necessary. Since dallis grass thrives in wet areas, draining or building up the lawn may be necessary.

DANDELION
Taraxacum officinale

■ *Description:* Dandelion's bright yellow flowers and stemless basal leaves are unmistakable. The weed grows from a single brownish taproot that often breaks—and can regrow—when you try to pull the plant out. It spreads by dispersing wind-borne seeds and by sprouting root crowns.

Flowering begins in spring and can often continue until frost; in mild weather, seeds can germinate year-round. The flower becomes a round, white seed head at maturity.

■ *Controls:* Proper turf maintenance procedures usually keep dandelions to a minimum. Pull out young plants before the taproot has a chance to grow deeply in the soil.

Apply MCPP in spring and fall. Spray isolated plants with glyphosate or another herbicide for broad-leaved weeds and reseed.

CURLY DOCK
Rumex crispus

■ *Description:* This broad-leaved perennial has long, narrow, dark green leaves with smooth, wavy edges. If not pulled, it sends up a tall, narrow spike of greenish flowers from the center of the plant.

■ *Controls:* Dock infestations are easy to identify and can be eradicated by hand-pulling or with the help of a small spade. For heavy infestations, use 2,4-D or dicamba in spring or fall.

KNOTWEED
Polygonum aviculare

■ *Description:* This annual, broad-leaved weed is usually light green, with small leaves growing sparsely on long,

trailing stems. However, the plants often grow close together, giving the appearance of thick foliage.

■ *Controls:* Knotweed infestations can be prevented by good maintenance practices, including dethatching and aeration. The favored chemical control is dicamba.

MALLOW, OR CHEESEWEED
Malva species

■ *Description:* This tough, low-flowering annual or biennial weed has rounded, fan-shaped green leaves at the top of a whitish stalk. There's a red spot at the base of each leaf. Mallow has a 6- to 8-month growing season, beginning in early spring.

Since the leaves stand an inch or two above the turf, the weed is easy to identify. Uncontrolled plants grow larger.

■ *Controls:* Hand-weeding is effective. Chemical controls include MCPP and dicamba.

OXALIS
Oxalis corniculata

■ *Description:* This aggressive, cloverlike weed spreads from a single taproot, which soon develops into a shallow, spreading root system. Plants may have green or reddish purple leaves and tiny, bright yellow flowers. Long, narrow, beaklike seed capsules explode like popcorn when ripe, shooting seeds as far as 6 feet.

■ *Controls:* A vigorous, well-fertilized lawn provides tough competition for oxalis. Once infestations occur, dig out small plants, tracing any runners back to the main plant. Or carefully spot-treat isolated plants with glyphosate and reseed. When weeds are gone, oryzalin is an effective preemergence control.

PLANTAIN
Plantago species

■ *Description:* This cool-season perennial weed grows in a rosette shape.

Broad-leaved plantain has broad, oval-shaped leaves 3 to 6 inches long. The flower stalk is long and slender and curls slightly at the top.

Buckhorn plantain plants have long, thin leaves and a conspicuously long (up to 12 inches) stalk with a ball-like blossom cluster at the end.

■ *Controls:* Hand-pull, or apply MCPP in spring or fall before flowers form.

QUACK GRASS
Agropyron repens

■ *Description:* This ungainly-looking, narrow-leaved perennial grass spreads aggressively by means of underground rhizomes. If left unmowed, it can grow from 1 to 3 feet tall. Narrow flower spikes rising from the plant resemble slender heads of wheat or rye.

■ *Controls:* Treat with glyphosate and reseed.

SPOTTED SPURGE
Euphorbia maculata

■ *Description:* This annual grows close to the ground in a thick, fast-spreading mat from a single taproot. Its small leaves are green with a red spot on the upper center. Cut stems exude a milky juice.

Spotted spurge grows aggressively in summer in almost all climates. Plants turn red orange and decline in fall as temperatures drop.

■ *Controls:* Control is difficult. Proper lawn maintenance will keep this weed to a minimum. Hoe out isolated plants early before they produce seed, or spray them with glyphosate and reseed. On lawns, use a preemergence herbicide such as DCPA (Dacthal).

Common Lawn Pests

Several different kinds of creatures can damage your lawn, some above the ground and others below ground. Different climates foster different problems: a worst offender in one region may be unknown in another.

A totally pest-free garden is neither possible nor desirable. Good maintenance procedures can go a long way toward reducing the threat of an insect infestation. Even releasing or encouraging beneficial insects can help. When you need to use insecticides, follow label directions exactly. Before you purchase a product, make sure you've correctly identified the problem. For help, contact a professional or your County Cooperative Extension office.

BILLBUGS
Sphenophorus species

■ *Description:* Billbugs are brownish black weevils with long snouts (hence, the name billbugs). The larvae are white and legless, measuring about ⅜ inch long when fully grown. They feed on roots and crowns.

■ *Susceptible plants:* All grasses, especially Bermuda grass. Old lawns in warm inland areas are most susceptible.

■ *Damage and detection.* Like white grubs, billbug larvae can destroy entire root systems if left unchecked. However, since they're active at shallower depths, the lawn cannot be rolled back, as it can after a white grub infestation, but pieces of turf can easily be picked up. To check for billbug infestations, examine the soil around browned grass roots and dig in the edges near green, healthy grass. If more than one grub per square foot is found, treat the lawn.

■ *Controls:* Diazinon and carbaryl (Sevin). Apply liquid formulations to moist turf, granular formulations to dry turf. Immediately after application, water well.

CHINCH BUGS
Blissus species

■ *Description:* Adults are dark gray to black insects that grow to less than ¼ inch long. When not in flight, the chinch bug's white wings fold flat over the body. Nymphs (immature insects) are red.

Chinch bugs crawl along grass blades and suck out the juices, leaving the lawn bleached and withered. The bugs thrive in hot weather.

■ *Susceptible plants:* St. Augustine and zoysia grasses are especially vulnerable to chinch bug infestations. Kentucky bluegrass and creeping bent grass are occasionally damaged.

■ *Damage and detection:* During infestations, yellowish patches appear in lawns, with the grass eventually dying. Sunny areas or portions under drought stress are particularly susceptible. The bugs can be found just at the edge of the damaged areas.

Check for chinch bugs by pushing a bottomless can into the soil just where the grass is beginning to turn brown. Fill the can with water. If the lawn is infested, the chinch bugs will float to the surface.

■ *Controls:* Diazinon and chlorpyrifos (Dursban). Mow and water before treatment; apply late in the day to moist turf. Do not water or mow for 24 hours.

CUTWORMS
Psudaletia species

■ *Description:* These thick-skinned, dark, 1- to 2-inch-long larvae often have spots or longitudinal stripes. When disturbed, they curl up, feigning death. At maturity, cutworms become nocturnal, brownish gray moths with a wingspan from 1 to 1½ inches.

■ *Susceptible plants:* All grasses and dichondra.

■ *Damage and detection:* The larvae feed off grass leaves and crowns, leaving small, brown, irregular patches in the grass. During the day, they hide in the thatch layer.

To detect cutworms, mix 1 tablespoon household detergent in 1 gallon water and pour evenly over a square yard of lawn area. Larvae will come to the surface. Treat when five or more larvae are found per square yard.

■ *Controls:* Thatch removal effectively eliminates the cutworms' hiding place. Chemical controls include acephate (Orthene), chlorpyrifos (Dursban), and diazinon. Mow and water before treatment; apply late in the day to moist turf. Do not water or mow for 24 hours.

FLEA BEETLES
Chaetocnema repens

■ *Description:* Adult flea beetles are black and very tiny and look somewhat like small fleas; they'll jump a foot or two into the air when disturbed. The larvae live in the soil and are rarely seen.

■ *Susceptible plants:* Dichondra.

■ *Damage and detection:* Although miniscule, these innocent-looking pests can devastate a dichondra lawn in a relatively short time. Adult flea beetles feed on the leaf's surface and remove the soft tissue. The remaining plant skeleton will twist and turn brown as though suffering from fertilizer burn or lack of water.

Upon close examination, you can spot the tiny beetles sitting on the plant leaves. When disturbed, the area will suddenly come alive with tiny, jumping insects.

■ *Controls:* Diazinon and chlorpyrifos (Dursban). Mow and water before treatment; apply late in the day to moist turf. Do not water or mow for 24 hours.

LEAFHOPPERS
Cicadellidae family

■ *Description:* Like tiny (⅛- to ¼-inch) grasshoppers, these pale green, gray, or yellow insects are very active. When disturbed, they may fly or hop short distances. Immature leafhoppers are the same colors as adults but lack wings.

■ *Susceptible plants:* All grasses. Dichondra is not usually attacked.

■ *Damage and detection:* Leafhoppers are easy to detect since they fly up in swarms as you walk through the lawn. They suck juices from the leaves and, if unchecked, can leave the lawn pale and dry.

■ *Controls:* Diazinon and carbaryl (Sevin). Mow and water before treatment; apply late in the day to moist turf. Do not water or mow for 24 hours.

SOD WEBWORMS (LAWN MOTHS)
Crambus sperryellus

■ *Description:* Sod webworms, slender gray caterpillars with black spots, are larvae of whitish or buff-colored moths that have a 1-inch wingspan. The webworms get their name from the silken tunnels they spin in thatch layers.

A silvery white stripe is easy to spot on the lawn moth's forewing. The moths hide in the grass during the day and fly in a zigzag pattern when disturbed. They usually fly at night, dropping their eggs while in flight. The larvae hatch and begin feeding on turf blades and stems.

■ *Susceptible plants:* All grasses. Especially vulnerable are bent grasses, bluegrasses, and all new lawns.

■ *Damage and detection:* Patchy brown areas on the lawn, often with pencil-size holes made by birds digging for the webworms, indicate an infestation. To detect webworms, bring them to the surface by mixing 1 tablespoon household detergent in 1 gallon water and pouring evenly over a 1-square-yard area. Treat when 15 or more webworms are found per square yard.

■ *Controls:* Proper lawn maintenance, including watering, aeration, and dethatching, will reduce the infestation. If necessary, treat with diazinon or chlorpyrifos (Dursban). Mow and water before treatment; apply late in the day to moist turf. Do not water or mow for 24 hours.

WHITE GRUBS
Cyclocephala species

■ *Description:* The larvae are large (from 1 to 1½ inches long) and C-shaped when at rest. Their most distinguishing feature is three pairs of legs. The adults are brown with reddish heads and are known as May beetles or June bugs (it's during those months that they emerge from the ground as adults). Japanese beetles also emerge in spring.

■ *Susceptible plants:* All grasses.

■ *Damage and detection:* White grubs feed beneath the surface, destroying grass roots. In areas where infestation is heavy, the roots are completely eaten away and the lawn can be rolled back like sod. Once the symptoms appear in late summer, most of the damage has been done.

To check for white grubs, dig up the soil under brown spots in mid-July. If more than one grub per square foot is found, treat the entire lawn by early August.

■ *Controls:* Diazinon and chlorpyrifos (Dursban). Apply liquid formulations to moist turf, granular formulations to dry turf. Immediately after application, water well.

Common Lawn Diseases

Most lawn diseases are the result of various fungi. But sometimes, unfavorable environmental conditions or poor maintenance practices can cause disease. The buildup of thatch creates favorable conditions for the development of fungal diseases, as do too much or too little fertilizer (or fertilizer applied at the wrong time of year) and poorly drained soil that stays moist for long periods of time.

Proper maintenance procedures are explained in this chapter. When disease persists, you may have to resort to a fungicide. As with any chemical, read the label carefully and follow directions to the letter.

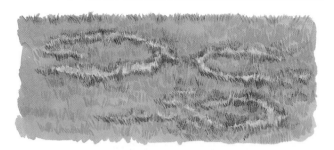

BROWN PATCH
Rhizoctonia solani

■ *Symptoms:* Brown patch is characterized by small, irregularly shaped brown spots that may enlarge as the disease strengthens. The centers of the spots may recover, exposing large brown circles (like smoke rings) in the lawn. The grass blades become water soaked, turn yellowish brown, and die.

■ *Susceptible grasses:* Bent grasses, Bermuda grasses, bluegrasses, fescues, ryegrasses, and St. Augustine grass.

■ *Controls:* Minimize shade and aerate the lawn. Irrigate 6 inches deep as needed. Avoid fertilizers high in nitrogen. Fungicidal controls include benomyl, chlorothalonil, and thiophanate.

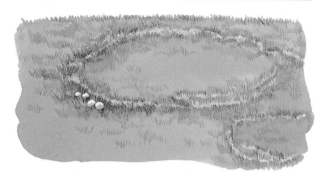

FAIRY RING
Marasmius oreades

■ *Symptoms:* Fairy ring appears as small, circular patches of dark green grass, often followed by dead grass. Mushrooms may or may not be present.

■ *Susceptible grasses:* All grasses.

■ *Controls:* Aerate the lawn, apply a fertilizer high in nitrogen, and keep the lawn wet for 3 to 5 days. There is no effective fungicidal control.

DOLLAR SPOT
Sclerotinia homeocarpa

■ *Symptoms:* Dollar spot attacks lawns in numerous small (about the size of a silver dollar) bleached or gray spots. When the fungus first starts, the infected areas have a water-soaked appearance. Sometimes, spots merge to make large, straw-colored areas.

■ *Susceptible grasses:* Bent grasses, Bermuda grasses, bluegrasses, fescues, and ryegrasses.

■ *Controls:* Dethatch the lawn and irrigate 6 inches deep as needed. Apply a fertilizer high in nitrogen. Fungicidal controls include anilazine, benomyl, and thiophanate.

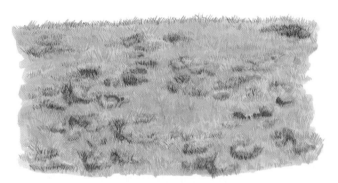

FUSARIUM PATCH
Fusarium nivale

■ *Symptoms:* Common in the central states and the Northeast, fusarium patch shows up as tan or brown spots 2 to 12 inches in diameter. Look for weblike threads in thatch or on dew-covered grass.

■ *Susceptible grasses:* Bent grasses, bluegrasses, fescues, and ryegrasses.

■ *Controls:* Minimize shade, aerate the lawn, and improve drainage. Avoid fertilizers high in nitrogen. Fungicidal controls include benomyl and thiophanate. Apply fungicide early in the fall.

GREASE SPOT
Pythium

■ *Symptoms:* Infected blades turn dark and become matted together, giving a greasy appearance in streaks through the lawn. Sometimes, a white, cottony mold appears on leaf blades.

■ *Susceptible grasses:* All grasses, particularly new lawns.

■ *Controls:* Minimize shade and aerate the lawn. Apply water early in the day and avoid excess watering. Control with chloroneb.

RUST
Puccinia

■ *Symptoms:* Small reddish pustules form in circular or elongated groups on older leaf blades and stems; the blades eventually shrivel and die. Rub a white cloth over a suspected infection: if the cloth picks up an orange color, it's rust disease.

■ *Susceptible grasses:* Bluegrasses and ryegrasses.

■ *Controls:* Apply a fertilizer high in nitrogen and water regularly. Triadimefon is the most effective fungicide. Anilazine and mancozeb are also helpful.

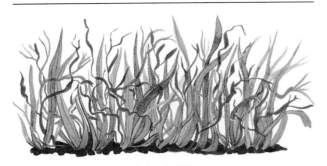

RED THREAD
Coricium fuciforme

■ *Symptoms:* Small patches of dead grass appear, followed by spiderlike webs of bright pink threads that bind blades together. The lawn yellows in patches 2 to 12 inches in diameter. This fungus likes cool, moist weather.

■ *Susceptible grasses:* Bent grasses, bluegrasses, fescues, and ryegrasses.

■ *Controls:* Apply a high-nitrogen fertilizer in late fall. Minimize shade on the lawn. Fungicidal controls include chlorothalonil and mancozeb.

SNOW MOLD
Typhula

■ *Symptoms:* As snow melts, snow mold appears as dirty white patches in the lawn. The margins between these patches are rather distinct, and the dead grass pulls up easily.

■ *Susceptible grasses:* Bent grasses, bluegrasses, and fescues.

■ *Controls:* Aerate the lawn and improve drainage, if possible. Try to reduce snow pileup. Fungicidal controls include benomyl and thiophanate (apply before the first snowfall).

Lawn Maintenance Calendar

	Cool-season Grasses	Warm-season Grasses
Spring 	**Seed** after ground warms. Lay sod anytime. **Mow** weekly. Towards end of season, raise cutting height to 2 inches. **Water** more as growth increases. **Fertilize** when temperature reaches 60°F and again about a month later. If lush growth doesn't result, add iron in West; adjust pH with lime in East. **Dethatch and aerate,** if needed, early in season. **Control weeds** with a preemergence herbicide, if necessary.	**Seed** or sprig after danger of frost has passed. Plant plugs before warming begins. Lay sod anytime. **Mow** more often as growth increases. **Water** more as growth increases. **Fertilize** early in season and again about a month later. If lush growth doesn't result, add iron in West; adjust pH with lime in East. **Dethatch and aerate,** if needed, late in season. **Control weeds** with a preemergence herbicide, if necessary.
Summer 	**Lay sod** anytime. Reseed late in summer. If seeding in fall, prepare soil. **Mow** regularly as temperatures rise, increasing cutting height to reduce weeds and improve drought and heat tolerance. **Water** slowly, deeply, and infrequently to discourage weeds and keep grass healthy. **Fertilize** no later than early June, if at all. **Aerate,** if needed, to improve water penetration. **Control weeds** and disease with regular mowing and deep, infrequent watering.	**Seed** early in season. Lay sod anytime. **Mow** regularly as temperatures rise, increasing cutting height. Leave grass clippings on lawn. **Water** slowly, deeply, and infrequently to discourage weeds and keep grass healthy. **Fertilize,** if necessary. **Aerate,** if needed, to improve water penetration. **Control weeds** and disease with regular mowing and deep, infrequent watering.
Fall 	**Seed** while soil is still warm. Lay sod anytime. **Mow** often if lawn is vigorous. **Water** less often unless lawn is new. **Fertilize** several times, about a month apart. **Dethatch,** if needed, early in fall; then fertilize. Aerate, if needed, to improve water penetration. **Control weeds,** if necessary, with a preemergence herbicide that prevents germination of winter weeds.	**Seed** only in very early fall. In mid-season, overseed with annual or perennial ryegrass or fescues for green winter lawns. Lay sod anytime. **Mow** as needed. **Water** less often. **Fertilize** early in season for a green lawn later in fall and earlier in spring. **Control weeds,** if necessary, with a preemergence herbicide that prevents germination of winter weeds.
Winter 	**Lay sod** in mild-winter areas. **Mow** as needed. **Water** as needed. **Fertilize,** if necessary, only in mildest winter climates. **Aerate,** if needed, to improve water penetration, but do not dethatch. **Control weeds** with a preemergence herbicide, if necessary. If snow mold damaged lawn last year, treat it now.	**Lay sod** anytime. **Mow** weekly if lawn is overseeded with annual ryegrass; otherwise, mow as needed. **Water** when needed. **Fertilize** in late winter if lawn stays green. **Aerate,** if needed, to improve water penetration. **Control weeds** with a preemergence herbicide, if necessary.

Ground Covers

Among the plants referred to as "ground cover" are plants so varied and so capable of thriving in diverse situations and climates that to describe them as versatile is an understatement. What they have in common is relatively low, dense growth, although ground covers range from prostrate woody shrubs to vines, and from spreading perennials to a few that are popularly thought of as bulbs.

Within the rich assortment of ground covers you can find plants that will stand in for lawn; but you'll encounter a far greater number that will prosper in lawn-defeating situations or where lawn maintenance would be an ongoing headache. Ground covers are the obvious solution to such less-than-perfect situations as deep shade, dry or poor soil, hot and dry expanses, steep slopes, and soil infiltrated by competing tree roots. And where water conservation is essential, certain ground covers are the only viable means of achieving an expanse of low verdure.

Assortment of heaths (Erica) provides uniform appearance but a variety of colors over a long flowering period.

Ground Covers at Work

Color through the Seasons

Many ground covers add spice to their utilitarian lives with a display of colorful flowers, some flamboyant, others restrained.

Sunshiny Carolina jessamine (Gelsemium sempervirens) predicts summer's warmth in late winter and early spring.

Trailing African daisy (Osteospermum fruticosum) puts on its most lavish display of color from late fall to early spring.

Colorful tapestry in harmonious shades combines several varieties of moss pink (Phlox subulata).

...Color through the Seasons

*A **good choice** for a small-scale ground cover, common thrift (Armeria maritima) comes in white and various shades of pink. To achieve a patchwork effect, choose plants when they're in flower.*

Ground Covers for Seasonal Color

PLANT	SPRING	SUMMER	FALL	WINTER	ZONES
Achillea		■	■		4–10
Agapanthus		■			9–10
Ajuga reptans	■	■			4–10
Arabis caucasica	■				6–9
Arctostaphylos	■			■	Vary
Arctotheca calendula	■	■	■	■	9–10
Arenaria balearica	■	■			6–10
Armeria maritima	■				3–10
Bergenia	■			■	3–10
Bougainvillea	■				10
Calluna vulgaris		■	■		5–9
Campanula	■	■			4–10
Carissa macrocarpa	■	■	■	■	9–10
Ceanothus	■				8–10
Cerastium tomentosum	■	■			3–10
Ceratostigma plumbaginoides		■	■		6–10
Chamaemelum nobile		■			3–10
Cistus salviifolius	■				8–10
Convallaria majalis	■				3–9
Convolvulus mauritanicus	■	■	■		8–10
Correa pulchella	■		■	■	9–10
Cotoneaster	■		■		Vary
Cotula squalida		■			6–10
Cytisus kewensis	■				6–8
Dalea greggii	■	■			9–10
Dampiera diversifolia	■	■			9–10
Epimedium	■				3–9
Erica	■	■	■	■	Vary
Erigeron karvinskianus	■	■	■		9–10
Erodium chamaedryoides	■	■	■		8–10
Galax urceolata		■			3–8
Gardenia jasminoides 'Radicans'		■			8–10
Gazania	■	■			9–10
Gelsemium sempervirens	■			■	8–10
Genista	■				6–9
Geranium	■	■	■		Vary
Grevillea	■	■			9–10
Hebe		■			Vary
Helianthemum nummularium	■	■			5–10
Helleborus	■			■	Vary
Hemerocallis	■	■	■		3–10
Hippocrepis comosa	■				9–10
Hosta	■	■			3–9
Hypericum calycinum	■	■			6–10
Iberis sempervirens	■				4–10
Ice plant	■	■			Vary
Jasminum polyanthum	■	■			8–10
Lantana	■	■			9–10
Laurentia fluviatilis	■	■			8–10
Liriope		■			Vary
Lonicera	■	■			5–10
Lotus berthelotii	■				9–10
Lysimachia nummularia		■			3–10
Mahonia	■				5–9
Mazus reptans	■	■			4–10
Myosotis scorpioides	■	■			4–10
Nepeta faassenii	■	■			4–10
Osteospermum fruticosum	■	■	■	■	9–10
Pelargonium peltatum	■	■	■		9–10
Phlox subulata	■				4–9
Polygonum	■	■			Vary
Potentilla	■	■			4–9
Pratia angulata		■			7–10
Pyracantha	■			■	Vary
Ranunculus repens 'Pleniflorus'	■				4–9
Rosa	■	■	■		Vary
Rosmarinus officinalis	■		■	■	7–10
Santolina		■			7–10
Saxifraga stolonifera	■				9–10
Scaevola 'Mauve Clusters'	■	■	■		9–10
Sedum	■	■			Vary
Stachys byzantina		■			4–10
Teucrium chamaedrys		■			6–10
Thymus	■	■			4–10
Trachelospermum jasminoides		■			9–10
Vancouveria planipetala	■				7–9
Verbena	■	■	■		Vary
Veronica	■				6–10
Vinca	■				Vary
Viola	■	■			Vary
Wedelia trilobata	■	■	■		9–10

Assertive color of this sunrose (Helianthemum nummularium) *is accurately captured in its variety name 'Fire Dragon'. White, shades of pink, copper, orange, and yellow are other available colors; foliage may be dark green or nearly gray.*

Bountiful in summer, *gazanias offer blossoms in shades of yellow and orange, as well as bronze, red, pink, cream, and white.*

Dalmatian bellflower (Campanula portenschlagiana) *unrolls its colorful purple carpet in spring and remains in bloom throughout summer.*

Water-thrifty Ground Covers

When water is limited, you can use drought-tolerant ground covers in all garden situations.

***Spartan Genista lydia** takes little water and poor soil in stride, furnishing an annual display of golden blossoms regardless of conditions.*

***Vivid and unthirsty duo** provides reliable display with little care. Gaudy red and pink flowers are trailing ice plant (Lampranthus spectabilis), highlighted by yellow blossoms of gazania.*

Sparkling, true blue shades are hallmark of wild lilacs (Ceanothus); C. griseus horizontalis is a favorite ground cover species.

Drought-tolerant Ground Covers

PLANT	ZONES
Achillea	4–10
Arctotheca calendula	9–10
Artemisia caucasica	5–9
Atriplex semibaccata	8–10
Baccharis pilularis	8–10
Ceanothus	8–10
Cistus salviifolius	9–10
Cotoneaster	Vary
Dalea greggii	9–10
Erigeron karvinskianus	9–10
Festuca ovina glauca	3–10
Genista	6–9
Grevillea	9–10
Hypericum calycinum	6–10
Ice plant (some)	Vary
Juniperus	Vary
Lantana	9–10
Mahonia	Vary
Polygonum cuspidatum compactum	4–10
Ribes viburnifolium	9–10
Rosmarinus officinalis	7–10
Santolina	7–10
Scaevola 'Mauve Clusters'	9–10
Teucrium chamaedrys	6–10

Rugged, adaptable Aaron's beard (Hypericum calycinum), at left and above, performs in sun or shade, with either little or regular garden watering.

...Water-thrifty Ground Covers

Reliable, undemanding junipers—
this one is Juniperus chinensis procumbens—
are valued for their unchanging good
appearance year-round.

Molten shades transform rock cotoneaster (Cotoneaster
horizontalis) each fall before leaves drop. Little water often results in
a more colorful foliage display.

A Preference for Shade

The coolness and reduced light intensity of shade offer preferred conditions for many ground covers.

Shaggy turf of mondo grass (Ophiopogon japonicus) gives a solid, grassy effect in shaded locations where real grasses languish.

Silvery gray leaves of Lamium maculatum 'Beacon Silver' (at right) brighten shady gardens throughout growing season.

...A Preference for Shade

PLANT	ZONES
Aegopodium podagraria	4–8
Ajuga reptans	4–10
Ardisia japonica	8–9
Asarum caudatum	5–9
Cornus canadensis	3–6
Duchesnea indica	3–10
Epimedium	3–9
Euonymus fortunei	5–9
Galax urceolata	3–8
Galium odoratum	5–10
Gaultheria	Vary
Hedera	Vary
Helleborus	Vary
Herniaria glabra	5–10
Hosta	3–9
Houttuynia cordata	6–10
Hypericum calycinum	6–10
Lamium maculatum	5–10
Liriope	Vary
Mahonia nervosa	5–9
Myosotis scorpioides	4–10
Ophiopogon japonicus	8–10
Pachysandra terminalis	4–9
Paxistima	5–9
Ranunculus repens 'Pleniflorus'	4–9
Rubus calycinoides	7–9
Sarcococca hookerana humilis	6–10
Saxifraga stolonifera	9–10
Soleirolia soleirolii	9–10
Taxus baccata 'Repandens'	6–10
Vancouveria planipetala	7–9
Viburnum davidii	7–10
Vinca	Vary
Viola	Vary
Wedelia trilobata	9–10

Versatile English ivy (Hedera helix) provides a lush, neat carpet of foliage year-round in exposures ranging from full sun to heavy shade.

Touches of white in foliage of variegated Bishop's weed (Aegopodium podagraria 'Variegatum') sparkle in sun or shade.

Hostas and shade are natural companions. Leaf colors, sizes, and shapes vary widely; this sea of greens is 'Frances Williams'.

Legendary fragrance emanates from violets (Viola odorata), which come in shades of blue, lavender, violet, pink, and white, as well as traditional purple.

Plants for "Living Carpets"

Ground-hugging plants offer the neatness and uniformity of turf grass without the lawn's need for frequent maintenance.

*Acting as **"living mortar,"** Irish moss (Sagina subulata) unites paving and rock outcrop with border of colorful annuals. Occasional footsteps leave it undamaged.*

Stepping-stones float *in a pool of blue star creeper (Laurentia fluviatilis); planting accepts moderate foot traffic.*

Undemanding goldmoss sedum *(Sedum acre) spreads springtime haze of yellow flowers over foliage cover of light green, fleshy leaves.*

Low-growing Ground Covers

PLANT	ZONES
Ajuga reptans	4–10
Arabis caucasica	6–9
*Arenaria balearica	6–10
*Chamaemelum nobile	3–10
Cotula squalida	6–10
Dampiera diversifolia	9–10
*Duchesnea indica	3–10
*Erodium chamaedryoides	8–10
Euonymus fortunei 'Minima'	5–9
Helianthemum nummularium	5–10
*Herniara glabra	5–10
*Hippocrepis comosa	9–10
Ice plant (some)	Vary
Lamium maculatum	5–10
*Laurentia fluviatilis	8–10
*Lotus	Vary
Lysimachia nummularia	3–10
*Mazus reptans	4–10
*Mentha requienii	7–10

PLANT	ZONES
*Phyla nodiflora	9–10
Polygonum capitatum	9–10
*Potentilla	4–9
Pratia angulata	7–10
*Sagina subulata	5–10
Saxifraga stolonifera	9–10
Scaevola 'Mauve Clusters'	9–10
Sedum	Vary
Soleirolia soleirolii	9–10
Stachys byzantina 'Silver Carpet'	4–10
Teucrium chamaedrys 'Prostrata'	6–10
Thymus praecox arcticus	4–10
Verbena	Vary
Veronica repens	6–10
Vinca minor	4–10
Viola	Vary
Waldsteinia fragarioides	5–10
*Zoysia tenuifolia	9–10

*Tolerates some foot traffic

Choices for Hillsides

Natural problem solvers, ground covers thrive on sloping sites that are hard to water, have shallow soil, or are exposed to harsh winds.

Two foolproof ground covers—juniper (Juniperus) and ivy (Hedera)—combine to cloak sloping ground with solid foliage cover. Roots of each help control erosion.

Ivy geranium (Pelargonium peltatum) is a warm-weather favorite for blanketing slopes with year-round color.

Warm-climate classic for hillside cover is trailing ice plant *(Lampranthus spectabilis). Gray green, fingerlike foliage is concealed beneath fluorescent flowers.*

Combined planting of heath (Erica) and Scotch heather (Calluna vulgaris) creates tumbling froth of foliage and flower colors.

Ground Covers for Hillsides

PLANT	ZONES	PLANT	ZONES
Arctostaphylos	Vary	Hemerocallis	3–10
Arctotheca calendula	9–10	*Hippocrepis comosa	9–10
*Arundinaria pygmaea	7–10	*Hypericum calycinum	6–10
Atriplex semibaccata	8–10	Ice plant (many)	Vary
Baccharis pilularis	8–10	*Juniperus	Vary
Bougainvillea	10	*Lantana	9–10
Calluna vulgaris	5–9	*Lonicera	5–10
Carissa macrocarpa	9–10	*Lotus corniculatus	5–10
*Ceanothus	8–10	*Mahonia	5–9
*Cissus	9–10	*Myoporum parvifolium	9–10
*Cistus salviifolius	8–10	Osteospermum fruticosum	9–10
Convolvulus mauritanicus	8–10	Pelargonium peltatum	9–10
Coprosma	9–10	*Polygonum cuspidatum compactum	4–10
*Coronilla varia	3–10	*Pyracantha	Vary
Correa pulchella	9–10	*Ribes viburnifolium	9–10
*Cotoneaster	Vary	Rosa	Vary
Cytisus kewensis	6–8	*Rosmarinus officinalis	7–10
Erica	Vary	Santolina	7–10
*Euonymus fortunei	5–9	Taxus baccata 'Repandens'	6–10
Genista	6–9	*Trachelospermum jasminoides	9–10
Grevillea	9–10	*Vinca	Vary
*Hedera	Vary	Zoysia tenuifolia	9–10

*Helps control erosion

Ground Covers—
The Basics

Success with ground covers starts with an assessment of your site: soil character, climate, the sun/shade ratio where you're planting, and the availability of water to the plants. Once you've collected this data, you can begin making your choices (see page 111).

Here we present the information you'll need to plant your ground cover, supply it with water, and care for it.

Design & Planting

Nature abounds in ground covers. Some are obvious—vast sweeps of prostrate manzanita in the mountains or at northern seashores, for example. Others, such as the mixed assortment of ferns, trilliums, and other semishade plants in an open woodland, are less frequently recognized as the ground covers they are.

Yet, to many people, ground covers only come to mind when the lawn is removed and the question arises about what to put in its place.

The Advantages of Ground Covers

Replacing turf grass with ground cover is just one of the practical uses of such plants. Many will, indeed, blanket large, flat expanses of ground while demanding less water and care than a comparable expanse of grass. And, by carefully choosing the appropriate ground cover, you can plant areas where a turf grass would be impractical or simply would not grow well.

Some ground covers will grow eagerly on slopes where a lawn is hard to care for; in addition, the ground cover can help prevent erosion and gullying. In dense shade, in areas where tree roots compete for water and nutrients, and in soils that are regularly too moist or too dry, some ground covers will thrive. Ground-hugging types are natural choices for planting between paving stones and garden steps.

Designing with Ground Covers

Ground covers have an artistic side as well as a practical one. They're particularly well suited for creating landscape patterns. Because ground covers are low and dense, you can spread them over the landscape as if they were brush strokes on a canvas: broad and flowing curves, discreet, geometric patches—whatever is appropriate in the overall design.

In addition, you can create a nearly infinite variety of contrasts and associations—ground cover with lawn, with

Potpourri of ground cover plants lends variety to landscape. Featured prominently are, left center, rock cotoneaster (Cotoneaster horizontalis) and, right center, Scotch heather (Calluna vulgaris).

other ground covers, with shrubs and vines, and with annuals and perennials.

Color and texture offer additional design choices. Foliage textures range from grassy to tropically bold; color encompasses subtle gray shades, soft to glossy green, bronze to purple, and variegated combinations of green to gray with yellow to white. And many ground cover plants provide some type of seasonal flower color— sometimes showy fruits as well.

Because ground cover plants are low growing, they can be used to create variety in the landscape without contributing bulk that would seem to close in on the space. Unlike turf grass, ground covers don't invite you to walk across them (although some can take limited foot traffic), so they can function as traffic barriers while offering no barrier to sight.

Soil Basics

Successful gardening—be it ground covers, vegetables, or roses—starts with an understanding of your garden's soil. Knowing the characteristics of your soil will influence your choice of plants, your approach to soil preparation, and your watering practices—how you apply water and how frequently you do it.

Soil Types

Soil is a dynamic relationship between soil particles, air, water, and organic matter. Initially, the nature of the soil particles—their sizes, shapes, and relative quantities—determines a soil's type and governs the air/water relationship within the soil. Organic matter enhances a soil's quality, affecting permeability (both of water and roots), drainage, and, to some extent, nutrient potential.

Clay and sand, the smallest and largest of the mineral particles in soil, give their names to two soil types. When both clay and sand particles are present along with silt, an intermediate-size particle, the soil is called loam. In reality, most soils fall somewhere in between those three types. You'll have to determine which one your soil most closely resembles.

Clay soil contains the smallest particles, each of which is flattened so that they fit closely together with little space between them for air and water (see illustration below). This is the "heavy" or "adobe" soil that's sticky when wet and cracks when dry. Squeeze a handful of wet clay soil and it will stay in a lump, the excess oozing between your fingers.

Water percolates slowly through clay, so this soil is considered poorly drained. But this slowness also means that it retains moisture the longest and thus can go without watering for greater lengths of time than other soil types. Dissolved nutrients also remain longer in clay.

Sandy soil is the opposite of clay. Particles are distinctly larger (up to 250 times the size of clay particles); because they're rounded rather than flat, they group together more loosely, with relatively large spaces between particles. Sandy soil feels gritty rather than sticky; squeeze a handful of wet sandy soil and it will fall apart when you release your grip or give it a slight prod.

Drainage in sandy soil is excellent, but water retention is poor; dissolved nutrients also leach away fairly rapidly.

For this reason, plants in sand need watering and fertilizing more often than those in clay.

Loam, touted as the ideal garden soil, contains both clay and sand particles as well as silt particles, considered intermediate in character between the two extremes; organic matter also is a component of loam.

This soil drains well but not too rapidly, so moisture retention is good. It leaches nutrients only moderately and contains enough air for healthy root growth.

Many gardens have soil that deviates from the "ideal" loam, but this is not a cause for despair. Many popular plants will prosper in a range of soils tending toward either extreme. Also, you can improve your soil by adding amendments when you prepare it for planting, as discussed on the facing page.

Acid or Alkaline Soil

Independent of soil type, soil may be acid, neutral, or alkaline; this is expressed in the pH scale that runs from 1 (extremely acid) to 14 (extremely alkaline), with 7 as the neutral point.

Soil Particles & Types

Clay
Less than 1/12500 in.

Silt
Up to 1/500 in.

Fine sand
Up to 1/250 in.

Medium sand
Up to 1/50 in.

Largest sand particles
1/12 in.

Clay

Sand

Loam

The majority of popular garden plants will thrive in soils that are moderately acid (about pH 6.5) to slightly alkaline (around pH 7.1); at higher and lower readings, certain nutrients may become unavailable to plants, thereby hindering growth. But some plants do have fairly specific pH needs, usually for acid soil (those that do are noted in the descriptions beginning on page 111).

A soil test will quickly reveal the acidity or alkalinity of your soil. Simple test kits, good enough to give you a close reading, are sold at nurseries and garden centers; professional soil laboratories can run more precise tests.

If your soil tests either highly acid or alkaline, check with your local County Cooperative Extension agent for advice on treatment appropriate for your region.

Preparing the Soil

Readying the soil for planting entails several steps, as outlined below.

Step 1: Weeding. Weeds—the bane of a gardener's existence—can easily spoil the appearance of a uniform ground cover. But weeds don't have to be a fact of your gardening life if you attend to some careful preparation.

Thoroughly clear all weeds from the area you intend to plant. A sharp hoe will dispatch shallow-rooted weeds easily. For the deep-rooted, perennial sorts (such as dandelions and Bermuda grass), you'll have to dig them out by hand to be sure of total control; make sure to pull out the weeds' roots as well as their tops.

If hoeing or hand-pulling is too daunting, you can rotary-till the ground and then rake out the dislodged weeds. Use this method only if annual weeds are the problem; tilling can actually help the spread of perennial weeds.

For thorough control of most annual and perennial weeds with minimum effort, you can spray the weeds with the systemic herbicide glyphosate and then prepare the soil after the weeds have been killed. Be sure to follow label directions to the letter and avoid getting herbicide on any desirable plants.

Step 2: Digging the soil. Dig or till the area to be planted—if the ground is level or only slightly sloping—to remove any foreign matter, such as rocks, roots, or buried construction debris. On distinctly sloping sites, it's better to leave the soil surface as undisturbed as possible so that erosion potential is minimized.

Step 3: Grading. Grade relatively level sites, if necessary, to eliminate humps and fill in hollows. A rake (either bow or level-head) should do the job.

Step 4: Adding amendments. Amend the soil (in level or gently sloping sites) with organic matter (see below) and any material needed to alter the pH. This is also the time to add phosphorus and potassium fertilizer to the soil, as these two nutrients are not readily soluble and must be dug into the soil where roots will take hold.

Spade or till all amendments and fertilizers into the soil to a depth of about 9 inches, rake the soil smooth, and water it. If low spots show up after watering, fill them in before you plant.

Using Organic Amendments

The decay of organic matter is part of a natural cycle that continually improves soil. Microorganisms break down plant and animal remains that fall to the soil or are dug into it; during the process, the bits of organic matter lodge between soil particles.

In clay soil, the decaying matter wedges between particles and groups of particles, opening up the soil so that water, air, and roots can penetrate more easily. In sand, the organic matter lodges in the relatively large spaces between particles, slowing the passage of water through the soil and rendering it more retentive of water and important nutrients.

Eventually, organic matter is completely reduced by soil microorganisms, depriving a soil of its benefits unless new material is added. With permanent plantings, you can't dig more organic matter into the root area, but an organic mulch (see page 105) will provide material for continued breakdown so that the upper portion of the soil will remain permeable.

Materials to use. Nurseries and garden centers routinely sell packaged organic materials such as peat moss, nitrogen-fortified wood products, and animal manures.

To calculate your needs, remember that a standard 2¼-cubic-foot bag will give a 3-inch layer over 9 square feet of soil. You may also be able to buy some materials—especially wood products and various by-products of regional agriculture—in bulk.

How to add organic amendments. The best way to add organic matter when planting is to dig it into the entire area you intend to plant.

Spread the organic matter over the soil and dig or till it in; use a quarter to a third the volume of organic matter to soil volume—for example, dig a 2-inch layer of organic matter into 6 to 8 inches of soil.

If you're planting ground covers from large (1- or 2-gallon) containers, you can simply add organic matter to the soil you return to the planting hole, providing your soil is sandy to sandy loam.

In heavier soils, however, organically amended backfill soil absorbs water more quickly than the surrounding soil can absorb it; the result can be plant death from waterlogged roots. In such soils, return the native soil to the planting hole; an organic mulch spread over the ground will help improve the top few inches in time.

Three Planting Methods for Ground Covers

To plant small plants from pots, packs, or flats, *dig a hole just deep enough for root ball. Top of ball should be even with surface.*

To plant from a 1- or 2-gallon container, *taper hole outward, creating a plateau for root ball. Top of ball should be slightly above grade.*

On a steep slope, *set a plant from a 1- or 2-gallon container on its own terrace with top of root ball high; dig a watering basin behind plant.*

Planting Techniques

You'll find plants for ground cover sold in several different ways. The spreading, root-as-they-go types such as ivy (*Hedera*) may be available in flats that contain numerous individual plants. Some perennial ground covers can be bought in packs (four, six, or eight plants in individual root balls) or in small pots. Many woody ground covers come in containers of 1- or 2-gallon size.

The illustrations above show planting methods for ground covers.

When to Plant

The best time of year to plant a ground cover is when it will have the longest possible time to become established before being stressed by unfavorable weather. In mild-winter regions, fall and winter are the best planting seasons: they allow root growth during the cool part of the year so the plants will be ready to grow vigorously at the onset of warm weather.

Gardeners in low- and intermediate-elevation deserts will want to plant just as soon as cool weather sets in. In cold-winter regions where snow can be expected and soil routinely freezes, plant in early spring just after the soil can be worked.

Summer—except in cool-summer areas—is the least desirable planting time. Plants are slower to establish when stressed by heat, and they need close attention to watering to forestall wilting.

Spacing Plants

The best planting distance between plants depends on the particular ground cover and, to some extent, on how quickly you want the area blanketed with growth.

The individual plant descriptions beginning on page 111 contain guidelines for spacing the plants. The chart below shows you how to calculate the amount of ground that will be covered by specified numbers of plants at various spacings between plants.

Watering

Some water is essential to the growth of any plant, even one that's drought tolerant. It follows, then, that you'll need to know how to satisfy your plants' water needs. And, in the process, you'll want to choose from among the several options available for supplying water to your ground cover plantings, as explained in the following sections.

Watering Guidelines

All ground covers need some watering at some time. But not all will need the same amount of water each time, nor

Spacing between Plants	Area Plants Will Cover			
	48 plants	64 plants	72 plants	100 plants
6 in.	10 sq. ft.	13½ sq. ft.	15½ sq. ft.	21½ sq. ft.
8 in.	18 sq. ft.	24½ sq. ft.	27½ sq. ft.	38 sq. ft.
10 in.	28½ sq. ft.	38½ sq. ft.	43 sq. ft.	60 sq. ft.
12 in.	41½ sq. ft.	55½ sq. ft.	62½ sq. ft.	86½ sq. ft.
15 in.	64½ sq. ft.	86 sq. ft.	97 sq. ft.	135 sq. ft.
18 in.	92 sq. ft.	123 sq. ft.	138 sq. ft.	192 sq. ft.
24 in.	165½ sq. ft.	220½ sq. ft.	248 sq. ft.	344½ sq. ft.

will they all need watering at the same time intervals.

The water requirements of each ground cover depend on a number of factors, including soil conditions, climate, and depth of roots. For information on the needs of each type, see the descriptions beginning on page 111.

How Much, How Often?

If you know your soil type and its characteristics (see page 98), you'll understand how water behaves when it contacts your soil. You'll be able to judge the rate of penetration (slow in clay, rapid in sand) and then estimate the amount of water you'll need to apply to gain the required penetration.

How often you should water depends first on your ground cover: does it need regular moisture or just infrequent watering? Your soil also influences intervals between watering; clay soil retains moisture the longest, sand the shortest.

Finally, climate and time of year affect the length of time a soil remains moist. Cool, moist climates (and times of year) stretch intervals between waterings; hot regions (and summers) impose greater frequencies.

Water Delivery Systems

For virtually all ground cover situations, there are two basic methods for applying water. One is to use a sprinkler head attached to the end of a hose; you place the sprinkler every time you water. The other is to use a water system with stationary points of water emission—an underground sprinkler system or a drip-irrigation system.

Hose-end sprinkling. With this watering method, you can choose from a wide array of sprinklers with differing modes of dispersing water. Sprinklers can be handy if one or two placements will cover all your ground cover. More than that, however, and moving the sprinkler becomes a nuisance. You also must be sure to overlap areas for even application to all parts of your planting.

Water waste is the inherent drawback to any hose-end sprinkler. Spray thrown into the air is subject to evaporation and wind drift; the volume of water delivered often is greater than soil can absorb easily, resulting in puddling and runoff after a short period of time, especially in heavier soils; and, if the sprinkler isn't carefully positioned, you can wastefully water paved surfaces along with your plants.

Stationary watering systems. If you want to set up a water delivery system with fixed-position watering heads, you have a choice between two types. One is the rigid-pipe, in-ground system with sprinkler heads— traditionally used for watering lawns. The more recent innovation is the drip-irrigation system, which features flexible plastic tubing laid on or just under the surface of the soil.

Because drip systems can be easily tailored to watering expanses of ground cover, detailed instructions for assembly are given, beginning on page 103.

Underground Sprinkler Systems

Some gardeners prefer a rigid-pipe underground system with fixed sprinkler heads for watering high, shrubby ground covers (some *Cotoneaster* species, for example) and those covers that form a solid mass of roots from countless plants, such as *Hypericum*. Risers elevate sprinkler heads just above the foliage; the spray of water moistens all the soil beneath.

Components of an underground system. Following are the basic components of such a system.

■ *Rigid polyvinyl chloride (PVC) pipe,* much easier to install and longer lasting than traditional galvanized pipe, is now the material of choice for underground watering systems. Pipes, which come in 10- or 20-foot lengths, are cut to length with pipe cutters or a hacksaw and are easily joined to each other or to special fittings with solvent.

■ *Sprinkler heads on risers* are positioned so that coverage overlaps and an even amount of water is distributed over the entire area.

You can choose from a variety of sprinkler heads; select the type that suits the shape of the area to be covered. Heads that produce a fountain of spray (or a partial fountain) water narrow plantings well; they also can be laid out in a grid pattern to cover large expanses.

If you'll be combining full- and partial-circle heads, look for matched-precipitation-rate heads that emit proportionate volumes (a head producing a 90° fan of spray delivers a quarter the amount of water of a full-circle head).

To minimize runoff potential, try low-precipitation-rate heads; these deliver water at a slower rate than normal heads.

For larger expanses of ground cover, good sprinkler choices are impact sprinklers and single-stream or multistream rotor types. These throw water a distance of 40 feet or more (depending on the model), so you need fewer heads. Most of these impact and rotor sprinklers have slow application rates (check the different models for precipitation rates) that allow the soil to absorb water with a minimum of runoff.

■ *Control valves equipped with antisiphon devices,* either integral or separate, operate circuits, each designed to serve plants with similar water needs.

■ *A manifold,* or a grouping of control valves, simplifies the operation of a multicircuit underground system and allows it to be operated automatically, if desired, when wired to a controller, or timer (see below).

■ *A controller,* the heart of an automatic system, can be programmed to turn each circuit on and off (for a description, see page 103).

Designing and installing a system. Manufacturers of underground sprinkler systems provide detailed instructions on designing and installing a system; look for their workbooks where irrigation equipment is sold. Pipes must be buried underground in trenches.

Although installing a system isn't difficult, digging trenches, laying pipes, and attaching the other equipment can take several days. If you prefer to hire a professional rather than do the work yourself, ask friends or neighbors for references. Or look in the Yellow Pages under "Irrigation Systems & Equipment," "Landscape Contractors," or "Sprinklers—Garden & Lawn."

Drip Irrigation

Many gardeners, particularly those living in regions where water conservation is paramount, prefer to water ground covers with some sort of drip-irrigation setup.

Unlike an in-ground sprinkler system, which uses high water pressure and volume to dispense water over a large area, drip irrigation delivers water at low pressure and volume to specific areas—often to individual plants; penetration is slow, its depth regulated by the length of time the system is on.

The result is well-watered plants with less use of water than with sprinklers. Drip emitters, which release water directly to the soil, waste virtually no water; even mini-sprays and mini-sprinklers, which spray water into the air, conserve much more water than ordinary sprinklers. The system can be connected to your water line or operated from a hose bibb or the end of a hose.

Look for drip-irrigation materials and fittings at irrigation supply stores.

Basic Components

A drip-irrigation system is easy to assemble and can be modified when your needs change. Most systems are made from polyvinyl tubing fitted with emitters or sprays. The components of a typical system are shown in the photograph above.

Tubing. The standard way to distribute water is through ½- or ⅜-inch flexible black poly tubing attached with plastic fittings and laid on the surface of the soil, where it can be obscured by a mulch

Components of a Drip-irrigation System

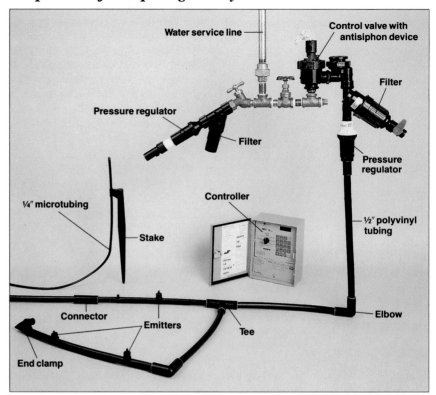

(see page 105) or by foliage. (For a sturdier but less flexible system, you can use PVC pipe for main lines and poly tubing for lateral lines.)

Thin, ¼-inch microtubing, often referred to as "spaghetti tubing," can run from the main line to individual plants.

Emitters and sprayers. You can choose from a variety of emitters, all of which deliver water through small openings at low flow rates. They're fitted directly into the main tubing or into the ends of microtubing. Add to these a choice of mini-sprayers and mini-sprinklers (see at right), and you have great latitude in design.

■ *Drip emitters* are best for watering individual plants, such as shrubby ground covers. Water placement is more precise than with mini-sprayers or mini-sprinklers, and the emitters can be completely hidden from view.

Some drip emitters are pressure-compensating, providing a steady flow

rate despite low or high pressure from the tap. Use these emitters if your setup spans an elevation change greater than 10 feet, if lateral lines exceed 200 feet, or if emitters on a line add up to more than 100 gallons per hour (gph).

■ *Mini-sprayers and mini-sprinklers* spread water over a wider area than drip emitters, but they still operate at low flow rates and low pressure. They're better for closely spaced perennial ground covers and those that root along spreading stems. You can also use them to water higher-growing, shrubby ground covers if you extend them above the foliage (drip emitters at ground level will give more efficient penetration with less waste, however).

Mini-sprayers are available in various spray patterns—from full circle to a fraction of a circle—so you can use them in tight or irregularly shaped spaces. The radius of coverage ranges from 4 to 10 feet; water output varies from 3 to 30 gph.

Mini-sprinklers emit larger droplets than mini-sprayers, so they're less affected by wind. All give full-circle coverage (with radii from 10 to 30 feet) at outputs ranging from 3 to 30 gph.

Valves. You'll need a valve that will turn the water on and off. If you design a hose-end system, you'll use the hose bibb. But if you connect directly to your water line, you'll need a valve with an antisiphon backflow preventer; the two come separately or as an integral unit.

Filter. Particulate impurities in water are the Achilles heel of drip systems; a good filter (installed just below the antisiphon device) will save you the time and frustration of cleaning clogged emitters.

A Y-filter with 150- to 200-mesh fiberglass or stainless steel screen is best for systems connected directly to a water source. For hose-bibb or hose-end systems, connect an in-line filter directly to the hose bibb; then add a pressure regulator (see below) and attach the system's main feeder line to it or to the end of a hose that connects between the pressure regulator and the drip system.

Pressure regulator. The components of a low-volume system are designed to operate best at water pressures between 20 and 30 pounds per square inch (psi). However, many household water lines operate at higher pressures. (To find out what your water pressure is, call your water department; or buy or borrow a gauge to measure pressure at the faucet. If your water pressure is over 75 psi, it's considered high.)

Most drip-irrigation systems need a pressure regulator, installed between the filter and the main drip line, for best performance. Preset to 20 or 30 psi, it reduces the pressure to a rate that the system can accept.

Optional Equipment

Three other devices are available for incorporation into a drip system. One operates the system for you, another expands the system's function, and a third helps you conserve water.

Controller. Popularly referred to as a timer, a controller is an electronic device that automatically regulates the operation of each system connected to it. Multiprogram controllers let you set up different watering frequencies and durations on different lines, so that plants with different water needs receive the right amounts of water—whether or not you're home.

Most new controllers are solid state, making them far more versatile than the older mechanical types. Before you purchase one, be sure that you can operate it easily and that it accommodates the needs of your system.

Fertilizer injector. Particularly useful with drip-irrigation systems, where water is applied directly to the soil, a fertilizer injector will add liquid fertilizer to your watering system.

You have a choice of types. For hose-end drip systems, you can use either a siphon attachment that sucks liquid fertilizer concentrate from a bucket and puts it into the system or a cartridge attachment that holds special dry but soluble fertilizers. Both devices attach between the hose bibb and the filter.

For drip systems connected directly to your household water line, you can install a fertilizer-injector canister in each system between the antisiphon device and the filter. The canister accommodates either liquid fertilizer (not fish emulsion, which can clog emitters) or dissolved dry fertilizer.

Automatic rain shutoff valve. Mounted out in the open, an automatic rain shutoff device measures rainfall and automatically inactivates your system when water reaches a certain level. This interruption of your programmed watering schedule prevents the watering of rain-soaked plantings—or automatic watering during rainfall. When the water evaporates, the system turns back on.

Design & Assembly

Advance planning is crucial to the success of a drip-irrigation system. Such planning includes overall concept, layout of lines, choice of emitters, and number of emitters placed on one line. Be sure you know your soil type, since water moves differently through different soils (see chart below).

Planning your system. Start by sketching the area (or areas) on paper. Pencil in water sources and any obstacles, such as patios or walkways, between the water source and the area to be served. Also mark any slopes or elevation changes—they can affect water distribution.

Next, determine the flow rate of water from your garden faucet. To do this, turn off all water indoors. Then turn on the faucet outdoors and accumulate water in a bucket for 30 seconds. Measure the number of gallons in the bucket and multiply that figure by 120. This will give you the gallons per hour (gph) your water lines will deliver.

Emitter Flow Rate	Amount & Pattern of Coverage		
½ gph 1 gph 2 gph	1 sq. ft. 5 sq. ft. 11 sq. ft.	5 sq. ft. 11 sq. ft. 18 sq. ft.	11 sq. ft. 18 sq. ft. 31 sq. ft.
	Sandy Soil	Loam	Clay Soil

A gallon of drip-irrigated water moves differently through three kinds of soil. Numbers for each give maximum horizontal coverage at different emitter flow rates (expressed in gallons per hour). Shading shows vertical wetting pattern.

From this figure you can calculate the number of emitters you can place on one drip-irrigation line, remembering that the emitters' total output (in gph) should not exceed 75 percent of available water flow at the faucet.

Laying out lines. Group plants on separate valves according to water needs. Be careful not to run lines too long or to put too many emitters on one line: the tubing has limits on how much water it can efficiently handle. Remember: Running a line uphill shortens the possible run, downhill increases it (for information about running lines on slopes, see below, at right).

You can either bury the lines 2 to 3 inches in the soil or leave them on the surface. Buried lines last longer, are less prone to disturbance, and don't affect the appearance of your garden. But lines left on the surface are easier to install, repair, and maintain. By adding a 2-inch layer of mulch over them, you create many of the same benefits that you have with buried lines.

Choosing and spacing emitters. The number and gallonage of emitters you use for each plant will depend on your soil and the plants you're watering.

As a rule of thumb, use higher-gpm emitters for ground covers in sandy soil, lower ones for shallow-rooted plants in clay soil. Also, space drip emitters closer together for shallow-rooted ground covers, such as many perennials and spreading root-along-the-stem kinds. Refer to the chart below for guidelines.

Spacing is greatly affected by the layout of the plants. If plants are spaced

Installation Tools

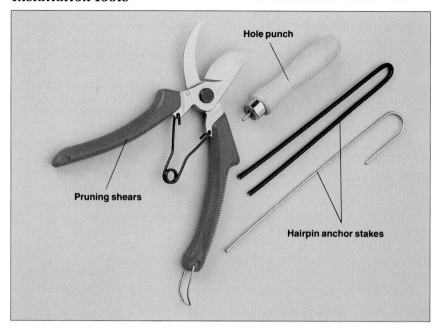

Hole punch

Pruning shears

Hairpin anchor stakes

less than about 2 feet apart in a confined bed, there's no need to design a system to suit each plant.

Systematizing a slope. Gravity slows the flow of water uphill and speeds it downhill. Therefore, if your lines will run on sloping soil, such as a bank or hillside, you'll want to plan to set valves and antisiphon backflow preventers at the top of the slope. Run main lines perpendicular to the slope and lateral lines parallel to it.

If you'll be watering shrubby ground covers with emitters, be sure to use the pressure-compensating kind. If you plan to use mini-sprayers, choose half-circle

sprays and position them so they spray downhill.

Installing the system. To assemble a drip system, you'll need some simple tools, shown above: pruning shears to cut tubing, a hole-punching device to install emitters, and a number of hairpin anchor stakes to secure the tubing to the ground.

Following the order shown in the photograph on page 102, assemble the valves, filter, and pressure regulator. If you're connecting your system directly to a water line, place a shutoff valve between your system and the water line; this will allow you to shut off the irriga-

Plants	Soil Type	Number & Size of Emitter
Low shrubs	Sandy soil	One 2-gph emitter next to plant
	Loam	One 1-gph emitter next to plant
	Clay soil	One ½-gph emitter next to plant
Ground covers spaced at least 2 feet apart	Sandy soil or loam	One 1-gph emitter at root ball
	Clay soil	One ½-gph emitter at root ball
Closer ground covers with less distinct root zones	Any soil	Overlapping mini-sprayers or mini-sprinklers
Beds of ground covers	Sandy soil	Several 2-gph emitters spaced about a foot apart in a row
	Loam	Several 1-gph emitters spaced about 1½ feet apart in a row
	Clay soil	Several ½-gph emitters spaced about 1½ feet apart in a row

tion system but still use the faucet. Wrap threaded connections with pipe tape before attaching them. Hand-tighten plastic fittings.

Connect the tubing to the valve assembly and lay out the main distribution lines; whenever possible, place them next to walls and edges of paths where they'll be easy to find and more protected from disturbance. Then attach lateral lines with tee and elbow fittings. Use hairpin stakes to secure all tubing in place.

Try not to get dirt in the system when assembling lines and installing emitters. Flush all lines before you close off the ends.

To punch holes in the tubing for emitters, hold the hole punch perpendicular to the tubing, squeeze the tube on each side with your fingers to keep it from flattening, and then push and twist straight down. Don't take a punch out and try to reinsert it—the hole may get so big it will leak.

If you're installing an automated system, mount the controller in a convenient place and wire the valves to it, following the instructions provided by the manufacturer.

Once the system is assembled, flush the lines again and then turn it on. To confirm that you have enough emitters in the right places, let the system run for its normal cycle, wait several hours, and then dig into the soil in several places to check the spread of moisture. If necessary, add or reposition some of the emitters.

Maintenance

To the gardener who is familiar with taking care of a lawn, the word "maintenance" immediately suggests weekly mowing.

But maintenance for ground covers—mulching, fertilizing, grooming, and controlling any pests or diseases—comes around far less often. In fact, a careful choice of plants can often reduce the need for any maintenance to once a year or less.

Mulches for Ground Covers

An aid to getting any ground cover off to a good start is a mulch over the bare earth between plants. Not only does this benefit the plants, but it also offers attractiveness—the mulch makes a uniform carpet that ties together the new planting.

The Advantages of Mulch

The traditional mulch is a layer of loose-textured organic material, 1 to perhaps 4 inches thick, spread over the soil. This layer retards the loss of surface moisture so the root zone stays moist for a longer period of time after watering. In hot weather, a mulch helps to lower soil temperature beneath its blanket.

These conditions favor good root growth and help plants establish themselves more quickly; eventually, the ground cover itself will form its own living mulch.

In addition, a mulch suppresses weed growth by effectively burying seeds and preventing their germination. Any weeds that do come up in the mulch can be pulled easily because of the mulch's loose texture.

A mulch also helps prevent erosion and gullying: it intercepts the force of rainfall (or watering); water percolates easily through a mulch instead of scouring the bare earth. This is especially important on gently sloping sites. Finally, an organic mulch, as it decomposes, improves the composition of the top few inches of soil.

Materials & Methods

You have a wide choice among potential mulch materials—from coarse to fine textured, and from long lasting to ephemeral. Aside from appearance, deciding factors will be cost and local availability. Whatever you choose, be sure it won't pack down into a sodden mass, repelling water rather than admitting it.

Because a mulch keeps the soil beneath cooler than if unmulched, it's best to delay applying mulch to new plantings until the soil has warmed. If applied early in the year when the soil is still cold, a mulch can slow root growth by keeping the ground too cool.

Here are some of the more generally available materials.

Wood products. Wood products, which include ground bark and sawdust, are sold bagged or in bulk form.

Ground bark may be from fir, pine, hemlock, or redwood; it's long lasting (especially redwood) and attractive, in tones of brown aging to gray. Textures range from fine to 2-inch chips.

Fine-textured sawdust needs nitrogen for its decomposition; otherwise, it will take available nitrogen from the soil for the process. Commercially packaged sawdust usually is nitrogen fortified; raw sawdust requires a nitrogen supplement: $\frac{1}{2}$ pound actual nitrogen for every 100 square feet of mulch spread 1 inch deep.

Straw. Although short-lived and coarse textured, straw is reasonably attractive, inexpensive, and widely available.

Animal manures. Also widely available, manure is sold both commercially packaged and in bulk. As a mulch its effective lifetime is about a year. Apply only aged or composted manures; fresh material can burn plant roots.

Agricultural by-products. These vary from region to region; lasting quality depends on the material. Most are sold in bulk rather than packaged. Examples are ground corncobs, mushroom compost, apple or grape pomace, hulls from various nut crops, and cotton gin trash.

Pine needles. Appearance is pleasant, permeability is excellent, and the needles will last for several years. Acid reaction may be a bonus in all but acid-soil regions.

Grass clippings. To be successful, these need careful management to prevent compaction into a smelly, water-repellent mat. Spread a thin ($\frac{1}{2}$- to 1-inch-deep) layer of clippings; let this layer dry before you add another thin layer.

Leaves from trees. Their main advantage is availability; their chief drawback is that they can be blown around by the wind. If you use leaves, choose those with thicker textures (such as the leaves of many oaks); they'll remain loose. Thin-textured leaves (maple, for example) can mat together when spread in layers and moistened.

Fertilizing

Nutrient needs vary from one ground cover to another. But the virtue of many of these plants is that they will perform well with little or no supplemental nutrition.

A workable rule-of-thumb is to assume that the woody, shrubby ground covers (especially those that are drought tolerant) have a fairly low nutrient need and may get along without any fertilizer at all. Perennial ground covers, on the other hand, often have a higher nutrient demand and may need at least an annual fertilizer application.

Soil type affects the need to fertilize. Heavier, claylike soils contain more nutrients (and hold dissolved nutrients from fertilizers longer) than do lighter, sandier soils. Ground covers in lighter soils, therefore, are more likely to need some periodic fertilizer boost.

What Fertilizer to Use

Plants need three major nutrients—nitrogen, phosphorus, and potassium. Most commercial fertilizers contain all three and are popularly known as "complete." Nutrient percentages are listed on the label—for example, 5-10-10, with nitrogen listed first, then phosphorus, and finally potassium.

Nitrogen is water soluble and is depleted by plant uptake, watering, and precipitation. Phosphorus and potassium do not leach through the soil; to be effective beyond the top few inches, they must be dug into the root zone—ideally before you plant.

For ground covers, you can use dry granules or liquid preparations.

Dry granular fertilizers. Most granular fertilizers are scattered onto the soil, lightly scratched in, and then watered. The effect may last from several weeks to several months, depending on the type of nitrogen the fertilizer contains.

Fertilizers containing nitrogen in nitrate form are the fastest acting (and shortest lasting); if nitrogen is in ammonium or organic form (or derived from urea), the fertilizer will be slower to act but more sustained.

Controlled-release fertilizers contain dry, soluble nutrients in small pellets covered with a permeable membrane; a small amount of nutrients is leached from each pellet every time you water or rain falls. Depending on the product, these fertilizers last from 3 to 8 months after being lightly scratched into the soil.

Liquid fertilizers. These provide nutrients immediately but, because they're already in solution, they leach through soil fairly soon after application. Some of these fertilizers are concentrated solutions that you dilute in water; others are dry concentrates that you dissolve in water. A fertilizer injector (see page 103) makes it easy to apply liquids over a large planting, especially if used in conjunction with a drip-irrigation system.

When to Fertilize

Your first opportunity to apply fertilizer is when you prepare soil for planting (see page 99). This is the best time to add phosphorus and potassium—the two major nutrients that do not leach into the soil from surface application. By digging such fertilizers into the soil, you put these nutrients where roots can contact them.

You can use a "complete" fertilizer, or you can add formulas that contain only phosphorus and potassium. Whatever your choice, follow package directions for the amount to apply.

For established ground cover plantings, the best time to apply supplemental nutrients is just before the growing season. Fertilizer applied then (or just as growth begins) will provide nutrients for the year's major growth push.

If your planting seems to be standing still, with little or no new growth and perhaps a pale or spindly appearance, lack of nutrients (usually nitrogen) may be the cause. An application of liquid fertilizer will give the quickest results.

Good Grooming Practices

Even though a ground cover requires less routine maintenance than a comparable patch of lawn, there's still a need for periodic grooming to keep the planting looking its best.

Listed below are the most commonplace grooming routines. Note that each one doesn't apply to all ground covers; therefore, your total maintenance list will be shorter. Most of these routines are seasonal in nature. What you do— and when and how often you do it— depend on the ground cover you're growing.

Weeding. This is an "as-needed" chore, one whose frequency can be greatly reduced by the use of some good gardening practices.

Before planting, thoroughly weed the area (for more information, see page 99). After planting, one of the most effective ways to control weeds is a mulch (see page 105) spread to a depth of an inch or more over the soil between plants. This layer prevents most weed seeds from germinating—essentially making them too deeply "planted" to sprout and grow.

If you're concerned that you'll get an ample weed crop regardless, apply a preemergence herbicide to the bare earth just after planting. It will inhibit the germination of weed seeds and stop the growth of the embryonic plants.

Some preemergence herbicides are granules you apply to the soil and disperse with water; others are liquid concentrates diluted in water and sprayed on the soil. Check labels for a list of weeds controlled as well as for directions and cautions.

After applying a preemergence herbicide, you can follow up with a mulch. If weeds persist, hand-pulling is the most effective control if the crop is light.

For a serious weed infestation, you may be able to use a selective herbicide as long as you're certain it won't harm your ground cover. Carefully read product labels to learn which ornamental plants are unaffected by a particular selective herbicide, as well as to determine which weeds will be killed.

Edging. A number of ground covers will attempt to expand their territories unless you restrict them from time to time. Shrubby ground covers with stems that grow horizontally will need to be headed back into bounds whenever they stray. The sooner you do this, the less apparent the pruning.

For ground covers that spread by underground stems or that stake out new territory by rooting along stems that touch soil, you may be able to control spread by trimming the edges with pruning or hedge shears.

But if growth goes significantly beyond bounds, a spade or shovel may be your best pruning tool. Slice back to the desired edge; then dig out portions that have grown too far.

Pruning to shape. Some shrubby ground covers, normally low growing, occasionally send out upright stems that spoil the evenness of the planting. As they develop, cut these stems back to the point of origin or to a horizontally growing lateral within the foliage mass.

Mowing. Some of the ground covers that root as they spread, or spread by underground stems into dense patches, become so thick and matted in time that only mowing will restore their attractiveness. Plants like ivy (*Hedera*) build up accumulated thatch beneath the foliage, noticeably raising the surface of the cover. Others, such as *Euonymus* and *Hypericum,* may become rangy and untidy.

Mow these ground covers with a heavy-duty power mower, set at 3 to 4 inches, just before the beginning of the growing season.

Rejuvenation. Various perennial ground covers may become crowded in time, causing a decline in performance (and attractiveness) as more and more plants in a given space compete for water and nutrients.

When this occurs, dig up the planting, amend the soil, and replant with the strongest divisions or with new plants. Do this at the best time of year for planting in your region (see page 100).

Pest & Disease Control

One criterion of a good ground cover is that it be relatively untroubled by pests or disease—or that any infestation will do little harm to health or appearance. Still, there may be times when a problem appears to be serious enough to call for some attempt at control.

First, realize that most pests have natural enemies that keep them in check most of the time. If you need to reduce an unusually heavy infestation, start with nonchemical controls that do the least harm to natural predators. Move on to a chemical preparation only if these first methods are ineffective.

If you resort to a chemical control, choose one that's known to treat your plant's particular problem. Follow the product's label directions exactly for application, disposal of any excess solution, and storage.

The chart below describes some of the most widespread pest and disease problems and lists some appropriate controls.

Dealing with Pests & Disease

Aphids		Up to ¼ inch in length, these soft-bodied insects may be green, pink, red, brown, or black. Some have wings, others are wingless. They appear, often in large numbers, on new growth, which they pierce to suck the plant's juices. **Nontoxic controls:** Water-wash or spray with an insecticidal soap solution. **Chemical controls:** Malathion, pyrethrins (contact); Orthene (systemic).
Caterpillars		These wormlike pests, the larvae of different moths, chew holes in leaves, often reducing them to skeletons. They may be difficult to spot because they may assume the color of the host plant's foliage. **Nontoxic controls:** Hand-pick small infestations; or spray with a *Bacillus thuringiensis* preparation. **Chemical controls:** Diazinon, Sevin (contact); Orthene (systemic).
Mites		Near-microscopic spider relatives, mites proliferate in hot weather, gathering on leaf undersides where they suck plant juices. Look for yellow-stippled, dry-looking leaves. Defoliation can result if the infestation is unchecked. **Nontoxic controls:** Water-wash leaf undersides or spray with an insecticidal soap solution. **Chemical controls:** Kelthane (if available), Plictran, Vendex.
Powdery Mildew		This widespread disease (actually many different mildew species) appears as a gray to white, furry to powdery coating on buds, leaves, and stems. Some mildews attack new growth, others mature leaves. Most thrive in humid air but need dry leaves to become established. Some plants are more susceptible than others. **Nontoxic control:** Water-wash. **Chemical controls:** Folpet (contact); benomyl, triforine (systemic).
Scale		Adult scale insects live beneath rounded, waxy shells which adhere to leaves and stems; underneath their coverings, the insects suck plant juices. Eggs hatch beneath the shells; in spring or summer, young insects crawl to other parts of the plant and form their own shells. **Nontoxic controls:** Hand-pick or scrape, or apply an oil spray. **Chemical controls:** Diazinon, Malathion, Sevin (contact); Orthene (systemic).
Slugs & Snails 		These related mollusks (a slug is essentially a shell-less snail) feed on a wide variety of plants, consuming leaves by means of rasping mouths on their bodies' undersides. They thrive in moist weather and are especially active during cool, damp nighttime hours and on moist, sunless days. **Nontoxic controls:** Hand-pick or use saucers of beer set with rim at soil level. **Chemical controls:** Slug and snail baits.

Ground Covers
A to Z

Enter the realm of ground covers and you'll discover a diverse and valuable assortment of garden problem solvers. On the following pages you'll find descriptions of the popular kinds that have proven their worth over many years in countless gardens. A few may be available primarily through specialty growers, but the majority are easy to obtain in the regions where they thrive.

Plants are listed in alphabetical order by their botanical names; beneath is the plant's common name, if it has one. In the first part of the detailed description that accompanies each entry, you'll find a complete plant profile—what the plant looks like, how tall and wide it grows, and how densely it covers. Popular hybrids and named varieties that differ in significant ways are also presented. Following that information are the plant's cultural and maintenance requirements.

For convenience in making a preliminary selection, consult the "thumbnail sketch" of each plant's cultural requirements, presented just below the name. This information can help you determine from the outset whether or not the ground cover is suitable for your particular situation.

■ *Zones* refers to the zones on the climate map on page 110 and specifies in which geographic regions the plant will grow.

■ *Type* tells you if the plant retains its leaves year-round (evergreen) or loses them over winter (deciduous). In addition, it specifies whether a plant has a permanent, woody structure (shrubs and most vines) or is a soft-stemmed perennial.

■ *Exposure* indicates whether the plant should receive sun, shade, or something in between. Degree of sun or shade tolerance can vary according to the climate; thus, the text may offer qualifications, for example, suggesting planting in partial shade where summer is hot. *Partial* shade—where the plant receives shade during part of a day (generally noon and afternoon)—has been differentiated from *light* shade, which indicates a bit of shade throughout the day.

■ *Water* needs vary, depending on the planting, your local climate, and your soil. Plants that must have a moist root zone need *regular* watering. If a plant will accept a bit of dryness between waterings, the need is *moderate*. Plants that require *little* water are the drought-tolerant individuals that will go for extended time periods between waterings.

■ *Spacing* refers to the recommended distances between plants, based on a plant's ultimate spread and its growth rate. The intervals should provide for complete cover in about 2 years.

Attractive entry landscape relies on just two ground covers: juniper (Juniperus) in foreground and, behind, a yellow-flowered carpet of spring cinquefoil (Potentilla tabernaemontanii).

109

Plant Hardiness Zone Map

The map shown below, devised by the U.S. Department of Agriculture, will help you determine the plants that will grow in your area. The zones are based on average expected low temperatures in winter; each zone encompasses a range of 10°F.

To use the map, locate the zone in which you live. Then consult the plant listings beginning on the facing page, noting the zone number or range given for the particular plant you're considering. That zone listing indicates the range of hardiness zones for which each plant is adapted. If your zone falls within the given range, the plant should grow in your region.

The map does have some obvious limitations. Any given hardiness zone will extend over a large geographical area.

For example, consider Zone 8, which includes the warm-humid North Carolina coast, the cool-humid Puget Sound, and the hot-dry Big Bend territory in Texas.

Moreover, a map such as this—based only on minimum expected temperatures—cannot possibly account for other significant aspects of climate that affect plant growth, such as humidity, expected high temperatures, and wind. Nor does it address variations in soils or the local microclimates that result from altitude, slopes, and morning and evening shadows from mountains.

Fortunately for the gardener, many plants will accept a variety of climates and still perform well. Where significant limitations do exist, such as in desert areas, we have noted them in the descriptions.

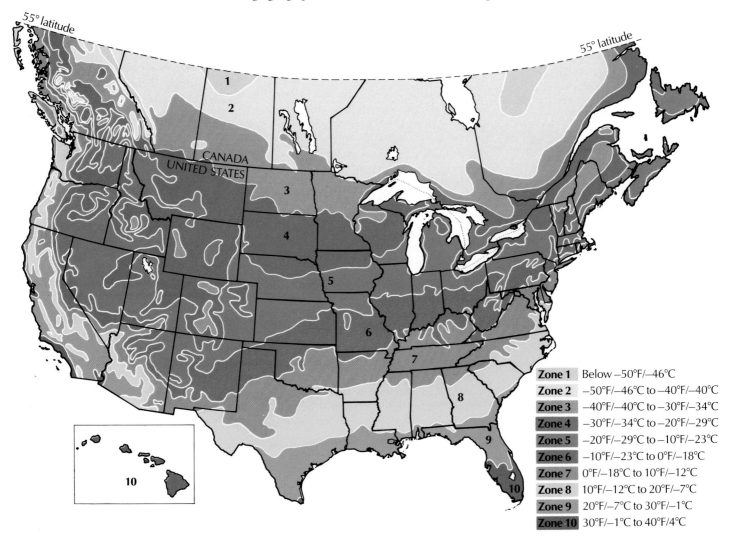

Zone 1	Below −50°F/−46°C
Zone 2	−50°F/−46°C to −40°F/−40°C
Zone 3	−40°F/−40°C to −30°F/−34°C
Zone 4	−30°F/−34°C to −20°F/−29°C
Zone 5	−20°F/−29°C to −10°F/−23°C
Zone 6	−10°F/−23°C to 0°F/−18°C
Zone 7	0°F/−18°C to 10°F/−12°C
Zone 8	10°F/−12°C to 20°F/−7°C
Zone 9	20°F/−7°C to 30°F/−1°C
Zone 10	30°F/−1°C to 40°F/4°C

ACHILLEA

YARROW

Zones: 4–10
Type: Evergreen perennials
Exposure: Sun
Water: Moderate
Spacing: 12 inches

The yarrows are easy, undemanding perennials, thriving in full sun and well-drained soil. In dry-summer regions, they appreciate moderate watering but can get by with less in cooler areas; established plantings will endure drought. Divide when plantings become overcrowded, showing diminished vigor or bare patches.

Foliage is finely cut to fernlike—gray or green and aromatic—forming low mats no higher than 4 to 6 inches. Tiny individual flowers are massed in flattened heads on stems rising above the foliage mass. Bloom starts in summer, lasting into fall. Shear off faded flowers to prolong bloom and keep appearance neat.

Greek yarrow (*A. ageratifolia*) forms a spreading mat of silvery leaves that may be lobed or nearly smooth edged. Stems 4 to 10 inches tall bear 1-inch clusters of white flowers. Silvery yarrow (*A. clavennae,* often sold as *A. argentea*) has silver gray, lobed leaves and ivory flowers in ¾-inch clusters atop 5- to 10-inch stems.

Woolly yarrow (*A. tomentosa*) has the lowest foliage of the three—a flat, dense mat of finely cut, furry, olive green leaves. Small clusters of bright yellow blossoms come on 6- to 10-inch stems; 'Primrose Beauty' has pale yellow flowers, while those of 'King George' are cream.

AEGOPODIUM PODAGRARIA

BISHOP'S WEED, GOUT-WEED
Pictured above and on page 90

Zones: 4–8
Type: Deciduous perennial
Exposure: Sun to shade
Water: Moderate
Spacing: 12 inches

Light green, divided leaves (each leaflet to 3 inches long) form a dense, even foliage mass about 6 inches high. "Ground elder," another common name, indicates

foliage resemblance to that of box elder (*Acer negundo*).

Most commonly planted is *A. p.* 'Variegatum', the leaves of which are irregularly margined in white. Slender stems rise up to 18 inches above foliage mass in summer, bearing small, flat-topped clusters of insignificant flowers.

Adaptability and vigor are bishop's weed's strong points. It grows rampantly in sun, a bit more slowly in partial to full shade. Although it will take regular watering and good soil, it also performs well under less than ideal conditions.

Plantings spread by underground runners and can become invasive if not curbed by a barrier of concrete, metal, or wood extending below ground level. Mowing two or three times during the growing season maintains a neat appearance.

AGAPANTHUS

LILY-OF-THE-NILE

Zones: 9–10
Type: Evergreen perennial
Exposure: Sun to light shade
Water: Regular watering
Spacing: 12 inches

Several small versions of normally 3-foot-plus lily-of-the-Nile make attractive ground cover plantings when massed together. All form fountainlike clumps of strap-shaped leaves, above which rise stems bearing trumpet-shaped summer flowers in heads that resemble bursts of fireworks.

Plants grow quickly, but clumps increase slowly enough that they need infrequent division to relieve overcrowding.

Smallest is 'Peter Pan', with foliage to 12 inches high and blue blossoms atop 12- to 18-inch stems. White-flowered 'Peter Pan Albus' and 'Henryi' are only slightly larger. 'Rancho White' (also known as 'Dwarf White' and 'Rancho') has foliage that can grow to 18 inches with flower stems to 2 feet.

Aegopodium podagraria 'Variegatum'

AJUGA REPTANS

CARPET BUGLE

Zones: 4–10
Type: Evergreen perennial
Exposure: Sun to shade
Water: Regular watering
Spacing: 6 to 12 inches (18 inches for large types)

One of the most widely planted ground covers, carpet bugle has good-looking foliage and flowers; it performs well in sun and shade. Dark green, lustrous leaves with a quilted appearance form a thick, low foliage mat; leaf size is larger in shaded plantings. Blue flowers in 6- to 9-inch spikes appear in spring and early summer.

Many named varieties are sold (some under more than one name), offering variations in foliage color and plant size. 'Purpurea' ('Atropurpurea') has bronze-tinted green leaves, while 'Bronze Ripple', 'Metallica Crispa', and 'Rubra' have purplish or bronze foliage. Leaves of 'Variegata' are edged and splashed with creamy yellow; 'Burgundy Lace' ('Burgundy Glow') features white and pink variegation on reddish purple leaves.

Varieties with "giant" or "jungle" in their names have larger leaves and taller

Arctostaphylos uva-ursi

flower spikes; they also form higher foliage masses. Green-leaved selections include 'Giant Green' and 'Jungle Green'. 'Giant Bronze' and 'Jungle Bronze' have bronze-tinted foliage.

Carpet bugle grows rapidly, given regular watering and an annual application of fertilizer. Plants need well-drained soil; root rot and fungus diseases can be a problem among thick plantings in heavy, waterlogged soils. You can mow plantings after flowering to remove stems and tidy up appearance. Divide and reset plantings when vigor declines and bare patches appear.

ARABIS CAUCASICA

WALL ROCKCRESS

Zones: 6–9
Type: Evergreen perennial
Exposure: Sun to light shade
Water: Moderate
Spacing: 8 inches

Gray green, tongue-shaped leaves with toothed edges form thick mats of foliage whorls to 6 inches high. In early spring, small white flowers nearly cover the plantings. Several named varieties offer variations on this theme. 'Variegata' has cream white margins on gray leaves. 'Floreplena' has double blossoms; those of 'Pink Charm' and 'Rosabella' are pink.

Wall rockcress is best used in small areas. It grows loosely enough to make a good cover for spring-flowering bulbs. In hot-summer regions, plant in light shade. Renew plantings from rooted pieces or cuttings when ragged, bare patches appear.

ARCTOSTAPHYLOS

MANZANITA
Pictured above

Zones: Vary (none in desert)
Type: Evergreen shrubs
Exposure: Sun to partial shade
Water: Moderate
Spacing: 3 to 4 feet

The manzanitas forego showiness in favor of year-round attractiveness. Leaves are thick and leathery, glossy and fresh looking; many of the species have smooth, red to purple bark on main stems.

Appearing in late winter to early spring are pleasing but unspectacular flowers—clusters of small (less than ½ inch), urn-shaped blossoms in white or pink. These may be followed by small, round fruits.

Nearly all manzanitas are native to western North America and rarely are successful in other regions. The popular exception, though, is *A. uva-ursi*—bearberry or kinnikinnick. It also hails from northern latitudes in Europe and Asia and will grow in Zones 3–10 (West) and 3–7 (East). Plants form a foot-high, dense mat that spreads widely at a moderate rate, rooting along its stems. Inch-long leaves are bright green, turning to red in winter. White or pink flowers are followed by bright red to pink fruits.

Nurseries offer various selected forms. 'Massachusetts' and 'Alaska' have smaller, rounded leaves. 'Point Reyes' has plentiful, dark green foliage and is the best choice in regions with hot, dry summers. 'Radiant' has lighter green foliage and usually bears a heavy crop of red fruits. Bearberry excels on hillsides and in coastal climates.

Best soil for bearberry (and other manzanitas, below) is acid to neutral, well-drained sand to loam. If you plant in heavier soil, be careful you don't over-water; waterlogged soil leads to root rot. While plants are becoming established, water often enough to keep soil moist. In subsequent years, plantings will need water about once or twice a month, depending on summer heat.

New plantings establish slowly. Be sure to mulch thoroughly, preferably with sawdust or another wood product (see page 105), to suppress weeds and to encourage rooting along stems.

Gardeners in western North America can plant several other low, carpet-forming manzanitas. Similar to bearberry (and possibly a hybrid of it) is *A. media* (Zones 7–10). It's fast growing to 2 feet high, with darker foliage and brighter red branches.

Little Sur manzanita—*A. edmundsii*, Zones 8–10—is available in several selected forms. 'Danville' has rounded, light green leaves on a red-stemmed plant 4 to 24 inches high; pink flowers come in early winter. Fast-growing 'Carmel Sur' has gray green leaves and pink flowers; plants grow well under ordinary garden conditions. Variety 'Little Sur' grows slowly and remains very low; its leaves always have some red tints. Pink flowers come in early spring.

A. 'Emerald Carpet' (Zones 8–10) is noted for its shiny, bright green leaves that are only ½ inch long but plentiful; pink flowers bloom in early spring. Growth is especially uniform, remaining about 12 inches high.

ARCTOTHECA CALENDULA

CAPE WEED

Zones: 9–10
Type: Evergreen perennial
Exposure: Sun
Water: Moderate to little
Spacing: 18 inches

So easy to grow and tough enough to be called indestructible, Cape weed excels in sunny locations where you need a low, fast-growing cover—even on hillsides and where soil is poor. Elongated, gray green leaves are deeply toothed, forming a thick cover under 12 inches high. Yellow, 2-inch, gazanialike flowers can appear throughout the year, with heaviest bloom in spring.

The rapidly spreading plants are not for confinement in small spaces; they can be invasive (but easy to remove) in some situations. After planting, give regular watering until plants become established. Thereafter, water needs are moderate to low. Plants may be damaged by frosts in Zone 9 but will recover rapidly.

ARDISIA JAPONICA

Zones: 8–9
Type: Evergreen shrub
Exposure: Shade
Water: Regular watering
Spacing: 18 inches

Elegant foliage and seasonal color recommend ardisia for small, shaded areas. Leathery, 4-inch, oval leaves are bright green and glossy, clustered toward branch tips on upright stems 6 to 18 inches high. In fall, tiny white flowers appear in small clusters among the leaves, then produce bright red, pea-size fruits that remain through winter untouched by birds.

Plants prefer acid to neutral soil, in which they will spread by underground stems at a slow to moderate rate.

ARENARIA BALEARICA

CORSICAN SANDWORT

Zones: 6–10
Type: Evergreen perennial
Exposure: Shade
Water: Regular watering
Spacing: 6 inches

Dense, ground-hugging growth of tiny leaves gives the appearance of a velvet carpet. Late spring and summer bring forth small, circular white flowers nestled on top of the foliage mat.

Stems root as they spread, sometimes becoming invasive under preferred conditions of shade and moisture. Best uses are as small-space lawn (it will endure light foot traffic) or as green filler between stepping-stones.

ARENARIA VERNA

(See Sagina Subulata)

ARMERIA MARITIMA

COMMON THRIFT, SEA PINK
Pictured below and on page 84

Zones: 3–10
Type: Evergreen perennial
Exposure: Sun
Water: Moderate
Spacing: 6 to 12 inches

Clumps of stiff, grasslike leaves form foliage mounds about 6 inches high and 12 inches across. Slender stems rise above the leaves, bearing tight, round clusters of pink or white flowers. Where frosts are rare or absent, plants can flower throughout the year. In other regions, bloom season is spring. The individual-clump effect resembles that of pink-flowered chives;

Armeria maritima

closely planted, foliage appears as a shaggy, flowering turf.

Root rot can be a problem if water lingers for any time at bases of plants. Well-drained soil is best, in which plants can take regular watering (even though they thrive with lesser amounts). In heavier soils, though, water moderately. After bloom season, shear off spent flowers.

ARTEMISIA CAUCASICA

SILVER SPREADER

Zones: 5–9
Type: Evergreen perennial
Exposure: Sun
Water: Moderate to little
Spacing: 12 to 24 inches

Silvery gray green, finely cut leaves glisten with a silken sheen on dense, spread-

Asarum caudatum

ing plants that grow no higher than 6 inches. Small yellow summer flowers are insignificant.

Silver spreader prefers well-drained soil; it tolerates heat, cold, and infrequent watering in summer. Established plantings are fire retardant.

ARUNDINARIA PYGMAEA

Zones: 7–10
Type: Evergreen perennial
Exposure: Sun to partial shade
Water: Regular watering
Spacing: 12 to 24 inches

Some nurseries still sell this bamboo as *Sasa pygmaea,* but under either name it is an aggressively spreading plant that grows no higher than 18 inches. Bright green leaves are narrow, to 5 inches long, borne on pencil-thick stems.

Due to its invasive nature, plants should be confined with sturdy underground barriers of concrete, metal, or wood. This invasiveness, though, makes it an excellent plant for controlling erosion on sloping land.

Plants from crowded containers will begin to colonize faster than will small, unestablished plants. If appearance becomes shabby or leggy in a few years, mow it to restore attractiveness.

ASARUM CAUDATUM

WILD GINGER
Pictured at left

Zones: 5–9 (West, except desert)
Type: Evergreen perennial
Exposure: Shade
Water: Regular watering
Spacing: 12 inches

When given the shade and moisture it prefers, wild ginger makes a handsome ground cover. Heart-shaped, dark green leaves are 2 to 7 inches across, each carried on a leaf stalk to 10 inches high; leaves overlap to form a lush, ground-concealing carpet. Unusual reddish brown, bell-shaped flowers appear in spring but are mostly hidden beneath the foliage.

Wild ginger needs ample moisture for good growth. Plants grow best in rich, moisture-retentive soil with regular watering, though they also will thrive in well-drained soils with plenty of water and periodic applications of fertilizer. Slugs and snails consider wild ginger a delicacy.

ASPARAGUS DENSIFLORUS 'SPRENGERI'

SPRENGER ASPARAGUS

Zones: 9–10
Type: Evergreen perennial
Exposure: Sun to light shade
Water: Regular watering
Spacing: 2 to 3 feet

Though it is most frequently seen as a container plant, Sprenger asparagus can serve well as a billowy, mounding ground cover. The many-branched stems, 3 to 6 feet long, fountain outward from a central root mass; each branch carries many bright green, needlelike "leaves" (which actually are modified branches) to 1 inch long, giving a distinctive feathery appearance. Small, pinkish white flowers form pea-sized berries that become bright red at maturity.

Sprenger asparagus thrives in full sun where summers are cool; in hot-summer regions, give it partial or light shade (too much shade, however, results in yellowed foliage).

Plants will withstand infrequent watering, but regular water produces the best appearance. In early spring, apply fertilizer and trim out old stems (or shear entire planting); new growth will quickly renew the planting.

ATRIPLEX SEMIBACCATA

AUSTRALIAN SALTBUSH

Zones: 8–10
Type: Evergreen shrub
Exposure: Sun
Water: Moderate to little
Spacing: 3 feet

Its ability to withstand heat, drought, and poor or alkaline soil—from desert to seashore—makes Australian saltbush a good ground cover candidate for hillside situations and garden fringe areas in dry-summer regions. Established plantings also are fire retardant. Gray green leaves to 1½ inches long densely clothe branches that rise to 12 inches high and spread to 6 feet or more. Flowers are insignificant.

BACCHARIS PILULARIS

COYOTE BRUSH,
DWARF CHAPARRAL BROOM
Pictured at right

Zones: 8–10 (West)
Type: Evergreen shrub
Exposure: Sun to light shade
Water: Moderate to little
Spacing: 2 to 3 feet

Although native to coastal California, coyote brush thrives in a wide range of soils and climates—from sandy soil and coastal fog to heavy or alkaline soil and desert heat. Mounding shrub reaches 8 to 24 inches high and may spread to 6 feet or more.

Glossy, ½-inch toothed leaves densely clothe the branches. Because female plants produce cottony seed heads (which can be messy as the wind disperses them), look for named selections which are propagated from seedless male plants. 'Twin Peaks' ('Twin Peaks #2') grows at a moderate rate, bearing small, dark green leaves. 'Pigeon Point' has larger, lighter green foliage; it grows

Baccharis pilularis

faster than 'Twin Peaks' and spreads farther.

Coyote brush will accept regular watering but doesn't require it. In coastal and inland areas, established plants will thrive during the dry months with no water; in regions with extremely hot summers, occasional watering may be needed.

Prune annually, before growth starts, to improve appearance. Remove upright or arching stems that disrupt evenness of planting's surface, and thin out old, woody branches.

BERGENIA

Pictured on page 116

Zones: 3–10 (except desert)
Type: Evergreen perennials
Exposure: Partial or light shade
Water: Regular to moderate
Spacing: 18 inches

Handsome, bold glossy leaves make a striking contrast to finer-textured plants.

Individual leaves are broad, rounded, and rubbery textured; they are carried on short leaf stalks that grow from clumping rootstocks. Foliage mass rises to 18 to 24 inches.

Two species are widely available. Rounded leaves of *B. cordifolia* reach 10 inches in length, with wavy, toothed edges and heart-shaped bases; clusters of 1½-inch pink flowers appear in spring on stems that are partially obscured by the foliage. Winter-blooming *B. crassifolia* features pink, lilac, or purple flowers on stems that rise above the foliage; individual leaves are broadly oval, to 8 inches long with wavy margins.

Bergenia plantings look best when they are grown in good soil and receive regular watering. But plants will endure poor soil and infrequent watering; in cool-summer regions, they will get through summer with little supplemental water even when planted in full sun.

Remove dead leaves annually; divide and replant when clumps become crowded and rootstocks rise well above the ground. Slugs and snails can be troublesome.

Bergenia crassifolia

BOUGAINVILLEA

Zone: 10
Type: Evergreen shrubby vine
Exposure: Sun
Water: Regular to moderate
Spacing: 6 to 8 feet

Although bougainvillea is most often grown as a vine, displaying flashy colors on walls, pergolas, and roofs, its vining habit can be put to use as a ground cover. Bougainvillea is particularly effective covering sloping land. Because of its thorns, it makes a fine barrier.

Stems are woody and sprawling, armed with needlelike spines; dark green leaves are oval to nearly heart shaped, 2 to 3 inches long. Showy spring and summer "flowers" actually are colorful, papery bracts surrounding the tiny, incon-spicuous real flowers. Familiar varieties feature bracts of red, violet, or purple, but new hybrids are available in yellow, bronze, pink, orange, lavender, white, and multicolor combinations. Some are shrubby rather than vining; for best ground cover, select a vining plant.

Planting requires particular care. Bougainvillea roots are sensitive to disturbance or exposure, and roots don't compact container soil into a firm mass.

If you're planting from a plastic container, cut out its bottom and place the container in the planting hole; then carefully slit one side and remove the plastic, filling in around the root ball with soil. If the container is metal, punch numerous holes in its sides and bottom, then plant the entire can; in time, the metal will rust.

Plants grow rampantly with regular watering but will thrive with moderate amounts. In midsummer, cut back on water to increase bloom production. Plants respond to applications of fertilizer in spring and again in summer. Try to train upward-growing shoots to a horizontal position; if that fails, cut them back to spreading stems.

CALLUNA VULGARIS

SCOTCH HEATHER
Pictured on pages 95 and 96

Zones: 5–9 (except desert)
Type: Evergreen shrub
Exposure: Sun to light shade
Water: Regular watering
Spacing: 12 to 18 inches

This species and its numerous varieties are true heathers; for a similar plant often incorrectly called heather, see *Erica* (heath) on page 123.

Fine textured is the term that describes Scotch heather. Tiny, scalelike, dark green leaves clothe branches of the mounded to spreading plants. Spikes of small, bell-shaped flowers appear at the tips of stems—usually in middle to late summer, although some varieties bloom in fall. Flowers come in pink, lavender, and purple shades, as well as white.

Among the many varieties available, plant habit varies from upright to mounding to spreading. Good choices among spreading kinds include 'Aurea', with purple flowers and gold foliage that turns red brown in winter; 'David Eason', red purple flowers in fall; 'J. H. Hamilton', double pink blossoms; 'Mrs. Ronald Gray', to 3 inches high with red purple flowers; and 'Nana', to 4 inches high with purple blooms.

Scotch heather needs acid, well-drained, moist soil. It performs best in regions that have cool, moist summer weather. You may be able to grow plants successfully in dry-summer areas if you water frequently so that soil never dries. With such regular watering, apply acid fertilizer in late winter and again in late spring. In hot-summer areas, the similar *Erica* is easier to grow.

CAMPANULA

BELLFLOWER
Pictured at right and on page 85

Zones: 4–10 (West), 4–9 (East)
Type: Evergreen perennials
Exposure: Sun to light shade
Water: Varies
Spacing: 12 inches

Of the many *Campanula* species, two are spreading plants that make excellent ground covers in small areas.

Dalmatian bellflower, *C. portenschlagiana* (often sold as *C. muralis*), forms a dark green foliage mass 4 to 7 inches high. Its long-stalked leaves are nearly round, with wavy, deeply toothed edges. From mid-spring through summer, foliage is nearly obscured by the inch-long, bell-shaped flowers of bright violet blue. The mounding plants spread at a moderately rapid rate.

Serbian bellflower, *C. poscharskyana*, spreads more rapidly with long, trailing, many-branched stems. Somewhat lighter green, its heart-shaped leaves vary from about 1 to 3½ inches long. From spring to early summer, star-shaped, blue to lavender blossoms dapple the plants; blooms up to an inch in diameter grow on stems that may reach 12 inches in height.

Both bellflowers perform best in good, well-drained soil with regular watering, although Serbian bellflower will endure infrequent watering (but at the expense of good appearance). They grow everywhere in partial or light shade but will take sunny locations wherever summer is cool or mild. Slugs and snails may be a problem.

CARISSA MACROCARPA

NATAL PLUM

Zones: 9 (warmest areas)–10
Type: Evergreen shrub
Exposure: Sun to shade
Water: Moderate
Spacing: 3 feet

In frost-free (or nearly frostless) regions, the low, spreading forms of Natal plum are among the most handsome and adaptable plants available for ground cover planting. Rich green, glossy, oval leaves to 3 inches long clothe stems that are armed with slender, sharp spines.

Highly fragrant, star-shaped, 2-inch flowers appear throughout the year, followed by 1- to 2-inch, plum-shaped green fruits that turn red when ripe; fruits (with cranberrylike flavor) are edible fresh or preserved. Because of its spines, Natal plum makes a good barrier planting.

Nurseries may offer several spreading varieties. 'Green Carpet' has small leaves on a plant that may reach 1½ feet high. 'Horizontalis' may reach 2 feet high, with more vinelike growth. 'Prostrata', despite its name, may reach 2 feet high, with occasional upright stems that should be cut out to keep planting low. 'Tuttle' (sometimes sold as 'Nana Compacta Tuttlei') is a mounding-spreading shrub to 3 feet high and 5 feet wide that produces a heavy crop of flowers and fruit.

Natal plum thrives in direct coastal conditions and is fairly drought tolerant in a coastal climate. Away from the coast, it will need moderate watering during dry months. Plants tolerate soils from sandy to claylike.

CEANOTHUS

WILD LILAC
Pictured on pages 87 and 118

Zones: 8–10 (West, except desert)
Type: Evergreen shrubs
Exposure: Sun to partial shade
Water: Moderate to little
Spacing: 3 to 5 feet

The wild lilacs of western North America (no relation to true lilacs) are cherished for their early spring contribution of blue shades to the landscape. Most are medium-size to large shrubs, but the naturally prostrate growth of two species has established them as ground covers.

Campanula poscharskyana

Point Reyes ceanothus, *C. gloriosus*, grows well in coastal and cool-summer areas but usually does not succeed where summer is hot. The basic species has inch-long, dark green, oval leaves with spiny margins; tiny, light blue blossoms are in rounded clusters 1 inch wide. The plant spreads widely but grows only 1 to 1½ feet high.

Variety 'Anchor Bay' is the same height but less spreading, with especially dense foliage cover and slightly deeper blue flowers. Deep violet blue blossoms distinguish *C. g. exaltatus* 'Emily Brown', which has hollylike, 1-inch leaves on a 2- to 3-foot-high plant.

Leaves that are glossy, 2-inch ovals give a different texture to Carmel creeper, *C. griseus horizontalis*. This fairly wide-spreading plant grows 1½ to 2½ feet tall, bearing 1-inch clusters of light blue flowers.

Pale blue-flowered 'Hurricane Point', an especially wide-spreading variety, grows to 3 feet high. 'Yankee Point' makes a high cover, 3 to 5 feet tall, clothed in slightly smaller, darker green leaves; its blossoms are medium blue.

In general, *Ceanothus* species are susceptible to root rot in poorly drained

Ceanothus

soils, especially in hot-summer regions. These ground cover types are more tolerant of normal garden conditions than most, particularly in coastal and cool-climate gardens, but the safest approach is to give them well-drained soil and moderate watering (after plants are established).

A notable exception to the general rule is 'Emily Brown', which will grow in heavy soil in coastal regions with regular watering.

CERASTIUM TOMENTOSUM

SNOW-IN-SUMMER

Zones: 3–10
Type: Evergreen perennial
Exposure: Sun
Water: Moderate
Spacing: 12 to 18 inches

Small, snowy white flowers nearly obscure this plant's foliage from late spring into summer, providing its descriptive common name. During the rest of the year, it's an attractive foliage mat 6 to 8 inches high, with tufts of narrow, silver gray leaves less than an inch long. Rapid growth may achieve a 2- to 3-foot spread from one plant in a year.

Snow-in-summer thrives in many climates, from cool coastal to simmering desert. Plants need well-drained soil to offset root rot; in hottest summer regions, plant in light shade. Plants grow most rapidly with regular watering but will tolerate considerable drought. Shear off flower stems or mow entire planting after blossoms have faded.

Snow-in-summer is not long-lived as a ground cover; plantings may begin to get patchy after several seasons. When that occurs, it's best to start over with divisions or cuttings.

CERATOSTIGMA PLUMBAGINOIDES

DWARF PLUMBAGO
Pictured on facing page

Zones: 6–10 (except desert)
Type: Deciduous perennial
Exposure: Sun to partial shade
Water: Moderate
Spacing: 18 inches

Dwarf plumbago provides a spot of vivid blue from midsummer to mid-autumn,

when cool tones are most welcome in the garden. Loose clusters of intense blue, ½-inch flowers appear at the ends of 6- to 12-inch, wiry stems; leaves are 3-inch ovals of bronze-tinted green that turn bronzy red with frost.

Best flower production is in regions having a long growing season. Plants spread fairly rapidly by underground stems to form a dense, soil-knitting cover.

Plants will grow in a wide range of soils from claylike to sandy, spreading more rapidly in lighter soils. After the flowering period, annual growth becomes shabby looking; shear or mow the planting before new growth begins. In time, overcrowding may cause plantings to decline in vigor or start to die out in patches. When this occurs, dig and replant with rooted stems.

CHAMAEMELUM NOBILE

CHAMOMILE

Zones: 3–10
Type: Evergreen perennial
Exposure: Sun to light shade
Water: Moderate
Spacing: 12 inches

Low, dense growth and finely cut, bright green leaves make chamomile useful as a lawn substitute and for growing between paving stones. Stems root as they spread along the ground, forming a solid cover. Aromatic foliage emits a pleasant scent underfoot.

Plantings may grow up to 12 inches high; in summer, they bear either small, buttonlike yellow flowers or, in some forms, small white daisy blossoms. Dried flowers were the source of traditional (rather bitter) chamomile tea. 'Treneague' is a nonflowering variety. Some nurseries still sell these plants under the old name *Anthemis nobilis*.

Plants grow well in light to heavy soil. An occasional mowing (particularly after the flowering period) keeps plantings neat. The flowerless 'Treneague' stays low and even without mowing.

CISSUS

Zones: 9–10
Type: Evergreen woody vines
Exposure: Sun to shade
Water: Moderate
Spacing: 5 feet

Several *Cissus* species—warm-climate relatives of familiar Boston ivy and Virginia creeper (*Parthenocissus* species)—make handsome ground and bank covers in regions where frost is light or nonexistent.

Kangaroo treebine, *C. antarctica,* has glossy, spear-shaped leaves to 3½ inches long with toothed edges and prominent veins; vigorous plants, with stems to about 10 feet long, make an elegant foliage cover.

Rampant *C. hypoglauca* may achieve a 15-foot spread in one season (established plants may reach 30 feet or more). Its highly polished, bronze-tinted leaves are divided into five rounded, leathery leaflets, each to 3 inches long; new growth is covered with rust-colored fuzz.

Delicate-appearing *C. striata* has foliage like Virginia creeper: leaves divided into three to five leaflets, each 1 to 3 inches long. The dark green, leathery foliage contrasts pleasantly with reddish stems on a plant that may reach 20 feet in spread.

None of the *Cissus* species is particular about soil. Growth generally is vigorous without supplemental fertilizer.

CISTUS SALVIIFOLIUS

SAGELEAF ROCKROSE

Zones: 8 (warmest parts)–10 (West)
Type: Evergreen shrub
Exposure: Sun to light shade
Water: Moderate to little
Spacing: 3 feet

A native of Mediterranean lands, sageleaf rockrose adapts well to dry-summer climates from seacoast to desert. Dense, shrubby growth reaches to 2 feet high, spreading to about 6 feet and rooting occasionally where stems contact soil.

Ceratostigma plumbaginoides

Wrinkled, wavy-edged leaves are light grayish green to an inch long. In spring, plants are covered with 1½-inch, yellow-centered white flowers. Each bloom lasts only a single day, but many buds keep a good display going for a month or more.

Sageleaf rockrose grows in a variety of soils—good or poor, claylike or sandy. It's a good choice for planting on sunny banks where its roots help control erosion. Although drought tolerant (needing just occasional summer watering in hot summer regions), it will take regular watering if soil drains well.

CONVALLARIA MAJALIS

LILY-OF-THE-VALLEY

Zones: 3–coldest parts of 9
(except desert)
Type: Deciduous perennial
Exposure: Shade
Water: Regular watering
Spacing: 6 inches (individual pips)

Lily-of-the-valley is renowned for its fragrant flowers—charming, pendant white bells in early spring on 6- to 8-inch stems. But the 8-inch, lance-shaped leaves are handsome in their own right. Plants will slowly spread into a thick cover that's an asset in a lightly shaded garden, in the deeper shade of north-facing walls, beneath deciduous trees (where they can endure root competition), or under choice evergreens, such as rhododendrons and pieris.

You can plant lily-of-the-valley from individual rootstocks (called pips), spacing them about 6 inches apart, or you can plant small clumps about 12 inches apart. Choose good soil and liberally amend it with organic matter. Give plantings an annual topdressing of leaf mold, compost, or other organic material after foliage dies down in fall and before spring growth begins.

CONVOLVULUS MAURITANICUS

GROUND MORNING GLORY

Zones: 8–10 (West, except desert)
Type: Evergreen perennial
Exposure: Sun
Water: Moderate
Spacing: 3 feet

Typical lavender blue, morning glorylike flowers adorn this 1- to 2-foot-high, spreading plant from late spring into mid-

Coprosma kirkii

fall. But unlike true morning glories (*Ipomoea*), these 2-inch flowers remain open during the day. Lax stems may extend to 3 feet or more, bearing softly hairy, rounded, gray green leaves to 1½ inches long.

Ground morning glory prefers light, sandy, or gravelly well-drained soil, although it can succeed in heavy soil if plants are not overwatered. Older plants may become woody and sparse; to prevent this, trim back older stems annually in late winter.

COPROSMA

Pictured above

Zones: 9–10 (West, except desert)
Type: Evergreen shrubs
Exposure: Sun to partial shade
Water: Moderate to little
Spacing: 2 feet

Two *Coprosma* species make fairly high, spreading ground covers bearing plentiful small, attractive leaves. Flowers are insignificant.

Inch-long, very narrow, yellow green leaves characterize *C. kirkii,* which

grows to 2 to 3 feet; its long branches angle upward from the base in a broad V-shape. Plants will control erosion on slopes and thrive in direct seacoast conditions. Slightly lower-growing *C. pumila* features broadly oval, shining, bright green leaves just under an inch long; 'Verde Vista' is a superior named variety.

Both species are drought tolerant when established and grow well in soils ranging from heavy to light. *C. pumila* will accept regular watering as well, although it doesn't need it.

CORNUS CANADENSIS

BUNCHBERRY

Zones: 3–6
Type: Deciduous perennial
Exposure: Shade
Water: Regular watering
Spacing: 12 inches

This ground-level dogwood is more exacting in its requirements than most other ground covers. But when conditions are suitable, it can cover great amounts of surface with an even carpet of broadly oval, 1- to 2-inch leaves in whorls atop 4- to 6-inch stems.

Spring flowers bloom at stem tips, the true flowers framed by four white, petal-like bracts that look like 1- to 1½-inch blossoms. Small, bright red, edible fruits appear in late summer to early fall. Foliage turns yellow in fall; then the entire plant dies back to ground level.

Basic requirements are moist, acid soil with plenty of organic matter. Given these conditions, bunchberry will spread by underground stems at a moderate rate. Sometimes, small pieces are hard to establish; for best success, transplant small clumps with a piece of rotten log with bark attached.

CORONILLA VARIA

CROWN VETCH

Zones: 3–10
Type: Deciduous perennial
Exposure: Sun to shade
Water: Moderate
Spacing: 12 inches

Use this clover relative on erosion-prone slopes and along the fringes of large gardens where its vigor and tenacity will outweigh its somewhat weedy appearance. It's not attractive for close-up planting, and its invasiveness will be a problem in well-organized gardens.

Spreading from underground roots, crown vetch sends up a thick cover of 2-foot, sprawling stems bearing compound leaves, each containing 11 to 25 oval, ½-inch leaflets. Clusters of small, pinkish lavender flowers form brown, fingerlike seed capsules. The entire plant dies down to roots for the winter.

Crown vetch performs best in full sun but will also grow satisfactorily in shade. It's not particular about soil type. For best appearance, mow planting in early spring; then fertilize and water to promote lush growth.

CORREA PULCHELLA

AUSTRALIAN FUCHSIA

Zones: 9–10 (West, except desert)
Type: Evergreen shrub
Exposure: Sun to partial shade
Water: Moderate
Spacing: 2 to 4 feet

Although not related to true fuchsias, these plants do have pendant, bell-shaped, 1-inch flowers that bloom at a distinctly unfuchsialike time of year: mid-fall to early spring. Three are suitable as ground covers, bearing rounded, inch-long leaves that have a dense, gray, feltlike covering on the undersides.

The most widely sold species is *C. pulchella,* which features light pink flowers. Plants grow to 2½ feet high and spread to 8 feet. 'Carmine Bells' has red blossoms on plants to 2 feet high; 'Ivory Bells' is similar except for flower color.

Good drainage is the key to success with Australian fuchsia. Sloping land and light soil (or poor, rocky soil) are entirely suitable. Plant in full sun where summer is mild; in hot-summer regions, plants may take full sun (although partial shade is safer), but they will not endure reflected heat from walls or pavement.

COTONEASTER

Pictured below and on pages 88, 96, and 122

Zones: Vary
Type: Evergreen and deciduous shrubs
Exposure: Sun to partial shade
Water: Moderate to little
Spacing: 3 to 5 feet

The rugged, undemanding cotoneasters provide special interest in two seasons. Springtime brings flattened clusters of small, wild roselike flowers in white or pale pink. In fall, bright red fruits (pea-size or larger) decorate the branches, usually remaining into winter.

All but one of the species described below have small (½- to 1-inch), oval leaves that range from bright to dark green on upper surfaces, gray to white beneath. In fall, the foliage of the deciduous species turns red.

Although cotoneasters will grow well in good soil with regular watering, they don't require such treatment. Poor soil and moderate watering are entirely suitable and, in fact, promote greater quantity of the decorative fruits.

All are best planted where they won't need frequent restrictive pruning; stubbed-off branch ends are unattractive. When pruning is necessary to limit spread, cut back to the branch juncture within the foliage mass so that the edge will retain an irregular, natural appearance. If vertical branches disrupt the desired horizontal plane, cut them back to their points of origin or to horizontal branches within the foliage.

Fireblight may cause a sudden wilting and blackening of cotoneaster stems and leaves; for remedies, see *Pyracantha,* page 147.

Two deciduous species offer distinctive growth habits. Creeping cotoneaster,

Cotoneaster microphyllus

C. adpressus (Zones 4–10), hugs the ground contours, growing slowly and remaining under 1 foot tall. Faster growing, to 18 inches high, with larger foliage and fruit, is *C. adpressus praecox* (sometimes sold as *C. praecox*).

Rock cotoneaster, *C. horizontalis* (Zones 4–10, except intermediate and low desert), has a very brief leafless period. Moderately fast growing, it may build to 3 feet high; the secondary branches along its main stems form a flat herringbone pattern. 'Variegatus' has white-edged leaves, while *C. h. perpusillus* is a lower-growing form with smaller leaves.

Among evergreen species, two spread widely but grow no higher than 6 inches. Bearberry cotoneaster, *C. dammeri* (sometimes sold as *C. humifusus*), Zones 5–10, grows rapidly, rooting as it spreads. The basic species has bright red fruits; selected varieties include 'Coral Beauty' (coral fruits), 'Royal Beauty' (deep red fruits), and 'Eichholz' (carmine red fruits and a scattering of colored leaves in fall). 'Skogsholmen' (Zones 6–10) has stiffer growth that can reach 1½ feet tall.

Narrow, willowlike leaves to 3½ inches long distinguish *C. salicifolius* 'Herbstfeuer' ('Autumn Fire') from the other ground cover types. Grown in Zones 6–10, it may lose part of its foliage over winter in the colder regions.

Similar to *C. dammeri* (and sometimes sold as a variety of it), *C.* 'Lowfast' (Zones 7–10) differs in several particulars: the ground cover reaches 1 foot high, its leaves are smaller, and growth is especially rapid. It's quite susceptible to fireblight in the warmest parts of the West Coast.

Taller still is rockspray cotoneaster, *C. microphyllus* (Zones 6–10). Main stems hug the ground, rooting as they spread, but secondary branches grow upright to 2 to 3 feet. Tiny, dark green leaves are slightly smaller than the rosy red fruits.

COTULA SQUALIDA

NEW ZEALAND BRASS BUTTONS

Zones: 6–10
Type: Evergreen to deciduous perennial
Exposure: Sun to light shade
Water: Regular watering
Spacing: 6 inches

Spreading plants with bronzy green, hairy, fernlike foliage hug the ground almost like turf. Against this fine-textured background come the summer flowers: petalless ¼-inch yellow daisies that look just like tiny brass buttons.

Reasonably rapid growth makes brass buttons suitable for large spaces as well as small; it also is attractive grown between paving stones. Plants may die to the ground over winter in Zones 6 and 7 but are evergreen in the warmer regions.

CYTISUS KEWENSIS

KEW BROOM

Zones: 6–8
Type: Deciduous shrub
Exposure: Sun
Water: Moderate
Spacing: 2 feet

Spreading, trailing green branches with tiny green leaves reach 4 feet or more in length but remain less than 12 inches high. In mid-spring, plants are decorated with a profusion of sweet pea-shaped, ½-inch blossoms in creamy white. If grown on a retained slope, branches will cascade, draping over the retaining wall.

Kew broom needs good drainage and will thrive in poor or sandy soils. Plants grow well in windy seashore gardens as well as inland locations.

Cotoneaster dammeri

DALEA GREGGII

TRAILING INDIGO BUSH

Zones: 9–10 (desert only)
Type: Evergreen shrub
Exposure: Sun
Water: Moderate to little
Spacing: 2 feet

This attractive desert native takes in stride the desert limitations of heat, dryness, and organically poor soils. Low, spreading branches are clothed with leaves consisting of small, pearly gray leaflets. Starting in spring and lasting until early summer, clusters of tiny lavender flowers decorate the gray surface. And good news for desert gardeners: the plant is not a favorite of rabbits.

Although established plants will tolerate drought, deep watering every other week encourages rapid growth.

DAMPIERA DIVERSIFOLIA

Zones: 9 (warmest parts)–10 (except desert)
Type: Evergreen perennial
Exposure: Sun
Water: Regular to moderate
Spacing: 12 to 18 inches

For small-scale use, even between paving stones, dampiera offers fine texture and arresting flower color. Ground-hugging plants consist of very narrow, inch-long leaves on trailing stems. In spring and summer, small, bright, deep blue blossoms that resemble those of the popular annual *Lobelia* appear.

Plants spread at a moderate rate both by underground stems and by rooting along stems that touch soil. Best growth is in well-drained sandy to loamy soil.

DUCHESNEA INDICA

INDIAN MOCK STRAWBERRY

Zones: 3–10
Type: Evergreen perennial
Exposure: Sun to shade
Water: Moderate
Spacing: 12 to 18 inches

At first glance, this ground cover would seem to be a strawberry: leaves are strawberrylike; plants spread by runners, rooting as they spread; and the ½-inch red fruits beg to be tasted.

But several details make the difference: the ½-inch flowers in spring and summer are yellow (not white), the fruits are nearly flavorless, and both flowers and fruits are carried above the foliage (whereas those of true strawberry nestle among or beneath the leaves). Foliage mass rises to about 6 inches in shade, lower in sun.

Growth is rapid and can be somewhat invasive, but it is easily controlled. Trim or mow annually in early spring to tidy up the appearance.

EPIMEDIUM

Zones: 3–9 (except desert)
Type: Evergreen perennial
Exposure: Shade
Water: Moderate
Spacing: 12 inches

A delicate tracery of handsome leaves and a pleasant display of spring flowers recommend the slow- to moderate-growing epimediums as small-scale ground covers. Use them in shaded or woodland gardens, along with rhododendrons, camellias, and other plants that prefer a somewhat acid soil.

From a dense network of underground stems rise wiry leaf stalks bearing leathery, 3-inch, heart-shaped leaflets— bronzy pink in new spring growth, turning bronze in fall. Flowers come in loose clusters, each blossom consisting of four sepals (in starlike arrangement) surrounding the small true flower, which usually has spurred petals.

Bishop's hat, *E. grandiflorum,* has flowers 1 to 2 inches across in a combination of red, lavender, and white; named varieties are available with flowers of white, pink, lavender, and red. Foliage and flowers reach about 12 inches high.

Yellow and red flowers distinguish *E. pinnatum,* which grows to 15 inches. Foot-tall *E. rubrum* has showy blossoms of crimson and yellow or white; named varieties with pink or white flowers are sold.

ERICA

HEATH

Pictured on pages 81 and 95

Zones: Vary (none in desert)
Type: Evergreen shrubs
Exposure: Sun
Water: Regular watering
Spacing: 18 inches

Closely related to true Scotch heather (see *Calluna vulgaris,* page 116), the heaths share a close resemblance and similar cultural needs. Leaves are small and needlelike on dense, mounding-to-spreading plants. Flowers are small and bell to urn shaped in large clusters or spikes.

Colors include lilac, purple, pink shades, rosy red, bright red, and white. Season of bloom varies, depending on species or variety; by careful selection you may have heath in flower nearly year-round. Some gardeners create colorful patchwork plantings by mixing species and varieties that have different colors and bloom seasons.

Heaths need soil that is both moist and well aerated. The best soils are the well-drained sandy to loam types liberally amended with organic matter. Root systems are dense and matted; they'll control erosion on sloping land but are shallow and won't tolerate drought. Most heaths also require acid soil; the exception is *E. carnea* and its varieties, which will also grow well in soil that's neutral to slightly alkaline.

Heaths perform best in regions where the air is cool and moist, such as the maritime areas of the Northeast and

Northwest. Drier and hotter inland climates limit the potential for success; in such regions, plants should be lightly or partially shaded during summer. Shear off flowering stems after blooms fade. Plants seldom need fertilizer except, perhaps, in the poorest of sandy soils.

The most adaptable heath, *E. carnea* (sometimes sold as *E. herbacea*), grows in Zones 5–10 (West) and 5–8 (East). Flowering usually begins in early winter and, depending on variety, may last until early summer.

The basic species has rosy red flowers on a prostrate plant that sends upright branches to 16 inches. Lower-growing varieties include fast-growing 'Springwood' ('Springwood White') with white flowers and light green foliage; pure pink 'Springwood Pink'; and carmine red 'Vivelli', which undergoes a foliage color change to bronzy red during winter.

Dorset heath, *E. ciliaris,* grows in Zones 7–9 (West) and 7–8 (East). Rosy red flowers appear from midsummer into fall on a plant with light green leaves; blooming at the same time are the darker-foliaged varieties 'Mrs. C. H. Gill' (deep red) and 'Stoborough' (white). Except for 18-inch 'Stoborough', plants grow no higher than 12 inches.

Purple-flowered twisted heath, *E. cinerea,* and its scarlet-blossomed variety 'Atrosanguinea' bloom from early summer into fall on mounding, spreading plants that grow no higher than 12 inches. Those plants thrive in Zones 7–9 (West) and 7–8 (East). Also growing well in those zones is *E. tetralix* 'Darleyensis'; it has salmon pink blossoms from early summer into fall on an 8-inch, spreading plant with gray green foliage.

Erica 'Dawn' is an easy to grow hybrid for Zones 7–10 (West) and 7–8 (East). The plant grows in a spreading mound to 1 foot tall; its new growth is a contrasting golden yellow. Deep pink flowers begin in early summer and continue into fall.

Erigeron karvinskianus

ERIGERON KARVINSKIANUS

MEXICAN DAISY,
SANTA BARBARA DAISY
Pictured above

Zones: 9–10 (West), 9 (East)
Type: Evergreen perennial
Exposure: Sun
Water: Moderate to little
Spacing: 12 inches

Fine texture and a graceful appearance belie the toughness of this plant. Mexican daisy grows in light or heavy soil, accepts root competition from trees and shrubs, and tolerates drought when established (but it will accept routine garden watering). Stems may root when they contact soil; combined with rapid growth, this can make Mexican daisy an invasive (but easy to curb) ground cover.

Slender to wiry branching stems bear narrow, toothed leaves to an inch long. Pinkish white daisy flowers appear over a long period from late spring into fall. Spreading plants may reach 10 to 20 inches high; if they become lumpy or straggly, shear them back after flowering is over.

ERODIUM CHAMAEDRYOIDES

CRANE'S BILL

Zones: 8–10 (except desert)
Type: Evergreen perennial
Exposure: Sun to light shade
Water: Regular watering
Spacing: 6 to 12 inches

Here's an example of a rugged ground cover with a delicate appearance. Each plant produces a thick carpet of foliage to 6 inches high and about 12 inches across.

Long-stalked, roundish leaves are about 1/3 inch long with scalloped margins. Cup-shaped, 1/2-inch flowers bloom from mid-spring to mid-fall in white or rose pink; petals are veined in dark rose. The slender, pointed seed capsule that develops from each blossom's center gives the plant its common name.

Crane's bill prefers well-drained soil, but water often enough so the soil doesn't dry out. Fairly slow growth recommends the plant for use in small-scale areas.

EUONYMUS FORTUNEI

WINTER CREEPER
Pictured at right

Zones: 5–9
Type: Evergreen woody vine
Exposure: Sun to shade
Water: Moderate
Spacing: 2 feet

Winter creeper shares its growth habit with another popular ground cover, ivy (*Hedera,* see page 129). Juvenile growth is trailing and vinelike; it will cover the ground, rooting as it spreads. When it encounters vertical surfaces, it climbs upward, attaching with rootlets along stems.

In time, the vertical growth sends out shrubby branches, and plants grown from these will be shrubs rather than vines. Therefore, some named varieties of *E. fortunei* are vines, and some are shrubs. The following vining ground covers are all dense and neat, with polished foliage.

Common winter creeper, *E. f. radicans,* has thick, oval leaves to an inch long, forming a spreading, sometimes undulating, cover. Purple-leaf winter creeper, *E. f.* 'Colorata', makes a more even ground cover; its foliage turns purple during fall and winter.

'Gracilis'—often sold as *E. radicans argentea variegata, E. fortunei variegata,* or *E. f.* 'Silver Edge'—is a good small-space ground cover; its leaves are variegated with white or cream that turns pinkish in cold weather. Smallest of all is 'Kewensis' ('Minima') with pea-size, dark green leaves.

The various winter creepers tolerate a wide range of conditions: sun to shade, sandy to claylike soil, and regular to moderate watering. Plantings give solid cover after several years.

Euonymus fortunei 'Gracilis'

FESTUCA OVINA GLAUCA

BLUE FESCUE

Zones: 3–10 (West), 3–9 (East)
Type: Evergreen perennial grass
Exposure: Sun to light shade
Water: Regular to little
Spacing: 6 to 12 inches

Although the fescues are best known as turf grasses, blue fescue is strictly an ornamental plant used for pattern planting and ground cover. Plants form tightly knit tufts of soft but tough, needlelike leaves 4 to 10 inches long; an individual clump resembles a blue gray shaving brush. Flowering stems and seed heads are inconspicuous.

Use blue fescue on level ground or slopes in well-drained soil. Because clumps don't spread to form a solid cover, density depends on the spacing of clumps.

Desert plantings need regular watering; elsewhere, occasional watering is sufficient. If plantings become shabby in appearance, mow or shear the clumps to 2 inches high at any time. Eventually, the clumps will become overgrown and decline in vigor. When this occurs, dig them up, separate each clump into small divisions, and replant.

FRAGARIA CHILOENSIS

WILD STRAWBERRY

Zones: 6–10
Type: Evergreen perennial
Exposure: Sun to light shade
Water: Regular to moderate
Spacing: 12 to 18 inches

This true strawberry is native to the Pacific coast of North and South America, where it thrives in full sun in the maritime climate. It will also succeed in hotter, drier regions, but in these areas, it needs light or partial shade and regular watering. The glossy, dark green leaves have three toothed leaflets—similar to commercial strawberries, of which it's an ancestor.

Inch-wide white blossoms appear in spring, rarely followed by small red fruits that are edible but second-rate in flavor. In winter, the foliage becomes tinted with red. Plants grow 6 to 12 inches high, spreading rapidly by runners.

Mow foliage annually in early spring, before growth begins, to keep plantings renewed and prevent stem buildup. Later in spring, apply fertilizer to ensure vigorous, lush growth. If leaves become yellowish in late summer, apply iron sulfate to restore normal green color.

GALAX URCEOLATA

Pictured on page 128

Zones: 3–8 (except desert)
Type: Evergreen perennial
Exposure: Shade
Water: Regular watering
Spacing: 12 inches

For shady garden situations, it's difficult to find a more handsome ground cover. Slowly spreading clumps feature long-stalked, heart-shaped glossy leaves to 5 inches across; except in deeply shaded plantings, foliage turns bronze in winter.

Foliage height ranges from 6 to 9 inches; in summer, flower stems rise to

2½ feet, bearing small white flowers in foxtail fashion at their extremities.

Galax prefers acid soil liberally amended with organic matter. Plant it under dogwood, rhododendrons, azaleas, and pieris—shrubs and trees that appreciate the same conditions.

GALIUM ODORATUM

SWEET WOODRUFF
Pictured below

Zones: 5–10 (except desert)
Type: Evergreen perennial
Exposure: Shade
Water: Regular watering
Spacing: 12 inches

Plantings of fine-textured sweet woodruff always have a fresh appearance. Dense growth consists of narrow, bright green leaves that appear in closely set whorls of six to eight on slender stems 6 to 12 inches high. Tiny white, four-petalled flowers spangle this feathery cover in late spring and summer. The "sweet" of the common name comes from the dried foliage, which is used to flavor May wine.

When given good, slightly acid soil and regular watering, sweet woodruff will spread rapidly. Its noncompetitive root system makes it a good companion for shade-loving shrubs and trees. Healthy plantings can become somewhat invasive—both from spreading and from seedling plants.

GARDENIA JASMINOIDES 'RADICANS'

Zones: 8–10
Type: Evergreen shrub
Exposure: Sun to shade
Water: Regular watering
Spacing: 18 to 24 inches

Although blossoms lack the opulence of florists' gardenias, flowers on this plant exude the familiar fragrance. Spreading plants extend 2 to 3 feet, rising only 6 to 12 inches high; their small, oval leaves are glossy dark green, frequently streaked with white. Inch-wide white flowers appear throughout summer.

To succeed with this gardenia, you must pay close attention to its cultural needs. Give plants well-drained soil containing plenty of organic matter; set root balls a few inches above soil grade to avoid root rot.

Plants need heat for best performance. Choose a location in full sun in mild coastal regions and light shade (although perhaps with morning sun) in warm to hot inland areas. Apply acid fertilizer monthly during the growing season for best results. If leaves become chlorotic (yellow, with veins remaining green), apply iron chelate or iron sulfate.

GAULTHERIA

Zones: Vary
Type: Evergreen shrubs
Exposure: Light shade
Water: Regular watering
Spacing: 12 inches

Two woodland natives—one eastern, one western—make attractive, small-scale ground covers when used with other plants that share their need for moist, acid soil amended with plenty of organic matter. Both spread slowly by underground stems that produce upright branches bearing leathery, broadly oval, dark green leaves.

Taller of the two species, to about 8 inches, is western *G. ovatifolia* (Zones 6–9, except desert). Tiny white to palest pink, urn-shaped summer flowers mature in fall into pea-size, edible berries with a wintergreen flavor.

Eastern *G. procumbens* (Zones 4–9, except desert) is known as wintergreen, checkerberry, or teaberry, from the flavor of its similar scarlet fruits. Small summer blossoms are white, on a plant to about 6 inches tall.

Galium odoratum

Gazania

GAZANIA

Pictured above and on page 85

Zones: 9–10 (West)
Type: Evergreen perennial
Exposure: Sun
Water: Moderate
Spacing: Varies

Gazanias embody the essence of summer; their 3- to 4-inch daisy flowers bloom in warm tones of yellow, orange, red, copper, pink, cream, or white, often with a contrasting dark central eye. The major flowering period is late spring into midsummer, although in mildest areas gazanias will flower sporadically throughout the year. Blossoms open on sunny days, close when evening approaches, and remain closed during cloudy or overcast weather (except as noted below).

You can buy two types of gazanias—those that form compact clumps and those that spread by trailing runners. Clumping kinds are good for small-scale ground covers on level ground; space plants about 12 inches apart. Leaves typically are long and narrow, green on the upper surface and gray beneath.

Nurseries sell various named strains of mixed colors; the Chansonette, Daybreak (which open at dawn), and Mini-Star plants are more compact than other types. Several named hybrids are widely sold: 'Aztec Queen' (multicolored yellow and bronze flowers), 'Burgundy', 'Copper King', and 'Fiesta Red'. 'Moonglow' has double yellow flowers that open even on sunless days.

Trailing gazanias, planted 12 to 18 inches apart, will spread quickly to cover large areas, even on sloping ground. Foliage generally is silvery gray; flowers may be white, yellow, orange, or bronze. Among named varieties are orange 'Sunburst', yellow 'Sunglow', and green-leafed 'Sunrise Yellow'.

Gazanias are not particular about soil type. In desert regions they may need regular watering, but in areas with less intense heat, moderate watering is sufficient. Plantings (especially of clumping kinds) may decline in vigor or become patchy after 3 to 4 years. If this occurs, you can dig, divide, and replant in early spring.

Galax urceolata

GELSEMIUM SEMPERVIRENS

CAROLINA JESSAMINE
Pictured on page 83

Zones: 8–10
Type: Evergreen woody vine
Exposure: Sun
Water: Regular watering
Spacing: 2 to 3 feet

In late winter and early spring, when floral displays are at a low ebb, Carolina jessamine covers itself with highly fragrant, 1- to 1½-inch, tubular yellow blossoms. During the rest of the year, an attractive appearance is maintained by the glossy, bright green, 1- to 4-inch oval leaves. Twining stems spread at a moderate rate. They'll try to climb any vertical supports they encounter—shrubs, trees, or fences.

As a ground cover, Carolina jessamine will mound up to 3 feet or more. Trim each year after flowering to help maintain the planting at an even height. Caution: All parts of the plant are poisonous.

GENISTA

BROOM
Pictured on page 86

Zones: 6–9 (except *G. lydia*)
Type: Deciduous shrubs
Exposure: Sun
Water: Little
Spacing: 2 feet

The various brooms offer an arresting display of small, sweet pealike yellow flowers in late spring. Tiny leaves may be oval or nearly needlelike and may not last through the growing season; however, the green stems give plants the appearance of being evergreen.

Smallest of the four ground cover species is *G. lydia* (sometimes sold as *Cytisus lydia*), which may reach 2 feet high with a spread to about 4 feet. It's also the least cold tolerant, growing in Zones 7–9 (except desert). Spanish broom, *G. hispanica,* grows 1 to 2 feet high and spreads widely; its spiny stems make it a good barrier plant.

Also wide spreading, to about 1½ feet high, is multibranched *G. pilosa,* which has gray green stems; selected for superior color and flower production is variety 'Vancouver Gold'. Winged branches of wide-spreading *G. sagittalis* give the foot-tall branches the appearance of being jointed. Its flowering period extends into summer.

The brooms are good choices for poor soil and for slopes or banks that receive little water. Plants thrive where summer is hot and dry (except for desert regions), as well as under coastal conditions.

GERANIUM

CRANESBILL

Zones: Vary
Type: Evergreen, deciduous perennials
Exposure: Sun
Water: Regular watering
Spacing: Varies

Although flowers are not as individually showy as those of the plants commonly called geranium (actually *Pelargonium*), the true geraniums offer a good show of color over a long period from spring to fall. Flowers are about an inch across, borne in clusters above a 6- to 10-inch cover of rounded leaves that are either lobed or finely cut.

Evergreen *G. incanum* grows in Zones 9–10 (except desert) but may be damaged by frost in colder parts of Zone 9. Finely cut foliage is the backdrop for magenta pink blossoms. Plants grow quickly, forming broad cushions; space them about 12 inches apart for cover.

Deciduous *G. macrorrhizum* (Zones 4–10) has aromatic, lobed leaves that take on tawny gold to russet shades in fall. Typical flower color is red, but with some searching you may find pink- or white-blooming varieties. Plants spread widely by underground stems; space them about 24 inches apart.

GREVILLEA

Zones: 9–10 (West, except desert)
Type: Evergreen shrubs
Exposure: Sun
Water: Moderate to little
Spacing: 3 to 4 feet

The two grevilleas suitable for ground cover are high, spreading shrubs. But large plantings escape appearing massive because of the fine texture created by the shrubs' needlelike leaves. Clustered flowers are narrow and tubular, with prominent stamens; hummingbirds find them enticing.

Woolly grevillea, *G. lanigera,* spreads to 10 feet, reaching 3 to 6 feet high. Gray green, ½-inch leaves are a good foil for the summer display of red and cream flowers.

Spring-blooming *G.* 'Noellii' features pink and white flowers against inch-long, bright green leaves. Plants may reach 4 feet high, spreading to 5 feet.

Although grevilleas will accept good, well-drained soil, they don't require it; they'll thrive in soils low in nutrients and organic matter.

Woolly grevillea excels in hot, sparingly watered situations; *G.* 'Noellii' needs moderate watering.

HEBE

Zones: Vary (West, except desert)
Type: Evergreen shrubs
Exposure: Sun to light shade
Water: Regular watering
Spacing: Varies

Wherever coastal weather dominates or influences a garden's climate, the hebes (sometimes still sold as *Veronica*) will flourish. And even in warmer, drier areas, they may succeed if planted in light shade. Plants need well-drained soil in all regions.

These ground covers bloom in summer; each blossom is tiny, with prominent, protruding stamens, but they appear grouped together in short spikes.

Taller of the two is *H. chathamica* (Zones 9–10), rising to 1½ feet and spreading to about 3 feet; space plants 18 inches apart. Lavender flowers appear against a backdrop of deep green, ½-inch oval leaves.

Creeping *H. pinguifolia* 'Pagei' (Zones 8–10) spreads to 5 feet but reaches only about 9 inches high; space plants 24 to 30 inches apart. Small, broadly oval, blue gray leaves are edged in pink; flowers are white, in plump spikes.

HEDERA

IVY
Pictured below and on pages 90 and 94

Zones: Vary
Type: Evergreen woody vines
Exposure: Sun to shade
Water: Regular to moderate
Spacing: 18 inches

If you need a rugged, adaptable ground cover that always appears neat and uniform and that will knit soil together with a multitude of roots (and control erosion on slopes), consider ivy.

When ivy is planted as a ground cover, the stems will root as they spread; if they contact vertical surfaces (for example, walls, fences, tree trunks, or shrubbery), they'll climb and cling with aerial rootlets. Ivy's leathery leaves are basically heart shaped with lobed margins; size and color vary.

Two species are widely available for ground cover planting. Algerian ivy, *H. canariensis,* is the larger of the two and grows in Zones 8–10. Its glossy leaves may reach 8 inches across; its variety 'Variegata' has green leaves edged with cream white.

Familiar English ivy, *H. helix,* grown in Zones 6–10, has dark green, nonglossy

Hedera canariensis

leaves to 4 inches across with conspicuous lighter veins. Nurseries may offer a few selected varieties; specialists will carry many more. 'Baltica' (a smaller-foliaged form whose leaves turn purple in winter) and 'Bulgarica' will grow in Zone 5.

'Hahn's Self-Branching' (sometimes sold as 'Hahn's Ivy' or 'Hahnii') has lighter green leaves and a more branching habit than the basic species. Other variations include those with small leaves, elongated foliage, and leaves with white, cream, or yellow variegation. Small-leafed types are effective as small-scale ground covers.

To get a planting off to a good start, prepare the soil as outlined on page 99. If you'll be planting on a slope, add organic amendment to each planting hole. When you plant, be sure that both the soil and the plants are thoroughly moistened.

Water regularly to get plants well established. Thereafter, Algerian ivy should receive regular watering. English ivy will have a better appearance in warm regions with routine watering, but plants are fairly tolerant of drought.

To keep plantings attractive and vigorous, apply a high-nitrogen fertilizer in early spring and again in midsummer. Hedge shears or a sharp spade will keep the edges of plantings neat.

After several years, a planting may build up a thick thatch of stems. When this occurs, you can shear back the ivy or mow it with a heavy-duty rotary mower; early spring is the best time, so new growth will quickly cover over.

Ivy is a notorious hiding and breeding place for slugs and snails, which may require control measures. In some areas, rodents take shelter in ivy plantings.

HELIANTHEMUM NUMMULARIUM

SUNROSE
Pictured on page 85

Zones: 5–10
Type: Evergreen shrublet
Exposure: Sun
Water: Moderate
Spacing: 24 to 30 inches

For small, sunny spaces (including sloping ground), sunroses offer fine-textured foliage spangled with a 2-month display of warmly colored flowers; bloom begins in middle to late spring, depending on the climate. Many varieties are sold; you can choose single or double flowers, and shades of pink, red, orange, copper, yellow, or white.

Each inch-wide blossom lasts only a day, but countless buds produce a good show throughout the bloom season. Narrow leaves, to an inch long, may be dark glossy green or nearly gray. Individual plants reach 6 to 8 inches high, spreading to about 3 feet.

Give sunroses well-drained soil and moderate watering in hot-summer regions, little water where summer is cool. Shear plants lightly after flowering to keep them dense and to encourage more blooms in late summer or fall. Where winter temperatures dip below freezing or where plants are exposed to wind and sun, cover plantings with evergreen boughs to prevent the leaves from drying out.

HELLEBORUS

HELLEBORE

Zones: Vary
Type: Evergreen perennial
Exposure: Shade
Water: Regular watering
Spacing: 12 to 18 inches

The elegant hellebores—including Christmas and Lenten roses—are clump-forming perennials that, when planted in mass, make handsome ground covers. Leaves are deeply lobed, each leaflet like the finger of an outstretched hand. Flowers resemble those of single roses,

blooming in open clusters (except for *H. niger*) on stems that rise above the foliage.

Smallest of the species is *H. foetidus* (Zones 3–10), which has very dark green leaves divided into seven to eleven long, narrow leaflets; plants reach 1 to 1½ feet high. Light green, purple-margined, inch-wide flowers appear in late winter and early spring.

Christmas rose, *H. niger* (Zones 4–8, except desert), may bloom in December in warmer regions, or in late winter or early spring where winter is colder. Greenish white, 2- to 3-inch flowers, one to a stem, turn pinkish purple as they age. Each leaf contains seven to nine narrow, 9-inch leaflets; foliage may rise 1½ feet high.

Flowering in late winter to early spring, Lenten rose, *H. orientalis* (Zones 4–9), is available in white, pink, green, and purplish shades. The 2- to 3-inch blossoms are often spotted with dark purple; usually, they become greenish as they age. Foliage is the largest of all—five to eleven broad leaflets up to about 10 inches long.

Hellebores grow best in good soil with regular watering and an annual fertilizer application in early spring. But plants are unexpectedly rugged, persisting and performing satisfactorily with nothing more than moderate watering. Clumps never require dividing.

HEMEROCALLIS

DAYLILY

Zones: 3–10
Type: Evergreen to deciduous perennial
Exposure: Sun to light shade
Water: Regular to moderate
Spacing: 18 inches

Legions of gardeners grow daylilies for their lavish display of lilylike flowers in a wide range of colors and color combinations. But the foliage also is a landscape asset: narrow, curved leaves (an individual plant resembles a young corn plant) form fountainlike foliage clumps.

Massed together, daylilies create a handsome foliage cover (1 to 3 feet high, depending on the variety) with an arresting show of blossoms in late spring—and again in late summer to fall, if you choose kinds that rebloom.

As the name implies, each blossom lasts just a day, but the slender, branched flower scapes rising above the foliage carry many buds to provide blooms for a month or more. Specialists offer long lists of named varieties in yellow, orange, red, bronze, purple, pink, lavender, cream, or near white; some kinds have contrasting dark or greenish central bands, or eyes.

The size of plant, flower, and foliage can vary from miniatures with foot-high leaves to those with foliage rising to 3 feet and flower stems reaching 6 feet. For best appearance with a ground cover planting, choose a single variety or select varieties of similar size.

Some daylilies are completely deciduous; others are semi-evergreen or completely evergreen. Deciduous varieties are the best to plant in Zones 3–5; evergreen daylilies are best adapted to Zones 7–10. Semi-evergreen kinds prosper in Zones 5–9.

Daylilies appreciate good, well-drained soil but will thrive in a wide range of soil types. Plants compete well with some shallow-rooted trees. Regular watering helps plants maintain a good appearance throughout the season, but they'll endure with moderate amounts of water—even very little—in cool-summer areas. Apply fertilizer to plantings just as growth begins in spring; repeat in midsummer.

When clumps become overcrowded and decline in vigor and flower quality, dig and divide in early spring (colder regions) or fall (milder areas).

HERNIARIA GLABRA

GREEN CARPET, RUPTURE WORT

Zones: 5–10
Type: Evergreen perennial
Exposure: Sun to shade
Water: Regular watering
Spacing: 12 inches

Green carpet's tiny green leaves on creeping stems no higher than 3 inches create a mosslike effect. But unlike mosses, this plant will grow in full sun as

Hosta undulata

well as in shade. Use it in small spaces—creeping around rocks, between paving stones, or as a pattern plant with other low ground covers. The plant's greenish flowers are insignificant. In the colder zones, leaves turn bronzy red over winter.

HIPPOCREPIS COMOSA

Zones: 9–10
Type: Evergreen perennial
Exposure: Sun
Water: Regular to moderate
Spacing: 12 inches

The fine texture and soft appearance of this low ground cover mask a tough constitution. Growing to 3 inches high and spreading widely, it can serve as a lawn substitute (even tolerating some foot traffic). Its roots will bind soil on sloping land, preventing erosion. And it will endure poor soil and little water.

Each leaf is composed of seven to fifteen tiny, bright green leaflets; the multibranched stems form a dense mat of foliage. Spring flowers are sweet pea-shaped, half-inch yellow blossoms in small clusters.

Despite its tolerance of adverse conditions, hippocrepis is better looking if planted in good soil and watered regularly. To keep a planting neat, mow it once a year after flowering is finished.

HOSTA

PLANTAIN LILY
Pictured below and on pages 91 and 131

Zones: 3–9 (except intermediate and low desert)
Type: Deciduous perennial
Exposure: Sun to shade
Water: Regular watering
Spacing: Varies

The many hostas (sometimes still sold under the old name *Funkia*) are premier foliage plants. Each makes a slowly expanding clump of long-stalked leaves that overlap in shingle fashion to become mounds of foliage. Slender stalks rise above the leaves (just barely above, in some varieties) in late spring or summer,

bearing small, bell-shaped blossoms of white or lavender.

This is the basic theme, but the variations are seemingly endless. Leaves may be nearly round, heart shaped, or lance shaped, with smooth or quilted surfaces. Some plants have glossy foliage; others are dusted with a grayish bloom.

Foliage colors range from gray and blue to light and dark green. Variegated combinations abound, mixing white, cream, or yellow with the other colors. Even leaf size varies—from "giants" with leaves 9 inches or more in length to miniature varieties that make clumps no greater than 9 inches across.

The best way to choose a hosta is to visit a well-stocked nursery or consult a specialty catalog. You can then select for the foliage effect you desire; or pick

several different kinds for a patterned planting.

All hostas prefer good soil and plenty of moisture. Plant in sun to moderate shade where summer is cool to moderately warm. In hot-summer regions, give plants, especially those with variegated foliage, light to medium shade. Clumps grow indefinitely without division and replanting, but you can easily extend plantings by dividing old clumps or by slicing out wedges with a spade.

Best performance is in regions that have definite winter chill and summer humidity (cool or hot). Slugs and snails are fond of hosta foliage.

HOUTTUYNIA CORDATA

Zones: 6–10 (West, except desert), 6–9 (East)
Type: Deciduous perennial
Exposure: Sun to shade
Water: Regular watering
Spacing: 18 inches

From a distance, houttuynia could be mistaken for English ivy. Heart-shaped, semiglossy leaves grow to 3 inches long, and the foliage forms an even cover to 9 inches high. The striking form 'Variegata' (sometimes sold as 'Chameleon') features splashes of cream, yellow, pink, and red on the outer portion of each leaf.

In cool-summer regions, you can grow houttuynia in sun; in all other areas, plant in light to deep shade. Plants spread by underground stems and can become somewhat invasive in the good, moist soil they prefer.

HYPERICUM CALYCINUM

AARON'S BEARD, CREEPING ST. JOHNSWORT
Pictured on page 87

Zones: 6–10
Type: Evergreen shrub
Exposure: Sun to shade
Water: Moderate
Spacing: 18 inches

Aaron's beard is both good looking and indestructible, forming a dense, even cover to 12 inches high. Arching stems

Hosta sieboldiana

bear pairs of oval leaves to 4 inches long that are rich green in sunny locations, lighter green in shade. In late spring to early summer, nearly every stem tip bears a 3-inch yellow blossom with prominent stamens.

Plants spread aggressively by underground stems; they can be invasive in some situations, unless restricted by a barrier to control the perimeter. On the positive side, the dense mat of roots and underground stems competes easily with surface-rooted trees and helps prevent erosion on sloping ground. Any soil is suitable.

Aaron's beard is fairly drought tolerant, but it grows more attractively with at least moderate watering. Mow or shear plantings about every 3 years in late winter or early spring to renew growth and maintain an even surface.

IBERIS SEMPERVIRENS

EVERGREEN CANDYTUFT
Pictured at right and on page 1

Zones: 4–10
Type: Evergreen perennial
Exposure: Sun to light shade
Water: Moderate
Spacing: 12 inches

At the peak of bloom, a planting of candytuft will be entirely white, with flattened clusters of tiny flowers completely obscuring the narrow, dark and glossy leaves. The major flowering period is early to late spring, but in mildest regions you may see flowers beginning in late fall. Each plant is a spreading hummock 8 to 12 inches high, spreading 12 to 18 inches.

Superior for ground cover use is the variety 'Snowflake', which has large flowers and foliage on a plant that spreads to 3 feet (and can be planted 18 to 24 inches apart). In warm-winter areas, it will bloom intermittently throughout the year.

After the spring flowering has finished, shear plants lightly to keep plants compact; this also encourages new growth and possible later bloom.

Iberis sempervirens

ICE PLANT

Pictured on pages 86, 95, and 134

Zones: Vary
Type: Evergreen perennials
Exposure: Sun
Water: Moderate to little
Spacing: Varies

Included under the common name "ice plant" are a number of succulent perennial plants once grouped together as *Mesembryanthemum* but now classified under different names. All have foliage that is thick and juicy, often with a powdery gray or crystalline surface. Most produce showy flowers—some almost blindingly brilliant—that resemble silky-petaled daisies; bees are attracted to the blooms.

Ice plants are not particular about soil; some of them will grow in nearly pure beach sand. Water just often enough to keep foliage from wilting or shriveling; overwatering can result in root rot or dieback, especially in heavier soils during hot weather. Fertilize lightly in mid-fall and again after flowering has finished.

Aptenia cordifolia; Zones 9 (warmest parts)–10. Succulent, bright green, inch-long leaves are heart shaped to oval; they grow on lax stems that trail to about 2 feet. Vivid purplish red, inch-wide flowers appear in spring and summer. The variety 'Variegata' has leaves margined in white. Use in small spaces, setting plants 12 to 18 inches apart.

Carpobrotus; Zones 9–10. Coarse-textured, trailing plants have thick, finger-like leaves and 2-inch, pastel blossoms. Plants will cover a considerable area on level or gently sloping ground; space new plants 18 to 24 inches apart. Avoid planting on steep banks where the weight of a rain-soaked planting could cause slippage.

C. chilensis has three-sided, straight leaves to 2 inches long; 3-inch, rosy purple flowers appear in summer. Far more common, *C. edulis* has curved leaves 4 to 5 inches long and pale yellow- to rose-colored blossoms.

Cephalophyllum 'Red Spike'; Zones 9–10. Individual plants reach 3 to 5 inches high and spread to 15 inches; bronzy red, spiky leaves point upward like slender fingers. The main display of the 2-inch, cerise red flowers comes in winter, but some bloom can occur throughout the year. Space new plants 12 inches apart; water sparingly during summer in desert areas to avoid root rot.

Delosperma; Zones vary. White trailing ice plant, *D.* 'Alba', grows in Zones 9–10. Bright green, rounded, fleshy leaves

Ice plant (Drosanthemum floribundum)

cover a low, trailing plant that roots as it spreads. Small white flowers in summer are noticeable but not showy. Space plants of this and the following two species 12 to 18 inches apart.

Protected by snow or winter mulch in the coldest regions, *D. cooperi* will grow in Zones 7–10. Plants reach 5 inches high, spreading to 2 feet, and are clothed in nearly cylindrical, fingerlike leaves. Glistening purple, 2-inch flowers appear throughout the summer.

D. nubigenum is even more cold tolerant, growing in Zones 5–10. Plants hug the ground, forming a thick carpet of cylindrical, bright green leaves that turn to glowing red in fall and remain that color until spring. Later in spring, 1- to 2-inch yellow blossoms cover the planting for about a month.

Drosanthemum; Zones 9–10 (except desert). Crystalline dots on leaves make these the most "icy" of ice plants. Rosea ice plant, *D. floribundum,* will cover large areas with a 6-inch mat of fine-textured foliage; of all the ice plants, this is the best for erosion control on steep slopes. In late spring, the planting becomes a solid sheet of cool, shimmering, light pink blossoms.

D. hispidum is a shrubbier plant, growing to 2 feet high and about 3 feet wide; it has cylindrical, inch-long leaves. Bright purple, 1-inch flowers make a fine display in late spring and early summer.

For quick cover, set plants of both species 18 inches apart.

Lampranthus; Zones 9–10 (except desert). Spreading, semishrubby plants with gray green, fingerlike leaves produce notably showy flowers from middle to late winter into spring. When planting, set plants 12 to 18 inches apart.

Brilliant orange, 2-inch flowers of *L. aurantiacus* come on bushy, compact plants to 15 inches high; variety 'Glaucus' has clear yellow flowers; those of 'Sunman' are golden yellow.

Growing to the same height but in a more spreading shape, *L. productus* has bronze-tipped foliage and inch-wide purple flowers. Trailing ice plant, *L. spectabilis,* grows to 12 inches high and produces especially showy flowers to 2½ inches across; color choices include lilac pink, rose pink, red, and purple.

Redondo creeper, *L. filicaulis,* differs in size and texture from the other three species. Thin, trailing stems and tiny leaves make a small, pink-flowered cover to 3 inches high. Plants spread slowly and grow best in small areas.

Malephora; Zones 9–10. Gray green, slender fingers of foliage form a dense backdrop to bright blossoms; the main flowering occurs in spring, but additional blooms appear throughout the year. Space new plants 12 to 18 inches apart.

Lower growing (to 6 inches) and trailing, *M. crocea* features 1½-inch flowers of red-shaded yellow. *M. c. purpureo-crocea* has salmon pink blossoms that harmonize with bluish green leaves; it can be used to control erosion on moderately steep land. *M. luteola,* a more compact plant that grows to 12 inches high, has gray green leaves and small yellow flowers.

JASMINUM POLYANTHUM

Zones: 8–10
Type: Evergreen woody vine
Exposure: Sun
Water: Regular watering
Spacing: 10 feet

Of the true jasmines that have fragrant flowers, this is the best species for ground cover use. (For the plant called star jasmine, see *Trachelospermum jasminoides,* page 154.) Twining stems reach out vigorously to 20 feet and bear leaves composed of five to seven narrow leaflets; the plant sheds some of its leaves in colder winter areas.

Clusters of deliciously scented, star-shaped flowers appear over an extended period—from late winter to midsummer in mild regions, mid-spring to midsummer elsewhere. Petal surfaces are white and backs are pink, giving flowers a rosy suffusion.

Plantings may become a bit tangled as stems twine among one another. When this occurs, thin out or cut back entangled growth before flowering begins.

JUNIPERUS

JUNIPER
*Pictured at right and on
pages 88, 94, 108, and 136*

Zones: Vary
Type: Evergreen shrubs
Exposure: Sun to partial shade
Water: Moderate
Spacing: 5 to 6 feet (see below)

Junipers are the universal (and seemingly ubiquitous) ground cover. You can find junipers that will flourish in the range of climates extending from Maine to California and from Minnesota to Florida. Eight species furnish prostrate forms for use as ground covers; available varieties are numerous, with new ones entering the nursery trade almost every year.

The lists below, grouped by species, highlight the most widely sold, proven kinds. Nurseries in your area may carry less well known but equally desirable varieties.

Juniper foliage is of two kinds: juvenile leaves are short, spiky needles; mature leaves are tiny, overlapping scales. Some varieties may bear only juvenile foliage, some only mature foliage, and others a combination of the two. Foliage colors range from silvery blue through many shades of green to yellowish green and variegated. Junipers are coniferous plants, allied to pine, fir, and spruce; but instead of bearing cones, junipers produce blue to black, berrylike "fruits."

One of juniper's strong points is its adaptability: plants will thrive in climates ranging from cool to hot, moist to dry, and in soils from light to heavy, acid to alkaline. But all are intolerant on one point: waterlogged soil, which can lead to root rot and plant death.

In many situations, junipers rate as drought tolerant. Where summers are cool to moderately warm, junipers growing in loam to claylike soils may need little or no summer watering. In hot-summer areas, moderate watering will see them through the dry season.

Where summer is hot, especially hot and dry, give a juniper planting partial shade. In cooler regions, plants will accept a bit of shade, but they will grow better in full sun.

Juniperus horizontalis 'Douglasii'

Even though junipers increase at a slow to moderate pace, you should space new plants 5 to 6 feet apart to avoid future overcrowding. Mulch well between plants to keep weeds under control. For seasonal interest during the early years, you can plant annuals in open soil between juniper plants. You'll achieve a faster cover by planting junipers 3 to 4 feet apart; but when they begin to crowd, remove every other plant.

The listing below describes the eight species and the most popular varieties of each.

Juniperus chinensis; Zones 4–10. *J. c. procumbens,* Japanese garden juniper, produces blue green, feathery foliage on a plant to 3 feet high, spreading 12 to 20 feet. Its variety 'Nana' has shorter needles on a plant to 1 foot high and 4 to 5 feet across.

J. c. 'San Jose' has both needlelike and scalelike foliage in dark sage green; plants grow to 2 feet high and 6 or more feet across.

Sargent juniper or Shimpaku, *J. c. sargentii,* has gray green, feathery foliage on a ground-hugging plant to 1 foot high and 10 feet across. Variety 'Glauca' has blue green foliage; that of 'Viridis' is bright green.

Juniperus communis; Zones 2–9. *J. c. saxatilis* reaches 1 foot high, trailing to 6 to 8 feet, with gray to gray green foliage; secondary branches point upward from prostrate main limbs.

Juniperus conferta; Zones 5–10. The shore juniper features soft, bright green needles on a trailing plant to 8 feet across and 1 foot high. Although native to a cool, moist climate, it will grow in dry, hot-summer regions if given well-drained soil and regular watering. Selected varieties include 'Emerald Sea' and heat-tolerant 'Blue Pacific' with blue green leaves.

Juniperus horizontalis; Zones vary. Two varieties will grow in Zones 4–10. Waukegan juniper, *J. h.* 'Douglasii', trails to 10 feet but rises no more than 1 foot

Juniperus horizontalis 'Wiltonii'

Juniperus scopulorum; Zones 4–10. The Rocky Mountain juniper has several prostrate forms, one of the best of which is *J. s.* 'White's Silver King'. Scalelike leaves are pale, silvery blue on a dense plant less than a foot high but spreading 6 to 8 feet. *J. s.* 'Blue Creeper' is similar but a bit less silvery and taller (to 2 feet).

Juniperus squamata; Zones 4–10. Slow-growing *J. s.* 'Blue Carpet' reaches a foot high and 5 feet across, with bright, blue gray foliage.

Juniperus virginiana; Zones 3–10. Fine-textured, feathery *J. v.* 'Silver Spreader' features silvery green foliage on an 18-inch plant with a 6- to 8-foot spread. Because this species is an alternate host for cedar-apple rust, it should not be planted in regions where apples are an important home or commercial crop.

LAMIUM MACULATUM

DEAD NETTLE
Pictured on page 89

Zones: 5–10
Type: Evergreen to deciduous perennial
Exposure: Shade
Water: Regular watering
Spacing: 18 to 24 inches

Varieties of dead nettle are suitable plants for brightening shaded situations. Prominently veined, heart-shaped leaves to 2 inches long are furry to the touch; sprawling stems root as they spread. Foliage mass reaches about 6 inches high. Small, hooded flowers (usually pink) bloom on short spikes in late spring or early summer.

Most widely sold are forms with variegated foliage. 'Variegatum' has dark green leaves with a silvery white stripe along the midrib of each. 'Beacon Silver' is almost totally silvery gray; only its leaf margins are green. 'White Nancy' is virtually identical except for its white flowers.

Similar to the dead nettles, but a larger plant, is the yellow archangel,

high; rich green new growth becomes steel blue, then turns plum color in winter.

Andorra juniper, *J. h.* 'Plumosa', has gray green foliage that also turns plum color in winter. Main limbs spread to 10 feet, the secondary branches growing upward to 1½ feet.

Three *J. horizontalis* varieties will grow in Zones 5–10. *J. h.* 'Bar Harbor' spreads quickly to 10 feet but grows no more than a foot high; its feathery foliage is blue gray, turning plum color in winter. As the plant ages, the foliage dies back in the center, exposing the main limbs.

With dense, gray green foliage, *J. h.* 'Blue Mat' is more compact—6 to 7 feet across and no more than 12 inches high. Varieties 'Emerald Spreader' and 'Turquoise Spreader' are low (about 6 inches), dense, and feathery, spreading only 4 to 6 feet; the foliage of the former is bright green, that of the latter a more bluish shade.

Blue carpet juniper—*J. h.* 'Wiltonii', sometimes sold as *J. h.* 'Blue Rug'—forms

long, trailing main branches with secondary stems rising no higher than 4 inches; color is a striking silver blue.

Juniperus sabina; Zones 4–10, with one exception. *J. s.* 'Blue Danube' is almost shrubby, spreading its lacy, blue green foliage to about 5 feet while rising to around 18 inches. Bright green *J. s.* 'Arcadia' has a similarly lacy apppearance but grows to 12 inches high, spreading to 10 feet.

J. s. 'Broadmoor' carries soft, bright green foliage on a dense, mounding plant to a bit more than a foot high and 10 feet wide. Slightly lower but also with soft green foliage, *J. s.* 'Calgary Carpet' will succeed in colder Zone 3.

J. s. 'Buffalo' offers feathery, bright green foliage on a plant that spreads only to 8 feet, rising no more than 12 inches. *J. s.* 'Scandia' presents fresh, bright green, lacy foliage on a compact plant to 8 feet across and a foot high.

Tamarix, or "Tam", juniper, *J. s.* 'Tamariscifolia' is an old favorite with the widest spread—to 20 feet; dense sprays of blue green foliage rise to 18 inches.

Lamiastrum galeobdolon. Its 3-inch leaves rise to 12 inches high; flowers are yellow. The variety 'Variegatum' has dark green leaves marbled with white.

LANTANA

Pictured on page 138

Zones: 9 (warmest parts)–10
Type: Evergreen shrubby vine
Exposure: Sun
Water: Moderate
Spacing: 3 feet

Where frost is rare or light, reliable, easy-to-grow lantanas provide color for most of the year. Small, individual flowers are packed into nosegaylike clusters about 1½ inches in diameter, borne atop dark green foliage with a crinkled, sandpaper texture.

The most familiar ground cover type is *L. montevidensis* (*L. sellowiana*), with lavender flowers on a wide-spreading plant that may reach 1 to 1½ feet high. It has been a parent (paired with a shrubby species) of numerous colorful hybrids, some of which have inherited its spreading habit.

The following varieties may reach 2 to 3 feet high, spreading to 6 to 8 feet: 'Confetti' (flowers of yellow, pink, and purple), 'Cream Carpet' (cream and yellow), 'Pink Frolic' (pink and yellow), 'Spreading Sunset' (orange red), 'Spreading Sunshine' (yellow), 'Sunburst' (golden yellow), and 'Tangerine' (orange).

Growing to about 2 feet high and spreading to 6 feet are 'Gold Mound' (yellow orange) and 'Kathleen' (pink and gold).

Lantanas have no soil preference and need only infrequent, deep watering. They're especially effective on sunny slopes, where they help control erosion. In early spring, cut out dead branches and old, woody stems to keep plantings low and well foliaged.

LAURENTIA FLUVIATILIS

BLUE STAR CREEPER
Pictured below and on page 92

Zones: 8–10 (West, except desert)
Type: Evergreen perennial
Exposure: Sun to light shade
Water: Regular watering
Spacing: 6 to 12 inches

With its tiny, bright green leaves and ground-hugging habit, blue star creeper gives the effect of moss as it blankets the soil, flows around rocks, or fills in between paving stones. But in unmosslike fashion, it has star-shaped, light blue blossoms (about the size of a pencil eraser) scattered over its surface in late spring and summer. Nurseries often sell it as *Isotoma fluviatilis.*

Where summers are hot, plant in light shade. For best appearance, water blue star creeper regularly and give it a light application of fertilizer monthly during spring, summer, and into fall.

Laurentia fluviatilis

LIRIOPE

LILY TURF

Zones: Vary
Type: Evergreen perennial
Exposure: Sun to shade
Water: Regular watering
Spacing: 8 to 12 inches

You can't walk on this "turf," but you can enjoy the illusion of coarse, shaggy grass with the bonus of attractive summer flowers that resemble grape hyacinth (*Muscari*).

Very narrow, strap-shaped leaves form thick clumps of arching foliage. It makes a particularly effective transition planting between lawn and trees or high shrubbery. Lily turfs are frequently used in Oriental-inspired landscapes. Two available species (and several varieties) give you a choice of heights.

Creeping lily turf, *L. spicata,* is the lower-growing species. Rather lax, dark green foliage rises to about 9 inches; clumps spread by underground stems to solidly colonize an area. Spikes of pale lavender to white flowers barely appear through the leaves. Variety 'Silver Dragon' has leaves striped in white.

Big blue lily turf, *L. muscari,* has stiffer but still arching foliage that can reach to 1½ feet. The plants form large clumps that don't spread. Typically, flowers are dark violet, borne on spikes rising above the foliage mass.

A number of varieties are available in nurseries (particularly in the southeastern United States). 'Lilac Beauty' has pale violet flowers. 'Majestic' carries its dark violet blooms in flattened, cockscomblike clusters. 'Silvery Sunproof' has more distinctly upright foliage, each leaf striped gold that ages to white; showy flowers are lavender.

New leaves of 'Variegata' (sometimes sold as *Ophiopogon jaburan* 'Variegata') are yellow edged during their first year, turning dark green thereafter; its violet blossoms are much darker than those of 'Silvery Sunproof'.

All lily turfs need well-drained soil; they look best with regular watering,

Lantana montevidensis

even though they will persist with some drought. Where summers are mild, you can plant in sun or shade; hot-summer regions call for at least partial or light shade (*L. m.* 'Variegata' is always best with some shade).

Plantings need some tidying up in late winter or early spring. Before new growth begins, mow or shear *L. spicata* plantings to get rid of shabby old leaves. With *L. muscari* and varieties, cut back brown and tired old leaves after new growth has started. Slugs and snails may require control.

LONICERA

HONEYSUCKLE
Pictured on facing page

Zones: 5–10
Type: Evergreen to deciduous woody vine; semi-evergreen shrub
Exposure: Sun to partial shade
Water: Moderate
Spacing: Varies

Two quite different honeysuckles can do service as ground covers. The first is

Hall's honeysuckle, *L. japonica* 'Halliana', an aggressively vigorous, twining vine that will quickly cover a large surface area if there's nothing for it to climb. Stems feature 3-inch, oval, deep green leaves in opposite pairs—evergreen in mild-winter zones, semi-evergreen to deciduous in progressively colder areas.

Notably fragrant flowers are tubular, flaring out to unequal petals, initially white but aging to yellow; season begins in late spring and lasts into summer.

Best uses are to cover slopes, control erosion, and blanket large expanses where the plant's vigor won't engulf other plants. Space plants 3 to 5 feet apart. Shear or mow plantings nearly to ground level annually in late winter; this prevents the buildup of dead stems that can be a fire hazard if allowed to accumulate.

The goldnet honeysuckle, *L. j.* 'Aureoreticulata', is less rampant and offers lighter green leaves prominently veined in yellow.

The second species is semi-evergreen privet honeysuckle, *L. pileata*, which is, by contrast, a spreading shrub 2 to 3 feet high; its stiffly horizontal branches are clothed in 1½-inch, oval leaves. Sweetly fragrant, small white flowers in mid-spring are followed by small purple berries.

Spaced 2 feet apart, plants form a neat, noninvasive cover for slopes or flat areas. They thrive in full sun in coastal gardens but prefer partial or light shade in hotter, drier climates. Performance is not satisfactory in the desert.

LOTUS

Zones: Vary
Type: Evergreen, deciduous perennials
Exposure: Sun
Water: Varies
Spacing: Varies

The two *Lotus* species used as ground covers differ markedly in appearance and garden use. Parrot's beak, *L. berthelotii*, is less cold tolerant (Zone 10 and warmer parts of Zone 9, but not desert) and is the showier of the two. Creeping stems with feathery, silver gray leaves form a soft-appearing carpet upon which float narrow-petalled, inch-long scarlet blossoms in early to midsummer.

Set 2 feet apart, plants will soon fill in; at the top of a retaining wall, foliage will spill over in a filmy curtain. Plants need well-drained soil and moderate watering; cut back occasionally to keep plants bushy.

Bird's-foot trefoil, *L. corniculatus,* grows in Zones 5–10; it becomes totally dormant in all but the warmest-winter regions. It excels as a lawn substitute (even with a bit of foot traffic), where it resembles a thick mat of clover. Dark green leaves contain three small leaflets in clover fashion; clusters of small yellow flowers resembling sweet peas appear in summer and fall. Its common name comes from the slender seed capsules that radiate from atop the flower stalks like the feet of a bird.

For a quick "lawn," sow seeds on ground prepared as for a turf lawn. Or set out plants 6 inches apart. Water regularly during the warm days of spring, summer, and early fall for a lush, lawnlike appearance. Once established, plantings need only moderate watering.

Occasionally mow lawn-substitute plantings to 2 inches to maintain an even surface. Plantings will regrow from the roots each year; new plants will germinate from seed.

LYSIMACHIA NUMMULARIA

MONEYWORT, CREEPING JENNY

Zones: 3–10 (except desert)
Type: Evergreen perennial
Exposure: Shade
Water: Regular watering
Spacing: 12 to 18 inches

A bit of shade and moist soil are all that moneywort needs to become a lush, low carpet of light green. In fact, it thrives in continually damp soil that will defeat most other ground covers.

Leaves are nearly round, less than an inch across, on rapidly spreading stems that root where leaf nodes contact soil. The variety 'Aurea' has yellow foliage. Summer brings a display of inch-wide, bright yellow flowers.

Lonicera japonica 'Halliana'

MAHONIA

Pictured below

Zones: 5–9 (West), 5–8 (East)
Type: Evergreen shrubs
Exposure: Varies
Water: Moderate to little
Spacing: 24 inches

The various mahonias are neat, tailored shrubs that retain their good looks throughout the year. Each leaf consists of oval leaflets with spiny, hollylike margins. Showy clusters of small, cup-shaped yellow flowers appear at branch tips in spring, followed by blue, pea-size berries. Plants spread at a moderate rate by underground stems.

Compact Oregon grape, *M. aquifolium* 'Compacta', is the most widely available. Leaves have from five to nine glossy, 3-inch-long leaflets; new growth emerges a bright copper color. Plantings, which may reach 2 feet high, grow best in partial to light shade where summer is hot.

Longleaf mahonia, *M. nervosa,* has as many as 21 glossy leaflets to nearly 4 inches long, with leaves clustered toward the branch tips. Plants generally remain about 2 feet high; cut back any tall stems to keep the planting even. For best appearance, plant in partial to light shade in all zones (it is not successful, though, in the desert). In cool-summer areas, it will grow very compactly in full sun.

Creeping mahonia, *M. repens,* reaches about 3 feet high. It bears dull, blue green leaflets to 2½ inches long that become bronze colored in winter. Plants will take full sun (except in desert gardens) as well as light shade.

Mahonia nervosa

MAZUS REPTANS

Pictured on facing page

Zones: 4–10 (except desert)
Type: Evergreen to deciduous perennial
Exposure: Sun to light shade
Water: Regular watering
Spacing: 6 to 12 inches

All aspects of this ground cover are small, but in this case "small" does not mean fragile. Creeping stems root along the ground, bearing light green, narrow leaves to an inch long on branches no more than 2 inches high. From spring into summer, plantings are dotted with small clusters of lobelialike flowers in dark lavender spotted with yellow and white.

If given good soil and ample water, dense, ground-hugging growth will quickly fill in between paving stones, flow among rocks, and solidly cover small areas. Plantings will even take light foot traffic. Evergreen in Zones 9–10, the plants die to the ground over winter in colder zones but will regrow in spring.

MENTHA REQUIENII

JEWEL MINT OF CORSICA

Zones: 7–10
Type: Evergreen perennial
Exposure: Sun to light shade
Water: Regular watering
Spacing: 6 to 12 inches

This ground cover invites foot traffic: when crushed, its leaves emit a pleasant minty or sagelike fragrance.

Creeping stems, which grow less than an inch high, bear tiny, round, bright green leaves and, in summer, equally small, light purple flowers. The mosslike effect is attractive in small areas—between paving stones, on earth steps, and alongside natural-earth pathways, for example.

In Zones 7, 8, and colder parts of 9, plants will freeze to the ground during winter but regrow in spring.

MYOPORUM PARVIFOLIUM

Zones: 9–10 (West, except desert)
Type: Evergreen shrub
Exposure: Sun
Water: Moderate
Spacing: 5 feet

Where coastal conditions influence the climate, gardeners value myoporum for ease of growth and attractive appearance the year around. Gardeners in hotter inland climates can derive the same satisfaction from the heat-tolerant variety 'Putah Creek'.

Leaves are narrow and thick, to an inch long, densely covering the trailing branches that root where they touch soil. Bell-shaped, white, ½-inch summer flowers are followed by small purple berries. The basic species grows 3 to 6 inches high; 'Putah Creek' may reach 1 foot.

A hybrid plant, *M.* 'Pacificum', grows especially fast, rising to 2 feet high and spreading to 30 feet. Space plants 12 to 15 feet apart.

Myoporum is a fine choice for planting on slopes and to control erosion, due to its fast, low, dense growth and multitude of roots from spreading stems. Plants need well-drained soil; in some beach communities, they thrive in nearly pure sand.

Near the coast, plants tolerate some drought but look better with periodic watering during summer. In hotter inland areas, give plantings moderate watering during the warmest months.

MYOSOTIS SCORPIOIDES

FORGET-ME-NOT

Zones: 4–10
Type: Deciduous perennial
Exposure: Shade
Water: Regular watering
Spacing: 6 to 12 inches

Forget-me-not's small flowers of purest light blue illuminate shaded and woodland gardens with an azure haze in spring and summer. Borne in elongated, curving clusters, blooms rise above spreading plants with narrow, bright green, 2-inch

Mazus reptans

leaves. Plants grow 6 to 12 inches high, spreading by creeping roots.

Forget-me-not will persist for years when given ample moisture and soil amended with organic matter. In colder zones, plants die to the ground over winter and regrow in spring.

NANDINA DOMESTICA

HEAVENLY BAMBOO

Zones: 8–10 (West), 8–9 (East)
Type: Evergreen shrub
Exposure: Sun to light shade
Water: Regular to moderate
Spacing: 12 to 18 inches

Nurseries offer several low-growing or dwarf varieties of the normally 6- to 8-foot-high heavenly bamboo. Of those,

'Harbour Dwarf' is the best ground cover, spreading at a moderate rate from underground stems. Plants grow 1½ to 2 feet high but have all the feathery grace of the basic species.

Upright stems carry leaves almost parallel to the ground, each leaf containing numerous narrow, pointed leaflets in groups of three. New growth in spring is pinkish green; in fall, cold weather turns leaves to shades of orange to bronze.

Best winter foliage color comes on plants growing in full sun, although in desert gardens and in hot-summer western valleys, light or partial shade is necessary. Chlorotic foliage may be a problem where soil is alkaline; treat the problem with iron chelate or iron sulfate.

Nepeta faassenii

its need is moderate. After blossoming is finished, shear off faded flower spikes to encourage a later flowering. Before new growth starts in late winter or early spring, cut back or shear plants by about half; new growth will fill in quickly.

OPHIOPOGON JAPONICUS

MONDO GRASS
Pictured on page 89

Zones: 8–10
Type: Evergreen perennial
Exposure: Sun to shade
Water: Regular watering
Spacing: 6 to 8 inches

This close relative of *Liriope* (see page 138) is even more grasslike than that plant. Dense clumps consist of lax, dark green leaves ⅛ inch wide and 8 to 12 inches long. Plants spread slowly by underground stems to form a solid, shaggy "turf" that rises 6 to 8 inches high.

Small, pale lavender flowers appear in summer on short spikes that are largely hidden among the leaves; round, pea-size blue fruits form after flowers fade. The variety 'Nana' ('Kyoto Dwarf') grows to about half the size of the basic species.

Plant mondo grass in well-drained soil. In cool-summer areas, you can plant in full sun; elsewhere, locate plantings in partial or light shade. Plants are somewhat drought tolerant, but water regularly for best appearance.

If the plants become shabby looking from an accumulation of old, dead foliage, you can mow or cut back in early spring before new growth begins.

NEPETA FAASSENII

CATMINT
Pictured above

Zones: 4–10 (West), 4–9 (East)
Type: Evergreen to deciduous perennial
Exposure: Sun
Water: Moderate
Spacing: 18 inches

A favorite foreground plant for perennial borders and herb gardens, catmint also serves well as a small-scale ground cover, providing a note of coolness to the late spring and early summer landscape.

Plants reach 6 to 8 inches high and spread to about 3 feet in diameter; catmint's many thin stems are set with small, oval, deeply veined, gray green leaves.

Loose clusters of ½-inch, lavender blue flowers rise 12 to 18 inches, creating a bluish cloud over the planting. The common name tells you that cats find this plant attractive, although not as enticing as the related catnip (*N. cataria*).

Catmint needs well-drained soil; it will accept regular watering, even though

OSTEOSPERMUM FRUTICOSUM

TRAILING AFRICAN DAISY
Pictured on facing page and page 83

Zones: 9–10 (West, except desert)
Type: Evergreen perennial
Exposure: Sun
Water: Moderate
Spacing: 2 feet

Trailing African daisy will bloom on sunny days throughout the year, but its

Osteospermum fruticosum

main flowering period begins in mid-fall and continues through winter; thus, when garden color is usually at its lowest ebb, these plantings will be covered by a sheet of flowers.

Each blossom is a purple-centered, 2- to 3-inch daisy; lavender petals fade to white but remain purple on their undersides. Nurseries may also offer several pure white and solid purple varieties.

Oval, gray green leaves 1 to 4 inches long cover fast-growing plants that root along stems as they spread. Each plant may grow to 4 feet in diameter in a year, rising to a height of 6 to 12 inches.

Trailing African daisy prospers both at the seashore and in hot-summer inland areas, but it does not grow well in the desert. Although they will tolerate drought, established plants look better with moderate watering in good, well-drained soil. With regular watering, a large planting can help retard fire.

When old plantings become untidy, cut back to healthy new growth after the main flowering period.

PACHYSANDRA TERMINALIS

JAPANESE SPURGE

Zones: 4–9 (except desert)
Type: Evergreen shrub
Exposure: Shade
Water: Regular watering
Spacing: 12 inches

Japanese spurge brings a touch of elegance to shade gardens. Foliage forms an even carpet about 10 inches high (lower in light shade) of lustrous, oval leaves carried in whorls toward the ends of upright stems.

In late spring or early summer, spikes of tiny, fluffy white flowers appear at stem tips; small white fruits often follow. Variety 'Variegata' has white leaf margins; use it to add extra sparkle to heavy shade.

Plants spread at a moderate rate by underground stems, even competing well with shallow-rooted trees. They grow best in good, somewhat acid soil with an annual fertilizer application in early spring.

PARTHENOCISSUS QUINQUEFOLIA

VIRGINIA CREEPER

Zones: 3–10
Type: Deciduous woody vine
Exposure: Sun to light shade
Water: Regular watering
Spacing: 3 feet

Gardeners in eastern North America know Virginia creeper as a rampant, scrambling vine renowned for its annual display of brilliant foliage. Glossy green in spring and summer, leaves turn blazing orange to red early in fall.

Each leaf contains five separate, oval leaflets to 6 inches long with distinct veins and sawtooth edges. Leaves are widely spaced along stems, providing a loose rather than dense cover. Variety 'Englemannii' has smaller and more closely spaced leaves.

Inconspicuous clusters of tiny flowers are followed by small, dark blue fruits. Stems easily cover flat ground or sloping land, rooting where they contact moist soil. When they encounter a vertical surface—tree trunk, fence, or shrubbery—they'll climb quickly, holding fast with clinging tendrils.

PAXISTIMA

Zones: 5–9 (except desert)
Type: Evergreen shrubs
Exposure: Sun to partial shade
Water: Regular watering
Spacing: 12 to 18 inches

Two North American species offer glossy, narrow foliage on dense, compact plants. They make good fillers or borders when used with showier large shrubs or in woodland settings.

The smaller of the two is *P. canbyi*, which grows at a slow to moderate rate to 12 inches high; the leaves, about an inch long and ¼ inch wide, become bronzy in the chill of fall and winter.

Oregon boxwood, *P. myrsinites*, has larger leaves and may reach 2 or more feet in height, especially in shaded locations; it can be kept low with periodic pruning.

Both species will grow in full sun where summers are cool or moderate, but they also thrive in light or partial shade. Some shade is necessary in hot-summer regions. Plant in well-drained soil that is somewhat acid.

PELARGONIUM PELTATUM

IVY GERANIUM
Pictured at left and on page 94

Zones: 9 (warmest parts)–10
Type: Evergreen shrubby perennial
Exposure: Sun
Water: Moderate
Spacing: 18 to 24 inches

Where frost is light or rare, ivy geranium is virtually unbeatable for providing plenty of color over a long period of time with minimal care.

Glossy, five-lobed leaves 2 to 3 inches across resemble the foliage of English ivy (*Hedera helix,* page 129), but they're thick and succulent. Trailing stems grow fairly rapidly, in time building up to about 12 inches high.

Individual flowers are single or double, about an inch across, in rounded clusters of five to ten. Flowering is heaviest from mid-spring to mid-fall but can occur the year around in frostless areas. Flower colors range from white, lavender, and pink shades to magenta and red; you can also find striped combinations.

Nurseries may sell named varieties or may offer plants labeled only as to color. Plants of seed-grown Summer Showers

Pelargonium peltatum

strain come in mixed colors. Specialist growers and some nurseries offer varieties with variegated foliage.

Ivy geraniums prefer well-drained or sandy soil; if soil is alkaline, add acid amendments such as redwood bark or peat moss. Water only when the upper inch of soil is dry.

Plants in reasonably good soil may not need fertilizer or, at most, only one application in late winter or early spring. Fertilize plants in sandy soil two or three times during the growing season.

PHLOX SUBULATA

MOSS PINK
Pictured at right and on page 82

Zones: 4–9
Type: Evergreen perennial
Exposure: Sun
Water: Moderate
Spacing: 12 to 18 inches

Moss pink is a favorite border and rock garden plant; the spreading, 6-inch-high plants are entirely covered with blossoms during the month-long season in late spring to early summer. Planted in mass as a ground cover, they'll form an arresting floral carpet.

Each flower is circular, to ¾ inch across; colors include white, pink shades, red, violet, and lavender blue. Nurseries sell plants labeled by color, or they may offer superior named varieties.

Creeping stems form dense mats of needlelike leaves to ½ inch long.

Plants thrive in well-drained soil with moderate watering. To encourage dense new growth, cut back or shear plants by about half after flowering has finished.

PHYLA NODIFLORA

LIPPIA
Pictured on page 146

Zones: 9–10
Type: Evergreen perennial
Exposure: Sun
Water: Regular to moderate
Spacing: 12 to 24 inches

Even though its appearance is not at all grasslike, lippia's ground-hugging growth

Phlox subulata

and ability to endure foot traffic have established its use as a lawn substitute. Creeping stems bear oval, grayish green leaves to ¾ inch long; in full sun this "turf" reaches no higher than 2 inches.

Tiny lavender to pink flowers clustered in rounded, ½-inch heads appear from spring to fall. The blossoms attract bees; to avoid this problem, mow periodically to remove flowers.

Lippia grows well in a wide range of soils. You can set established clumps 2 feet apart or plant rooted sprigs at 12-inch intervals. Plants perform well in desert gardens, although susceptibility to nematodes hampers growth in areas where soils are infested.

Appearance is unattractive during the winter dormant period. Fertilize plants in early spring to encourage fresh new growth.

POLYGONUM

KNOTWEED

Zones: Vary
Type: Evergreen, deciduous perennials
Exposure: Sun to light shade
Water: Moderate
Spacing: Varies

Used where their invasive growth won't infiltrate other plantings, the knotweeds serve well as good-looking, low-maintenance ground covers.

Lower growing of the two species is evergreen *P. capitatum,* which forms a thick, spreading cover to 6 inches high. The 1½-inch, oval leaves are dark green when new but become tinged with pink as they age, combining well with the cloverlike heads of pink flowers (carried on

Phyla nodiflora

POTENTILLA

CINQUEFOIL
Pictured on facing page and page 108

Zones: 4–9 (West), 4–8 (East)
Type: Evergreen perennials
Exposure: Sun to light shade
Water: Moderate
Spacing: 12 inches

Growth habit and general appearance suggest strawberry (see *Fragaria chiloensis,* page 125), but each cinquefoil leaf contains five leaflets (as the name suggests) instead of the strawberry's three. In spring and early summer, small yellow flowers that resemble single roses dot the foliage cover.

Both species described below prefer average soil, moderate watering, and full sun (except where summer is hot).

Foliage color easily distinguishes *P. cinerea:* each wedge-shaped leaflet is gray and hairy, with a white, woolly underside. Half-inch, pale yellow flowers nestle against the leaves; spreading, matted stems grow at a moderate rate to build a foliage mass 4 inches high.

In contrast, spring cinquefoil, *P. tabernaemontanii* (sometimes sold as *P. verna*), has glossy green leaflets and butter yellow blossoms. Growth is more rapid, building to 6 inches high; if you wish, mow occasionally to even up the surface.

PRATIA ANGULATA

Zones: 7–10
Type: Evergreen perennial
Exposure: Sun to shade
Water: Regular watering
Spacing: 6 to 8 inches

Pratia's dense, lush carpet of foliage has the succulent greenness of baby's tears (*Soleirolia soleirolii,* page 152), combined with rounded, ½-inch leaves similar to those of dichondra. Creeping stems spread at a moderate rate, rooting at the joints, to form a glossy, dark green mat. White or blue white summer flowers resemble the related *Lobelia.*

pink stems) that are present throughout the warmer months.

Foliage will be damaged or killed at 28°F/-2°C, but roots will survive into Zone 8 temperatures. Plants seed themselves freely and will grow as an annual ground cover in colder regions. Set plants 12 inches apart in sun or shade; water regularly for best appearance.

Deciduous *P. cuspidatum compactum* (often sold as *P. reynoutria*) is taller (10 to 24 inches high) and will grow in Zones 4–10. Wiry, red, upright stems bear light green, red-veined leaves; these are lance to heart shaped and 3 to 6 inches long. Small, light pink flowers in fluffy heads open from red buds in late summer. Foliage turns bright red in fall; then the entire plant dies back to the ground.

This species, which spreads by underground stems, is a good choice for controlling erosion on sunny hillsides that receive little water. Set plants 2 feet apart and water moderately until established; thereafter, give moderate to little water.

Give pratia good soil and ample water. Where summers are cool, you can plant in sun; in warm to hot regions, locate plantings in light or partial shade. Despite its perishable appearance, pratia will grow in the desert when its cultural needs are met.

PYRACANTHA

FIRETHORN

Zones: Vary
Type: Evergreen shrubs
Exposure: Sun
Water: Moderate
Spacing: Varies

The large, shrubby firethorns are a staple of the nursery trade; they're widely planted for their springtime show of small, fragrant white flowers and striking fall display of orange to red, pea-size berries.

A number of prostrate, low, and spreading varieties, available for ground cover use, provide the same seasonal interest. All have small, glossy, oval leaves and grow at a moderate to rapid rate. The needlelike thorns make firethorn an effective barrier plant.

Three firethorns will grow in Zones 7–10. Orange-fruited *P. angustifolia* 'Gnome' has dense foliage on a spreading, nearly prostrate plant; space individual plants 3 feet apart. *P. coccinea* 'Lowboy', with similar growth and orange fruits, is the best choice for the coldest parts of Zone 7.

For red fruits, look for *P.* 'Walderi' (sometimes sold as *P.* 'Walderi Prostrata'). Growth is wide spreading, to 1½ feet high; plant 4 to 5 feet apart.

Gardeners in Zones 8–10 can consider two additional varieties. *P.* 'Ruby Mound' is well described by its name— bright red fruits appear on rounded, spreading plants that reach about 1½ feet high and 3 feet wide; set plants 2 feet apart. Red-fruited *P.* 'Santa Cruz' (*P.* 'Santa Cruz Prostrata') is spreading rather than mounding and easily kept below 3 feet high; plant 4 to 5 feet apart.

All firethorns are easy to grow but are susceptible to pests. Scale, spider mites, and woolly aphids may be problems.

Fireblight, which kills branches, leaving them blackened and sooty appearing, may appear following a moist spring. Cut out infected branches 4 to 6 inches below the obvious infection. If you make more than one cut, disinfect shears between cuts for 20 to 30 seconds with rubbing alcohol or a 10 percent solution of household bleach.

RANUNCULUS REPENS 'PLENIFLORUS'

CREEPING BUTTERCUP

Zones: 4–9
Type: Deciduous perennial
Exposure: Shade
Water: Regular watering
Spacing: 12 to 18 inches

In shaded situations with moist soil, creeping buttercup is a rapidly spreading ground cover; stems root at the joints. Plants will invade other plantings, or even spread into a lawn, if not checked periodically.

Long-stalked, glossy, rounded leaves are deeply cut into numerous segments; foliage cover is dense and about 12

Potentilla tabernaemontanii

inches high. In spring, button-shaped, double yellow flowers rise above foliage on 1- to 2-foot stems.

The basic species, *R. repens,* has showy, single yellow flowers. Plants spread more aggressively than those of the double variety.

RIBES VIBURNIFOLIUM

CATALINA PERFUME, EVERGREEN CURRANT

Zones: 9–10 (West, except desert)
Type: Evergreen shrub
Exposure: Sun to shade
Water: Moderate to little
Spacing: 3 feet

Rosa 'Etain'

Catalina perfume is chiefly valued for its ability to thrive in shaded locations that receive little water, although it will also grow in sunny situations in coastal gardens. The low, scrambling shrub has reddish brown stems that root wherever they contact moist soil.

Rounded, 1-inch leaves of lustrous dark green appear attractively fresh and clean even during the heat and dryness of summer. Foliage is pleasantly aromatic after a rainfall or when crushed. Short, upright clusters of small, light pink to purplish flowers appear from late winter to mid-spring; small red berries often follow.

Widely spreading plants may reach 3 feet high but can be kept lower with judicious pruning.

ROSA

ROSE
Pictured below

Zones: 6–10 (except where noted)
Type: Evergreen to deciduous shrubs
Exposure: Sun
Water: Regular watering
Spacing: 8 to 10 feet

A number of diverse climbing roses have traditionally been used as ground covers, some of them naturally sprawling, others with canes limber enough to be pinned to the ground. Most of these were roses that flowered only in spring—many of them hybrids of *R. wichuraiana,* described below.

In recent years, rose breeders have sought to develop roses that could serve as ground covers and flower repeatedly during the warm months. All the roses described below, except as noted, will blossom from spring through summer and into fall, climate permitting.

Roses grow most vigorously in good soil with regular watering. Unlike ordinary bush roses, these ground covers won't need an annual pruning, but they should be thinned of old, unproductive, and dead wood every so often.

Apply fertilizer in late winter or early spring. One attribute of a first-rate ground cover rose is its resistance to foliage diseases; however, various pest controls may be needed from time to time.

'Etain'. This has the glossy leaves and lax canes of a wichuraiana rambler, but the plant flowers repeatedly throughout the season. From apricot pink buds come 3-inch, pale pink blossoms in clusters.

'Fiona'. Small, semidouble, rich dark red blossoms appear on a spreading, moderate-size plant with small, semiglossy foliage.

'Max Graf'. This once-blooming hybrid of *R. wichuraiana* (below) features large, single pink flowers. Plant has trailing stems with especially handsome, glossy foliage.

'Mermaid'; Zones 8–10. This very large-growing, shrubby climber with evergreen, glossy foliage has large, single yellow flowers. You may need to pin down canes to achieve low cover. Stout, sharp thorns make it a useful barrier.

Rubus calycinoides

'Nozomi'. A climbing miniature rose with trailing growth and small, glossy leaves, plant presents single, light pink flowers in clusters.

'Ralph's Creeper'. Light-centered, nearly single, 2-inch, bright red blossoms fade to pink. Spreading, moderate-size plant has matte green foliage.

'Rote Max Graf'. Large, single flowers resemble a red version of 'Max Graf' (above). Moderate-size, spreading plant has small, leathery, matte-finish leaves.

'Sea Foam'. Small, glossy leaves cover a mounding, spreading plant that bears clusters of medium-size, very double blossoms of white to cream.

'Swany'. Very double, flat white flowers adorn a trailing, medium-size to large plant with glossy, bronze-tinted foliage.

'White Meidiland'. Clusters of very double white flowers shine against a backdrop of dark, glossy leaves on a medium-size, spreading plant.

R. banksiae; Zones 8–10. Once-blooming species features small, very double blossoms in earliest spring; white and yellow forms are sold. This plant grows very large and bears evergreen foliage with narrow leaflets on thornless stems. Pin canes to the ground to achieve a low cover.

R. wichuraiana. This naturally prostrate species bears very glossy foliage; single white flowers bloom only in late spring. Plant is wide spreading and will root along stems as it spreads. Old-rose specialists may offer hybrids (wichuraiana ramblers) that have double flowers in white and pink shades; the best are those with French names, which have disease-resistant foliage. Avoid mildew-prone 'Dorothy Perkins'.

ROSMARINUS OFFICINALIS

ROSEMARY
Pictured on page 150

Zones: 7–10 (West), 7–8 (East)
Type: Evergreen shrub
Exposure: Sun
Water: Moderate to little
Spacing: 2 feet

Culinary rosemary is a variable species; several of its selected forms make durable, dense, low-maintenance ground covers. All have narrow, almost needlelike, leaves of medium to dark green with gray undersides; leaves are pungently scented and slightly sticky to the touch.

Small blue flowers appear from fall into spring, with peak display varying according to the variety. Stems root as

Rosmarinus officinalis 'Prostratus'

they spread, so that one plant becomes a colony of many individual but interconnected plants.

'Prostratus' is the most widely sold variety. Growth hugs the ground at first, but secondary stems arch, curve, or twist, giving a tumbled appearance to a mass planting. Growth may reach 2 feet high, but it can be kept lower with selective pruning. Planted at the edge of a raised bed, stems will trail over the side in waterfall fashion. Light gray blue flowers appear in late winter or early spring.

A similar plant is 'Lockwood de Forest', distinguished by blue flowers and lighter, brighter green foliage. 'Collingwood Ingram' is noted for its bright, violet blue flowers in early spring; plants grow 2 to 3 feet high, with stems curving outward and upward. 'Huntington Carpet' is the lowest growing of all, to 1½ feet high; its late winter flowers are an intense, bright blue.

Rosemary grows best in well-drained (even poor) soil; if not overwatered, it will prosper in heavier soils as well.

Water plants moderately during the first year until they become established; thereafter, water needs are minimal.

In cool-summer gardens, plants will remain attractive throughout the year with little or no supplemental water. In hot-summer regions, water rosemary occasionally in summer to keep plants looking fresh. In the desert, plants need periodic summer watering to survive.

RUBUS CALYCINOIDES

Pictured on page 149

Zones: 7–9
Type: Evergreen shrub
Exposure: Sun to light shade
Water: Moderate
Spacing: 2 feet

This blackberry relative boasts handsome foliage instead of tasty fruits. Individual leaves are round in general outline, 1 to 1½ inches across, with three to five broad lobes and ruffled margins. The lustrous, dark green upper surface has a rough texture; the gray white underside is feltlike.

Foliage covers the creeping, thornless stems, which spread at a moderate rate to make a dense cover to about a foot high. Hidden in the foliage are small white flowers that resemble strawberry blossoms. Nurseries may offer the superior selection 'Emerald Carpet'.

Give plants well-drained soil. They'll take light shade in all regions and will also thrive in full sun where summers are relatively cool.

SAGINA SUBULATA

IRISH MOSS, SCOTCH MOSS
Pictured on page 92

Zones: 5–10 (except intermediate and low desert)
Type: Evergreen perennial
Exposure: Sun to partial shade
Water: Regular watering
Spacing: 6 inches

Especially favored for planting among paving stones and rocks, these "mosses" can also be used to cover small areas in a green, velvetlike carpet.

Actually, there are two plants, *Arenaria verna* and *Sagina subulata,* so similar that they're interchangeable in the garden. (*Arenaria* has tiny white flowers

in clusters; blossoms of *Sagina* appear singly.) Green forms of both are sold as Irish moss; each also has a yellowish green variety 'Aurea' that may be sold as Scotch moss.

Choose good, well-drained soil for Irish and Scotch mosses. Plants are usually sold in flats. Cut squares from the flat and plant them so that the edges of the squares are at the same level or slightly lower than the soil surface; this helps prevent lumpiness.

In time, plantings will form humps; when this happens, cut out narrow strips and press the remaining turf into the soil.

SANTOLINA

Pictured on facing page

Zones: 7–10 (West), 7–8 (East)
Type: Evergreen shrub
Exposure: Sun
Water: Moderate to little
Spacing: 3 feet

Adaptability is a trait shared by both *Santolina* species described below. They grow easily in climates ranging from cool and dry to hot and moist. Established plants are quite tolerant of drought but will accept regular watering as long as the soil is reasonably well drained.

Left alone, a plant will spread widely; its many stems send up branches that arch upward to produce a billowy effect. But plants can be clipped or sheared to an even surface; one species, *S. chamaecyparissus,* is often grown as an ankle-height clipped hedge in formal herb plantings.

More common of the two species is lavender cotton, *S. chamaecyparissus,* with gray white foliage. Each leaf is very narrow and about an inch long; its margin is finely divided into feathery segments. Buttonlike, ½-inch yellow flowers (like daisies without petals) cover unsheared plants in late spring.

In contrast, *S. virens* has needlelike, bright green leaves about twice as long as lavender cotton's; its buttonlike flowers are creamy chartreuse.

In both species, foliage is pleasantly aromatic.

Without shearing or trimming, plants may grow 2 feet high. If older plantings become shabby, showing bare patches, cut back or shear plants heavily in early spring; dense new growth will fill in soon. For neatest appearance, shear off spent flowers after the flowering period.

SARCOCOCCA HOOKERANA HUMILIS

Zones: 6–10 (except desert)
Type: Evergreen shrub
Exposure: Shade to partial shade
Water: Regular watering
Spacing: 2 to 3 feet

Although this boxwood relative looks quite different, it shares boxwood's qualities of neatness and polish. Narrow, pointed-oval leaves are very dark green and glossy; they grow 3 inches long, closely set on the branches.

Plants may reach 1½ feet high and spread at a fairly slow rate by underground runners to 8 or more feet. Hidden among the leaves in winter or early spring are tiny, highly fragrant white flowers; these are followed by glossy, blue black fruits.

Best growth is in good soil liberally amended with organic matter. Plants prosper in shade everywhere, but they'll take sun where summer weather is cool and moist.

SAXIFRAGA STOLONIFERA

STRAWBERRY GERANIUM

Zones: 9–10 (except desert)
Type: Evergreen perennial
Exposure: Shade or partial shade
Water: Regular watering
Spacing: 12 to 18 inches

The common name of this ground cover comes both from the leaves, which resemble those of some true *Geranium* species, and from the plant's habit of spreading rapidly, in strawberry fashion, by long runners.

Fleshy leaves are nearly round, to 4 inches across, attractively veined in white with contrasting pink undersides. Foliage mass may reach 6 inches high. In spring,

slender stems grow to 2 feet and bear loose clusters of small white flowers.

Although plants should be watered regularly, they also need soil that drains well so that the roots won't rot.

Use this fine, small-scale ground cover with azaleas, rhododendrons, and other plants with similar moisture and drainage requirements.

SCAEVOLA 'MAUVE CLUSTERS'

Zones: 9–10 (West, except desert)
Type: Evergreen shrubby perennial
Exposure: Sun
Water: Moderate
Spacing: 3 feet

Where frost is rare or light, 'Mauve Clusters' excels as a trouble-free and nearly everblooming low ground cover. Spreading stems are densely clothed with oval, dark green leaves ¼ to ½ inch long; foliage mass may reach 6 inches high.

Sprinkled over the foliage are small clusters of ½-inch, bluish lilac flowers, each in an unusual fan or semicircular shape; plants flower nearly year-round in milder areas.

Once established, plants perform well in ordinary soil with infrequent watering. To enhance flower color, fertilize with iron sulfate.

SEDUM

STONECROP
Pictured on pages 93 and 152

Zones: Vary
Type: Evergreen succulent perennials
Exposure: Sun to partial shade
Water: Moderate
Spacing: 12 inches

Here are some of the best low-growing stonecrops, selected from the many species of *Sedum,* for use as ground covers. Foliage size, shape, and color vary, but all have thick, succulent leaves that are easily crushed.

Clustered small flowers, shaped like stars, are quite showy in some cases. All thrive in ordinary soil with no special care. New plants are easy to start from stem cuttings or from detached leaves.

Five stonecrops are cold tolerant enough to be grown in Zones 4–10. Goldmoss sedum, *S. acre,* has tiny, mosslike,

Santolina virens

light green leaves; yellow flowers bloom in late spring. Trailing stems send up branchlets 2 to 5 inches tall. Use gold-moss sedum to fill in between paving stones, among rocks, or as small-scale cover.

Equally low-growing S. album has nearly cylindrical, ½-inch leaves that are sometimes tinted red. Clusters of white to pinkish white flowers appear above the foliage in early summer.

For mosslike, dark green foliage, choose S. anglicum; spring flowers are pinkish white.

A larger plant, S. lineare (often sold as S. sarmentosum) grows to a foot high, bearing inch-long, narrow, light green leaves ('Variegatum' has leaves edged in white). Clusters of yellow flowers appear in late spring and early summer.

The thick, rounded leaves of S. spurium are an inch long and nearly as wide, carried in loose rosettes on trailing stems. Dense clusters of showy pink flowers appear in late summer. Popular variety 'Dragon's Blood' features bronze foliage and rose red flowers.

Several additional stonecrops are useful in warm areas of Zones 9–10.

Mexican sedum, S. confusum (often sold as S. amecamecanum), forms spreading clumps of upright stems 6 to 12 inches high. Rubbery, tongue-shaped leaves to 1½ inches long are bright, light green; leaves cluster in rosettes toward stem ends. Spring flowers are yellow, growing in dense clusters.

Mediterranean native S. sediforme (often sold as S. altissimum) has narrow, thick, blue gray leaves to 1½ inches long, closely set on stems that may reach 16 inches high. Summer flowers are greenish white.

A similar plant is S. reflexum, but its leaves are only ½ inch long and its blossoms are yellow.

Popular pork and beans, S. rubrotinctum, has cylindrical, nearly inch-long leaves packed tightly on sprawling stems to make a cover 6 to 8 inches high. Each green leaf is tipped in reddish brown; the foliage may be totally bronze red in full sun. Spring flowers are yellow tinted with red.

Sedum spurium

SOLEIROLIA SOLEIROLII

BABY'S TEARS, ANGEL'S TEARS

Zones: 9–10
Type: Evergreen perennial
Exposure: Shade
Water: Regular watering
Spacing: 12 inches

Countless tiny, emerald green leaves on threadlike, interlacing stems create an undulating carpet that looks both cool and soft.

Baby's tears grows to 4 inches high in the shadiest locations, but it will remain lower in light or partial shade. Its tiny flowers are inconspicuous. Nurseries sometimes offer a variety with chartreuse gold foliage.

Under favorable shade and moisture conditions, baby's tears spreads quickly; it can become invasive, because even small pieces of stems will take root wherever they touch soil. Juicy leaves and stems are easily injured by foot traffic, but fast growth soon repairs any damage. Hard frosts turn plants into a black mush, but the onset of warmer weather initiates regrowth from the roots.

STACHYS BYZANTINA

LAMB'S EARS
Pictured on facing page

Zones: 4–10
Type: Evergreen to deciduous perennial
Exposure: Sun
Water: Moderate
Spacing: 18 inches

It's hard to resist touching the furry-surfaced, gray white leaves of lamb's ears. Thick, pointed-oval leaves reach 4 to 6 inches long, forming a solid cover of foliage from creeping stems that root as they spread.

Plants maintain an even cover about 8 inches high except in early summer, when branched 12- to 18-inch flower stalks bear small, pinkish purple flowers in tiered whorls. Specialty nurseries may offer 'Silver Carpet', a form that produces no flowering stems.

Lamb's ears is undemanding, requiring only well-drained soil, but it's best used as a small-scale cover because it needs periodic grooming. Subfreezing weather will damage or kill the foliage; if this occurs, remove dead foliage in late winter or early spring before new growth starts.

After flowering ceases, cut out the flower stalks to restore neatness. (This also prevents the formation of seed, which can self-sow prolifically.) When bare patches begin to appear after several years, dig and divide plants; replant well-rooted divisions.

TAXUS BACCATA 'REPANDENS'

SPREADING ENGLISH YEW

Zones: 6–10 (except desert)
Type: Evergreen shrub
Exposure: Sun to shade
Water: Regular to moderate
Spacing: 3 feet

Spreading English yew, although botanically related to the familiar junipers (see page 135), produces a softer foliage effect in the landscape. Leaves are needlelike, about ½ inch long, and are borne in featherlike fashion on opposite sides of branches.

Growth is rather slow. Horizontal stems spread widely, forming a solid cover in time. You can keep it low—to several inches high—by shearing or clipping, or you can allow branches to build up to around 2 feet. Foliage color is rich green, but the variety 'Repandens Aurea' produces golden yellow new growth.

In fall, small, berrylike red fruits form on the branches if there's a pistillate (male) English yew planted nearby.

Plants prosper in soils ranging from acid to slightly alkaline, as long as the soil

Stachys byzantina

drains well. Growth is equally good in sun or shade, even dense shade beneath trees. Avoid planting against south- or west-facing walls where the foliage can burn from reflected heat and light.

TEUCRIUM CHAMAEDRYS

GERMANDER
Pictured on page 154

Zones: 6–10 (West), 6–7 (East)
Type: Evergreen shrubby perennial
Exposure: Sun to partial shade
Water: Moderate to little
Spacing: 18 to 24 inches

Trouble-free germander consistently provides a dark green carpet, even when soil

is poor or watering is infrequent. Plants have many spreading stems and ascending branches that rise to about 12 inches; stems bear oval leaves nearly an inch long with prominently toothed edges. Variety 'Prostratum' grows only 4 to 6 inches high, spreading widely.

In summer, loose spikes of small, pinkish purple or white flowers appear at stem ends.

Germander isn't fussy about soil quality, but too much moisture is an enemy. Plants grown in well-drained soil will take regular to little watering; in heavy, clay-like soil, water infrequently. If plants become straggly, shear back to encourage lower, branching growth.

Teucrium chamaedrys

THYMUS

THYME

Zones: 4–10
Type: Evergreen perennials
Exposure: Sun to light shade
Water: Moderate
Spacing: 12 inches

Several of the aromatic thymes can provide attractive cover between paving stones and in small patches in rock gardens. These include caraway-scented thyme, *T. herba-barona,* and furry, gray-leafed woolly thyme, *T. pseudolanuginosus.*

For larger expanses, the best choice is *T. praecox arcticus* (sometimes sold as *T. serpyllum* or *T. drucei*), popularly called creeping thyme or mother-of-thyme. Its initial stems form a flat mat; above it rise upright branches 2 to 6 inches high bearing tiny, rounded, pleasantly pungent leaves. In late spring and early summer, rounded clusters of small, lilac purple flowers blossom at branch tips. Some nurseries also offer 'Reiter's', which has rosy red blossoms, as well as a white-flowered variety.

All thymes prefer well-drained, nutrient-poor soil that's fairly dry. In hot-summer regions, however, plants need periodic watering during the warmest months. If a planting becomes straggly, you can shear or cut back stems.

TRACHELOSPERMUM JASMINOIDES

STAR JASMINE, CONFEDERATE JASMINE
Pictured on facing page

Zones: 9–10
Type: Evergreen vine
Exposure: Sun to partial shade
Water: Regular watering
Spacing: 3 feet

Although not a true jasmine, star jasmine possesses a similar and equally penetrating perfume.

The handsome plant is a twining vine that, when unsupported, will cover the ground at a moderate rate, building to a depth of about 2 feet. When star jasmine is grown in a raised bed or on a retained hillside, its stems will spill gracefully over the side of the confining wall.

Leathery, glossy leaves are pointed ovals to 3 inches long, maturing from light green new growth to dark green foliage. Against this polished backdrop, clusters of 1-inch, pinwheel-shaped white flowers bloom in summer (late spring in the desert); their intense fragrance carries for some distance.

A similar species is *T. asiaticum;* its leaves are smaller and less glossy, and flowers range from yellow to cream in color.

Star jasmine thrives in average, well-drained soil; where summer is especially hot, and certainly in the desert, locate plants in partial shade. Fertilize at the start of the growing season and again after flowering to encourage lush growth. Chlorosis may develop in alkaline soil; if this occurs, treat with iron chelate or iron sulfate.

VANCOUVERIA PLANIPETALA

INSIDE-OUT FLOWER

Zones: 7–9 (except desert)
Type: Evergreen perennial
Exposure: Shade
Water: Regular to moderate
Spacing: 12 to 18 inches

The curious common name refers to the odd shape of this plant's flower, which looks as though its petals had been swept back in a strong wind. A lesser-known name, redwood ivy, aptly describes its foliage. Individual leaflets resemble shallowly lobed ivy leaves carried on wirelike leaf stalks that grow from a thick mat of creeping underground stems. This carpet of overlapping foliage may reach as high as 2 feet.

In late spring, large, open flower clusters rise above the foliage on slender stems, each cluster comprised of 25 to 50 individual white blossoms less than ½ inch across.

Nurseries specializing in western native plants may carry other *Vancouveria* species that will be equally useful in shaded gardens.

VERBENA

Zones: Vary (West only)
Type: Evergreen perennial
Exposure: Sun
Water: Moderate
Spacing: 12 to 18 inches

Few ground covers surpass the verbenas for amount of color provided over an extended period of time. Flat-topped clusters of brightly colored small flowers nearly hide the foliage at the peak of summer bloom.

These low, spreading plants grow rapidly in sunny situations from coast to desert; hot summer weather actually encourages top performance. Plants are not particular about soil and need only moderate watering. In late winter or early spring, shear or cut back established plantings; then apply fertilizer.

Most verbenas are rather short-lived perennials; you may need to replace them after several years.

The basic type of ground-hugging *V. peruviana* (Zones 9–10) offers vivid

scarlet flowers on a vigorous plant with small, oval leaves. Nurseries also carry numerous hybrid varieties—some sold by name, others labeled only by color—that have slightly larger foliage and grow to about 12 inches high. In addition to red, available colors include pink, magenta, purple, blue, and white.

Garden verbena, *V. hybrida* (Zones 9–10), is often planted as an annual but will persist for several years. Spreading plants grow 6 to 12 inches high and are clothed in oblong green or gray green leaves 2 to 4 inches long. Colors are the same as listed for *V. peruviana*, above; named strains are available. Plants are somewhat subject to mildew; to minimize the problem, water deeply and infrequently.

Two verbenas native to the Southwest make effective ground covers in Zones 5–10. Plants of *V. bipinnatifida* grow 8 to 15 inches high, bearing very finely divided leaves and clusters of blue flowers. Reaching several inches taller, *V. goodingii* features pinkish lavender flowers above deeply cut foliage. Both species perpetuate themselves in the garden by reseeding.

VERONICA

SPEEDWELL

Zones: 6–10
Type: Evergreen to deciduous perennials
Exposure: Sun to partial shade
Water: Regular watering
Spacing: 12 inches

The speedwells form low carpets of small, pointed leaves from which rise upright spikes or small clusters of sparkling blue or white flowers. Use these plants in small areas (they'll provide good cover for spring-flowering bulbs) and between paving stones.

Creeping speedwell, *V. repens*, forms a low mat of shiny foliage. Plants are evergreen in Zones 9–10; in colder areas, they lose their leaves in fall and regrow them in spring. Small clusters of ¼-inch lavender or white flowers appear in spring.

A slightly larger, higher plant, *V. prostrata* (*V. rupestris*) has mintlike leaves to 1½ inches long. Light blue flowers cluster atop 8-inch stems; lower-growing 'Heavenly Blue' has flowers of a darker, more intense shade.

Trachelospermum jasminoides

VIBURNUM DAVIDII

Zones: 7–10 (except desert)
Type: Evergreen shrub
Exposure: Shade to partial shade
Water: Regular to moderate
Spacing: 18 inches

Although springtime brings small clusters of white flowers, it's the foliage that makes this viburnum a garden ornament. Pointed-oval leaves may reach 6 inches long; they're dark green and glossy, with prominent veins that run from base to tip.

Plants spread slowly to form small clumps 1 to 2 feet high; the elegant foliage makes a solid cover. In a mass planting, attractive metallic blue fruits will form after the flowers fade.

Best-looking foliage comes on plants grown in good soil and watered regularly, although plants in cool climates or heavy soil may thrive with moderate watering. Control height by cutting back any stems that grow too tall.

VINCA

PERIWINKLE, MYRTLE
Pictured below

Zones: Vary
Type: Evergreen perennials
Exposure: Sun to shade
Water: Moderate
Spacing: 18 inches

Ease of growth and general attractiveness are assets of both *Vinca* species; the drawback is potential invasiveness—particularly in shade and with *V. major.*

Plants send out spreading or arching green stems bearing pairs of shiny, oval leaves. Stems may root at the joints or even at the tips when they touch moist soil; each newly rooted part is then capable of sending out additional stems. Flowers that resemble single phlox blossoms appear in spring.

Plants are undemanding and willing to grow in any soil; they even compete well with surface tree roots. In cool-

summer regions, the periwinkles can take full sun as well as shade; where summers are hot, partial shade to shade produces the best appearance.

If plantings mound up too high or become too layered with old stems, shear or mow them in late winter to bring on new growth close to the ground.

V. major (Zones 8–10), the larger of the two species, has broadly oval leaves to 3 inches on stems that may build up a planting to about 2 feet high. Lavender blue (often called periwinkle blue) flowers, 1 to 2 inches across, are scattered over the foliage. To enliven shaded plantings, use the variety with creamy white variegated leaves.

Dwarf periwinkle, *V. minor* (Zones 4–10), resembles a miniature version of *V. major.* However, growth is lower and more prostrate, and the narrower leaves are spaced more closely on the stems. Flowers are an inch across, their greater abundance making a showier display than *V. major.*

Available varieties have flowers of white and various shades of blue; some even have double blossoms. You'll also find a form with variegated leaves.

VIOLA

Violet
Pictured on facing page and page 91

Zones: Vary
Type: Evergreen, deciduous perennials
Exposure: Sun to shade
Water: Regular watering
Spacing: 12 inches

The fragrant purple violets used in a romantic nosegay are just one of several different violets available for ground cover use. All have rounded leaves, borne at the ends of slender leaf stalks, that make solid, low carpets of foliage. Flowers rise in great profusion just above the foliage mass.

For best growth, plant in good soil and water regularly. Apply fertilizer in early spring to enhance bloom production and general appearance. Where sum-

Vinca minor

mers are cool, violets can grow in sun, but in hot-summer regions they need at least afternoon shade.

Evergreen sweet violet, *V. odorata* (Zones 6–10), is the beloved fragrant species; it begins to bloom in late winter or early spring, depending on winter cold. Purple is considered the traditional color, but specialists carry many named varieties with flowers of blue, lavender, violet, pink, or white. Plants spread in strawberry fashion, forming new plants at the ends of runners.

Deciduous Confederate violet, *V. sororia* (sometimes sold as *V. priceana*), grows in Zones 6–10; it forms clumps of thick rootstocks. Unless spent flowers are removed, plantings will self-seed profusely. Spring flowers resemble small pansies in white, heavily veined with blue.

Australian violet, *V. hederacea*, thrives in Zones 8–10 (except desert). When temperatures drop to 30°F/-1°C, the plant goes deciduous. Late spring to summer flowers are blue or violet, broadly edged in white; the effect is of white flowers with a dark central patch. Plants spread slowly by stolons.

Viola hederacea

WALDSTEINIA FRAGARIOIDES

BARREN STRAWBERRY

Zones: 5–10 (except desert)
Type: Evergreen perennial
Exposure: Sun to light shade
Water: Regular watering
Spacing: 12 inches

One of three strawberrylike ground covers (see also *Duchesnea indica*, page 123, and *Fragaria chiloensis*, page 125), this plant also forms a thick carpet of strawberry-lookalike leaves 2 to 3 inches high. But this plant spreads more slowly than the other two and is less likely to overgrow its confines.

Small clusters of ¾-inch, single yellow flowers appear in spring but form no fruits. Fall brings another show of color when the glossy green leaves turn to bronzy red.

WEDELIA TRILOBATA

WEDELIA

Zones: 9 (warmest parts)–10
Type: Evergreen perennial
Exposure: Sun to shade
Water: Regular watering
Spacing: 18 inches

Within the limits of its cold tolerance, wedelia is remarkably adaptable, growing well at the seashore and in the low desert. Basic needs are only well-drained soil and regular moisture. Frost will kill wedelia to the ground, but if freezes are not sustained, the plant will regrow quickly with the onset of warmer weather.

Glossy, fleshy leaves to 4 inches long make a thick, lush carpet; for most of the year, it's decorated with inch-wide yellow flowers that resemble single marigolds. Plants spread rapidly and extensively by creeping stems that root as they spread. When older plantings become too thick or uneven, shear or cut them back heavily.

ZOYSIA TENUIFOLIA

KOREAN GRASS

Zones: 9–10
Type: Evergreen perennial grass
Exposure: Sun to light shade
Water: Moderate
Spacing: 8 to 12 inches

An established planting of Korean grass resembles a piece of rumpled velour. Tiny blades of rich green are densely packed into a mounding, undulating turf that never needs mowing and will accept some foot traffic. You can use it in moderately large expanses or in small spaces; between paving stones it forms a velvety green "mortar."

Korean grass prefers well-drained soil but will grow in claylike soil if not overwatered. Leaf blades turn brown with the first frost; they'll return to green at the onset of warm weather in spring.

Plant Index

Aaron's beard. See *Hypericum calycinum*
Achillea, 111
Aegopodium podagraria, 111
Agapanthus, 111
Ajuga reptans, 111
Angel's tears. See *Soleirolia soleirolii*
Arabis caucasica, 112
Arctostaphylos, 112
Arctotheca calendula, 113
Ardisia japonica, 113
Arenaria balearica, 113
Arenaria verna. See *Sagina subulata*
Armeria maritima, 113
Artemisia caucasica, 114
Arundinaria pygmaea, 114
Asarum caudatum, 114
Asparagus densiflorus 'Sprengeri', 115
Atriplex semibaccata, 115
Australian fuchsia. See *Correa pulchella*
Australian saltbush. See *Atriplex semibaccata*

Baby's tears. See *Soleirolia soleirolii*
Baccharis pilularis, 115
Barren strawberry. See *Waldsteinia fragarioides*
Bellflower. See *Campanula*
Bergenia, 115
Bishop's weed. See *Aegopodium podagraria*
Blue fescue. See *Festuca ovina glauca*
Blue star creeper. See *Laurentia fluviatilis*
Bougainvillea, 116
Broom. See *Genista*
Bunchberry. See *Cornus canadensis*

Calluna vulgaris, 116
Campanula, 117
Cape weed. See *Arctotheca calendula*
Carissa macrocarpa, 117
Carolina jessamine. See *Gelsemium sempervirens*
Carpet bugle. See *Ajuga reptans*
Catalina perfume. See *Ribes viburnifolium*
Catmint. See *Nepeta faassenii*
Ceanothus, 117
Cerastium tomentosum, 118
Ceratostigma plumbaginoides, 118
Chamaemelum nobile, 118
Chamomile. See *Chamaemelum nobile*
Cinquefoil. See *Potentilla*
Cissus, 119
Cistus salviifolius, 119
Common thrift. See *Armeria maritima*
Confederate jasmine. See *Trachelospermum jasminoides*
Convallaria majalis, 119
Convolvulus mauritanicus, 119
Coprosma, 120
Cornus canadensis, 120
Coronilla varia, 120
Correa pulchella, 121

Corsican sandwort. See *Arenaria balearica*
Cotoneaster, 121
Cotula squalida, 122
Coyote brush. See *Baccharis pilularis*
Crane's bill. See *Erodium chamaedryoides*
Cranesbill. See *Geranium*
Creeping buttercup. See *Ranunculus repens* 'Pleniflorus'
Creeping Jenny. See *Lysimachia nummularia*
Creeping St. Johnswort. See *Hypericum calycinum*
Crown vetch. See *Coronilla varia*
Cytisus kewensis, 122

Dalea greggii, 123
Dampiera diversifolia, 123
Daylily. See *Hemerocallis*
Dead nettle. See *Lamium maculatum*
Dichondra, 22
Duchesnea indica, 123
Dwarf chaparral broom. See *Baccharis pilularis*
Dwarf plumbago. See *Ceratostigma plumbaginoides*

Epimedium, 123
Erica, 123
Erigeron karvinskianus, 124
Erodium chamaedryoides, 124
Euonymus fortunei, 125
Evergreen candytuft. See *Iberis sempervirens*
Evergreen currant. See *Ribes viburnifolium*

Festuca ovina glauca, 125
Firethorn. See *Pyracantha*
Forget-me-not. See *Myosotis scorpioides*
Fragaria chiloensis, 125

Galax urceolata, 125
Galium odoratum, 126
Gardenia jasminoides 'Radicans', 126
Gaultheria, 126
Gazania, 127
Gelsemium sempervirens, 128
Genista, 128
Geranium, 128
Germander. See *Teucrium chamaedrys*
Gout-weed. See *Aegopodium podagraria*
Green carpet. See *Herniaria glabra*
Grevillea, 129
Ground morning glory. See *Convolvulus mauritanicus*

Heath. See *Erica*
Heavenly bamboo. See *Nandina domestica*
Hebe, 129
Hedera, 129
Helianthemum nummularium, 130
Hellebore. See *Helleborus*
Helleborus, 130
Hemerocallis, 130
Herniaria glabra, 131
Hippocrepis comosa, 131
Honeysuckle. See *Lonicera*
Hosta, 132
Houttuynia cordata, 132
Hypericum calycinum, 132

Iberis sempervirens, 133
Ice plant, 133
Indian mock strawberry. See *Duchesnea indica*
Inside-out flower. See *Vancouveria planipetala*
Irish moss. See *Sagina subulata*
Ivy. See *Hedera*
Ivy geranium. See *Pelargonium peltatum*

Japanese spurge. See *Pachysandra terminalis*
Jasminum polyanthum, 134
Jewel mint of Corsica. See *Mentha requienii*
Juniper. See *Juniperus*
Juniperus, 135

Kew broom. See *Cytisus kewensis*
Knotweed. See *Polygonum*
Korean grass. See *Zoysia tenuifolia*

Lamb's ears. See *Stachys byzantina*
Lamium maculatum, 136
Lantana, 137
Laurentia fluviatilis, 137
Lily-of-the-Nile. See *Agapanthus*
Lily-of-the-valley. See *Convallaria majalis*
Lily turf. See *Liriope*
Lippia. See *Phyla nodiflora*
Liriope, 138
Lonicera, 138
Lotus, 139
Lysimachia nummularia, 139

Mahonia, 140
Manzanita. See *Arctostaphylos*
Mazus reptans, 140
Mentha requienii, 140
Mexican daisy. See *Erigeron karvinskianus*
Mondo grass. See *Ophiopogon japonicus*
Moneywort. See *Lysimachia nummularia*
Moss pink. See *Phlox subulata*
Myoporum parvifolium, 141
Myosotis scorpioides, 141
Myrtle. See *Vinca*

Nandina domestica, 141
Natal plum. See *Carissa macrocarpa*
Nepeta faassenii, 142
New Zealand brass buttons. See *Cotula squalida*

Ophiopogon japonicus, 142
Osteospermum fruticosum, 142

Pachysandra terminalis, 143
Parthenocissus quinquefolia, 144
Paxistima, 144
Pelargonium peltatum, 144
Periwinkle. See *Vinca*
Phlox subulata, 145
Phyla nodiflora, 145
Plantain lily. See *Hosta*
Polygonum, 145
Potentilla, 146
Pratia angulata, 146
Pyracantha, 147

Ranunculus repens 'Pleniflorus', 147
Ribes viburnifolium, 148
Rosa, 148
Rose. See *Rosa*

Rosemary. See *Rosmarinus officinalis*
Rosmarinus officinalis, 149
Rubus calycinoides, 150
Rupture wort. See *Herniaria glabra*

Sageleaf rockrose. See *Cistus salviifolius*
Sagina subulata, 150
Santa Barbara daisy. See *Erigeron karvinskianus*
Santolina, 150
Sarcococca hookerana humilis, 151
Saxifraga stolonifera, 151
Scaevola 'Mauve Clusters', 151
Scotch heather. See *Calluna vulgaris*
Scotch moss. See *Sagina subulata*
Sea pink. See *Armeria maritima*
Sedum, 151
Silver spreader. See *Artemisia caucasica*
Snow-in-summer. See *Cerastium tomentosum*
Soleirolia soleirolii, 152
Speedwell. See *Veronica*
Spreading English yew. See *Taxus baccata* 'Repandens'
Sprenger asparagus. See *Asparagus densiflorus* 'Sprengeri'
Stachys byzantina, 152
Star jasmine. See *Trachelospermum jasminoides*
Stonecrop. See *Sedum*
Strawberry geranium. See *Saxifraga stolonifera*
Sunrose. See *Helianthemum nummularium*
Sweet woodruff. See *Galium odoratum*

Taxus baccata 'Repandens', 153
Teucrium chamaedrys, 153
Thyme. See *Thymus*
Thymus, 154
Trachelospermum jasminoides, 154
Trailing African daisy. See *Osteospermum fruticosum*
Trailing indigo bush. See *Dalea greggii*

Vancouveria planipetala, 154
Verbena, 155
Veronica, 155
Viburnum davidii, 156
Vinca, 156
Viola, 156
Violet. See *Viola*
Virginia creeper. See *Parthenocissus quinquefolia*

Waldsteinia fragarioides, 157
Wall rockcress. See *Arabis caucasica*
Wedelia. See *Wedelia trilobata*
Wedelia trilobata, 157
Wild ginger. See *Asarum caudatum*
Wild lilac. See *Ceanothus*
Wild strawberry. See *Fragaria chiloensis*
Winter creeper. See *Euonymus fortunei*

Yarrow. See *Achillea*

Zoysia grass, 24, 26

General Subject Index

Acid soil, 35, 98–99
Adobe soils. *See* Clay soils
Aeration, 66
  techniques, 66
  when to aerate, 66
Agricultural by-products, 105
Agropyron cristatum. See Crested wheatgrass
Agropyron repens. See Quack grass
Agrostis palustris. See Creeping bent grass
Agrostis tenuis. See Colonial bent grass
Alkaline soil, 35, 98–99
Amending soil
  for ground covers, 99
  for lawns, 35–37
Amendments
  for ground covers, 99
    applying, 99
    organic, 99
  for lawns, 35–37
    applying, 37
    inorganic, 37
    organic, 36–37
Ammophila breviligulata. See Beach grass
Anatomy of grasses, 17
Animal manures, 105
Annual bluegrass, 70. *See also* Weeds
Annual ryegrass, 25
Aphids, 107
Architects, landscape, 32
Athletic surfaces. *See* Play surfaces
Automatic rain shutoff valve, 103
Automatic sprinkler systems. *See* Underground sprinkler systems
Automatic tensiometers, 50

Bahia grass, 19, 24
Balance, in landscape design, 30
Basins, catch, 34
Beach grass, 27
Beetles
  flea, 75
  Japanese. *See* White grubs
  May. *See* White grubs
Benderboard edgings, 38
Bent grasses
  colonial, 19
  creeping, 19
Bermuda grasses
  common, 20, 24
  hybrid, 20, 24
  weed, 70. *See also* Weeds
Billbugs, 74
Blends, grass, 18
Blissus species. *See* Chinch bugs
Blue grama, 27
Bluegrasses
  annual, 70. *See also* Weeds
  Kentucky, 20
  rough-stalk, 22
Bouteloua gracilis. See Blue grama
Brick-in-soil edgings, 38
Broadcasters, 65
Broad-leaved plantain, 73. *See also* Weeds
Broad-leaved weeds, 68
Brown patch, 77
Buchloe dactyloides. See Buffalo grass
Buckthorn plantain, 73. *See also* Weeds
Buffalo grass, 27

Calendar, lawn maintenance, 79
Catch basins, 34
Caterpillars, 107
Centipede grass, 22
Chaetocnema repens. See Flea beetles
Channeling excess water, 33
Cheeseweed (mallow), 72. *See also* Weeds
Chemical problems, 35
Chewings fescue, 23
Chickweed, 71. *See also* Weeds
Chimneys, drainage, 33
Chinch bugs, 74
Chlorosis, 35
Cicadellidae family. *See* Leafhoppers
Circuits, plotting, 54
Clay soils, 34, 47–48, 98
Climate considerations, 17
  for watering, 48
Climate map for grasses, 21
Cold-tolerant grasses, 18. *See also* Cool-season grasses
Collecting excess water, 33–34
Colonial bent grass, 19
Color, seasonal, with ground covers, 83–85
Combination products, for lawn care, 64
Common Bermuda grass, 20, 24
Concrete edgings, 38, 40
Cone sprayers, 59
Contractors, landscape, 32
Controllers, 52–53, 101, 103
  installing, 58
Control valves, 51–52, 103
Cool-season grasses, 17
  annual ryegrass, 25
  chewings fescue, 23
  colonial bent, 19
  creeping bent, 19
  creeping red fescue, 23
  hard fescue, 23
  Kentucky bluegrass, 20
  perennial ryegrass, 24, 26
  rough-stalk bluegrass, 22
  tall fescue, 24, 25
Cornicium fuciforme. See Red thread
Crabgrass, 71. *See also* Weeds
Crambus sperryellus. See Sod webworms
Creeping bent grass, 19
Creeping red fescue, 23
Crested wheatgrass, 27
Crop seed, 39
Cultivars, 17–18
Curly dock, 72. *See also* Weeds
Cutworms, 75
Cyclocephala species. *See* White grubs
Cynodon. See Hybrid Bermuda grass
Cynodon dactylon. See Bermuda grass, weed; Common Bermuda grass

Dallis grass, 71. *See also* Weeds
Dandelion, 71–72. *See also* Weeds
Dead spots, 69
Design
  ground cover, 97–98
  lawn, 14–15, 30–31
Designers, landscape, 32
Dethatching, 65–66
  techniques, 66
  when to dethatch, 66
Dichondra, 22
Dichondra micrantha. See Dichondra
Digitaria species. *See* Crabgrass
Disease-resistant grasses, 18
Diseases, fungus
  ground cover, 107
  lawn, 69, 76–78
Dock, curly, 72. *See also* Weeds
Dollar spot, 77
Drainage
  chimneys, 33
  improving, 33–34

Drainpipes, flexible, 33
Drip irrigation, 102–105
  basic components, 102–103
  design and assembly, 103–105
  optional equipment, 103
Drop-spreaders, 65
Drought-tolerant grasses, 18. *See also* Native grasses
Drought-tolerant ground covers, 86–88
Dry granular fertilizers, 64, 106
Dry wells, 33–34

Edgers, 63
Edging ground covers, 107
Edgings, 37–38, 40
  masonry, 38, 40
  wood, 38
Electronic sensors, 50
Emitters, 102
Eremochloa ophiuroides. See Centipede grass
ET (evapotranspiration), 49
Euphorbia maculata. See Spotted spurge
Evapotranspiration (ET), 49

Fairy ring, 77
Fertilizer injector, 103
Fertilizers
  for ground covers, 106
    choosing, 106
    when to apply, 106
  for lawns, 63–65
    techniques, 65
    understanding, 64
    when to apply, 64–65
Fertilizing
  ground covers, 106
  lawns, 65
Fescues
  chewings, 23
  creeping red, 23
  hard, 23
  tall, 24, 25
Festuca arundinacea. See Tall fescue
Festuca longifolia. See Hard fescue
Festuca rubra commutata. See Chewings fescue
Festuca rubra rubra. See Creeping red fescue
Filter, 103
Finish grading, 37
Fittings, pipe, 52
Flea beetles, 75
Flexible drainpipes, 33
Flushing pipes, 56
Formal lawns, 6–7
Fungus diseases
  ground cover, 107
    powdery mildew, 107
  lawn, 69, 76–78
    brown patch, 77
    dollar spot, 77
    fairy ring, 77
    fusarium patch, 77
    grease spot, 78
    red thread, 78
    rust, 78
    snow mold, 78
Fusarium nivale. See Fusarium patch
Fusarium patch, 77

Gardeners, professional, 32
Germination percentage, 39
Gophers, 69
Grading
  for ground covers, 99
  for lawns, 32–33, 37
Granular fertilizers, dry, 64, 106
Grass
  clippings, 105–106
  seed label, reading a, 39

Grasses. *See also* Lawns
  anatomy of, 17
  choosing, 18
  climate map for, 21
  cool-season. *See* Cool-season grasses
  descriptions of, 19–27
  maintaining, 61–79
  native, 27
  planting, 29–45
  for play surfaces, 10, 24
  warm-season. *See* Warm-season grasses
  watering, 47–59
Grassy weeds, 68
Gravel-filled trenches, 33
Grease spot, 78
Grooming ground covers, 106–107
Ground covers, 80–157
  descriptions of, 109–157
  design, 97–98
  drought-tolerant, 86–88
  ground-hugging, 92–93
  for hillsides, 94–95
  maintaining, 105–107
  planting, 100
  preparing soil for, 99
  for seasonal color, 83–85
  shade-tolerant, 89–91
  watering, 100–105
Grubs, white, 76
Gumbo soils. *See* Clay soils
Gypsum. *See* Inorganic amendments

Hard fescue, 23
Hardiness zone map, plant, 110
Hardpan, 35
Heat-tolerant grasses, 18. *See also* Warm-season grasses
"Heavy" soils. *See* Clay soils
Herbicides, 68
Hillsides
  ground covers for, 94–95
  lawns for, 11, 12
Hose-end sprinklers
  for ground covers, 101
  for lawns, 59
Hoses, 58–59
  materials, 58–59
  sizes, 59
  storing, 59
Hybrid Bermuda grass, 20, 24
Hydroseeding, 40, 42

Impact sprinklers, 59
Impulse sprinklers, 59
Inert matter, 39
Innovations, turf, 13
Inorganic amendments, 37
Insects, 69
Iron deficiency. *See* Chlorosis

Japanese beetles. *See* White grubs
June bugs. *See* White grubs

Kentucky bluegrass, 20
Knotweed, 72. *See also* Weeds

Label, grass seed, reading a, 39
Landscape
  architects, 32
  contractors, 32
  designers, 32
  drama, 14–15
Landscaping principles, 30
Lawn moths, 76
Lawns, 4–79
  design primer for, 30–31
  formal, 6–7
  grasses for, 17–27
  innovations for, 13
  for landscape drama, 14–15
  maintaining, 61–79
  planting, 29–45
  as problem solvers, 10–12
  small-scale, 8–9
  watering, 47–59

Leafhoppers, 75
Leaves, 106
Legal considerations, 32
Lime. See Inorganic amendments
Liquid fertilizers, 64, 106
Loam, 34, 47–48, 98
Lolium multiflorum. See Annual ryegrass
Lolium perenne. See Perennial ryegrass
Low-growing ground covers, 92–93

Maintenance
  for ground covers, 105–107
    fertilizing, 106
    grooming, 106–107
    mulches, 105–106
    pests and disease, controlling, 107
  for lawns, 61–79
    aeration, 66
    calendar, 79
    dethatching, 65–66
    fertilizing, 63–65
    fungus diseases, controlling, 69, 76–78
    lawn renovation, 66–68
    mowing, 61–63
    pests, controlling, 68–69, 74–76
  of underground sprinkler systems, 58
  weeds, controlling, 68, 70–73
Mallow, 72. See also Weeds
Malva species. See Mallow
Manifold, 56, 101
Manual tensiometers, 50
Maps
  climate, for grasses, 21
  plant hardiness zone, 110
Marasmius oreades. See Fairy ring
Masonry edgings, 38, 40
May beetles. See White grubs
Mildew, powdery, 107
Mini-sprinklers and mini-sprayers, 102–103
Mites, 107
Mix percentages, grass seed, 39
Mixtures, grass, 18
Moisture sensors, 49–50
Moles, 69
Mowers, 61–62
  purchasing, 62
  types of, 61–62
  using and maintaining, 62
Mowing
  ground covers, 107
  lawns, 61–63
    new, 63
    mowers for, 61–62
    strips, 37–38
    techniques, 63
    trimming and edging, 63
    when to mow, 62
Mulches, 105–106

Native grasses, 27
Natural-material amendments. See Organic amendments
New lawns, mowing, 63
Noxious weeds, 39
Nursery personnel, 32

Organic amendments
  for ground covers, 99
  for lawns, 36–37
Organic fertilizers, 64
Oscillating sprinklers, 59
Overseeding, 18
Oxalis, 72–73. See also Weeds
Oxalis corniculata. See Oxalis

Paspalum, seashore, 25
Paspalum dilatatum. See Dallis grass

Paspalum notatum. See Bahia grass
Paspalum vaginatum. See Seashore paspalum
Perennial ryegrass, 24, 26
Permits. See Legal considerations
Pest-resistant grasses, 18
Pests
  ground cover, 107
    aphids, 107
    caterpillars, 107
    mites, 107
    scale, 107
    slugs, 107
    snails, 107
  lawn, 68–69, 74–76
    billbugs, 74
    chinch bugs, 74
    cutworms, 75
    flea beetles, 75
    leafhoppers, 75
    sod webworms, 76
    white grubs, 76
pH, soil. See Chemical problems
Physical problems, 35
Pine needles, 105
Pipe fittings, 52
Pipes, 52, 101
  laying, 56
  working with, 55
Plantago species. See Plantain
Plantain, 73. See also Weeds
Plant hardiness zone map, 110
Planting
  ground covers, 99–100
    preparing soil, 99
    spacing, 100
    when to plant, 100
  lawns, 29–45
    amending soil, 35–37
    drainage, 33–34
    edgings, 37–38, 40
    grading, 32–33
    lawn design, 30–31
    laying sod, 42–44
    plugging, 45
    preparing soil, 34–35
    seeding, 40–42
    sprigging, 44–45
    working with professionals, 29, 32
Plastic netting for sod, 43
Play surfaces, 10, 24
Plugging, 45
Plugs
  buying, 45
  planting, 45
Poa annua. See Annual bluegrass
Poa pratensis. See Kentucky bluegrass
Poa trivialis. See Rough-stalk bluegrass
Polygonum aviculare. See Knotweed
Portable tensiometers, 50
Powdery mildew, 107
Pressure regulator, 103
Probes, soil, 50–51
Problem solvers, lawn, 10–12
Professionals, lawn, 29–30
Proportion, in landscape design, 30
Pruning, 197
Psudaletia species. See Cutworms
Puccinia. See Rust
Puddling, 69
Pythium. See Grease spot

Quack grass, 73. See also Weeds

Rain shutoff valve, automatic, 103
Red thread, 78
Reel mowers, 61
Reinforced rubber-vinyl hoses, 59
Reinforced vinyl hoses, 59
Rejuvenation, for ground covers, 107
Renovation, lawn, 66–68
Repair, for underground sprinkler systems, 58
Revolving-arm sprinklers, 59

Rhizoctonia solani. See Brown patch
Ride-on mowers, 62
Risers, 52, 101
  installing, 56
  replacing, 58
Root depth, grass, 18
Rotary mowers, 61–62
Rough grading, 32–33
Rough-stalk bluegrass, 22
Rubber hoses, 58
Rumex crispus. See Curly dock
Rust, 78
Ryegrasses
  annual, 25
  perennial, 24, 26

St. Augustine grass, 26
Salinity, 35
Salty soil. See Salinity
Sampling tubes. See Soil probes
Sandy soils, 34, 47–48, 98
Scale, 107
Sclerotina homeocarpa. See Dollar spot
Seashore paspalum, 25
Seasonal color, with ground covers, 83–85
Seed
  choosing, 40
  hydroseeding, 40, 42
  label, grass, reading a, 39
  sowing, 40, 41
  versus sod, 44
Seedbed, preparing, 32–40
Sensors, moisture, 49–50
Service line, tapping in, 55–56
Shade-tolerant grasses, 18
Shade-tolerant ground covers, 89–91
Shallow soil, 35
Slugs, 107
Small-scale lawns, 8–9
Snails, 107
Snow mold, 78
Sod
  laying, 44
  shopping for, 42–44
  versus seed, 44
  webworms, 76
Soil
  acid, 35, 98–99
  alkaline, 35, 98–99
  amending
    for ground covers, 99
    for lawns, 35–37
  chlorosis, 35
  -coring tubes. See Soil probes
  preparing
    for ground covers, 99
    for lawns, 34–37
  probes, 50–51
  problems and remedies, 34–35
  salinity, 35
  shallow, 35
  tests, 34–35
  types, 34, 47–48, 98
Solid-lumber edgings, 38
Sowing seed, 40, 41
Sphenophorus species. See Billbugs
Spots, on lawns, 69
Spotted spurge, 73. See also Weeds
Sprayers, 102
Sprays, fertilizer, 65
Sprigging, 44–45
Sprigs
  planting, 45
  shopping for, 45
Sprinkler heads, 52, 101
  attaching, 57
  locating, 54
  repairing, 58
  replacing, 58
Sprinklers, hose-end
  for ground covers, 101
  for lawns, 59
Sprinkler systems, underground
  for ground covers, 101–102
  for lawns, 51–58

Spurge, spotted, 73. See also Weeds
Stellaria media. See Chickweed
Stenotaphrum secundatum. See St. Augustine grass
Straw, 105
Synthetic fertilizers, 64

Tall fescue, 24, 25
Taraxacum officinale. See Dandelion
Tensiometers, 49–50
Tests, soil, 34–35
Thatch. See Dethatching
Timers. See Controllers
Tolerance chart, for grasses, 18
Topsoil, adding, 35
Trenches
  backfilling, 58
  digging, 55
  gravel-filled, 33
Trimmers, 63
Tubing, 102
Turf innovations, 13
Typhula. See Snow mold

Underground sprinkler systems
  for ground covers, 101–102
    components, 101
    design and installation, 101–102
  for lawns, 51–58
    components, 51–53
    installation, 37, 55–58
    maintenance, 58
    planning, 53–55
    repair, 58
Unity, in landscape design, 30
Unreinforced vinyl hoses, 58

Valves, control, 51–52, 103
Variety, in landscape design, 30
Vinyl hoses, 58–59

Warm-season grasses, 17
  Bahia, 19, 24
  centipede, 22
  common Bermuda, 20, 24
  dichondra, 22
  hybrid Bermuda, 20, 24
  St. Augustine, 26
  seashore paspalum, 25
  zoysia, 24, 26
Water-efficient lawn, tips for a more, 48
Watering
  ground covers, 100–105
    drip irrigation, 102–105
    guidelines, 100–101
    hose-end sprinkling, 101
    underground sprinkler systems, 101–102
  lawns, 47–59
    guidelines, 47–51
    hoses and sprinklers, 58–59
    underground sprinkler systems, 51–58
Water pressure and gpm, measuring, 53
Water-thrifty ground covers, 86–88
Wear-resistant grasses, 18. See also Play surfaces
Webworms, sod, 76
Weeds
  in ground covers, 106–107
    eradicating, 99
  in lawns, 68, 70–73
Weed seed, 39
White grubs, 76
Wood edgings, 38
Wood products, 105

Yellowing, of lawns, 69

Zone map, plant hardiness, 110
Zones, climate, for grasses, 21
Zoysia grass, 24, 26
Zoysia species. See Zoysia grass